THE IMMACULATE INNING

THE IMMACULATE INNING

UNASSISTED TRIPLE PLAYS, 40/40 SEASONS, AND
THE STORIES BEHIND BASEBALL'S RAREST FEATS

JOE COX

GUILFORD, CONNECTICUT

To the men who starred in the Negro Leagues, who by all rights should have their accomplishments celebrated in this book. The statistics don't allow their inclusion, but this book is dedicated to them, and to their baseball feats, many of which were equal or superior to those chronicled here.

Also, to Pap, have missed you many times in the last two decades, but never more than during Game 7 of the 2016 World Series. They finally did it!

An imprint of The Rowman & Littlefield Publishing Group, Inc.
4501 Forbes Blvd., Ste. 200
Lanham, MD 20706
www.rowman.com

Distributed by NATIONAL BOOK NETWORK

Copyright © 2018 by Joe Cox

First Lyons Press paperback edition 2020

British Library Cataloguing in Publication Information available

Library of Congress Cataloging-in-Publication Data available

ISBN 978-1-4930-4807-6 (paperback)
ISBN 978-1-4930-3213-6 (e-book)

♾™ The paper used in this publication meets the minimum requirements of American National Standard for Information Sciences—Permanence of Paper for Printed Library Materials, ANSI/NISO Z39.48-1992.

CONTENTS

FOREWORD

When Joe Cox asked me if I could write a few words to lead off *The Immaculate Inning*, I was excited to share a few thoughts about some of the more amazing parts of baseball history. The more that Joe and I talked about the book, the more I felt like what he's doing here and what I do for ESPN on *Sunday Night Baseball* have a lot in common. We're getting at the inside stories behind the game, and tracking accomplishments and feats. Of course, Joe got to think about and plan out exactly which stories he wanted to tell, whereas many times, on ESPN, we find ourselves working on them on the fly.

My very first *Sunday Night Baseball* game was the first no-hitter in the 30-year history of *Sunday Night Baseball*. I walk into the booth, I'm nervous, trying to figure out who I'm working with, just trying to get through the game, and Jake Arrieta throws a no-hitter against the Dodgers and it becomes this historic moment, out of nowhere in an early September game. In many ways, that embodies the reality that any time you go to the ballpark, you could see something amazing happen.

The Immaculate Inning reminded me of being in Chicago when Willson Contreras homered on his first pitch he saw in the big leagues. That was magical, the way the moment was building. He comes on deck, and our *Sunday Night Baseball* crew is actually set up in the seats—we do that two or three times a year—and the entire place starts to come to their feet, just while he's on deck. He's a big prospect, and the entire Chicago fan base gets to its feet, just to see him on deck. You can feel the anticipation and hear the cheering begin before he even steps into the batter's box. It's like a movie script. If you're watching the movie, you're going, "Come on!" The movie wouldn't even have been written in that way—it's the first pitch, he hits it out of the park. And wow, to hear that place explode—it was like the World Series. It felt like that.

That story is in *The Immaculate Inning*, but so are a lot of other stories from players and games that are long before my time—and any of the readers' times as well. I love the story about Bobby Lowe hitting four home runs after a big fish dinner and going back to the restaurant and eating there again, having the same meal until he got sick of it. Reading that story, I pictured Lowe running back to the restaurant, and in my mind's eye I see that maybe the restaurant ends up with a sign on the wall that Bobby Lowe ate here and hit four home runs. Those kind of stories *are* baseball to me. I grew up in Los Angeles listening to Vin Scully and all those great stories. I love the beautiful way that baseball allows you the time to delve into things, and to mention the context of who this person is and the background of where they come from. All of a sudden, you paint a picture of someone that's not just a number of whatever they're chasing or doing.

That said, the chase of numbers is also a big part of baseball. We've lived through that with the 2017 Indians and their big winning streak. We've seen it with this amazing 2017 rookie class, with Cody Bellinger and Aaron Judge and Rhys Hoskins, and all the historic "first time in baseball history" moments with those guys. I'm seeing that more than any other time in my life, and it's incredible when historic numbers are reached and passed.

Those historic numbers are really important in providing historical context. For example, I think about Ted Williams hitting .400. We've got some hitters right now with players like José Altuve and Daniel Murphy, who stand out as guys who get hit after hit and are at the top of batting races consistently year after year. And then you think about how far their numbers are from .400, and it's unbelievable. To think about what Ted Williams did, it's the kind of stuff that gives me a craving to go back in time and watch—and have it not be black and white—not even for just the numbers, but for the context. What was playing in that time like? We don't have a time machine, but the stories are a pretty good substitute to help us know different eras and styles of baseball.

As the first woman to regularly work national baseball telecasts, I get asked a lot about my legacy in the profession. To be honest, I don't do a good job of stepping back—I'm in the moment, thinking about the next game, so it's more getting my brain on how can I break down

Daniel Murphy's at-bats or talk about Cody Bellinger. It helps me stay where I'm at and not think too much about any of it. But I do know that as long as I can be, I'll be out there tracking the historic moments, telling the inside stories. Those stories—the stories that Joe Cox tells here, the stories that I'm looking forward to telling in the next game—they're what makes baseball great, and they're absolutely necessary for baseball to continue to be great.

Jessica Mendoza
September 2017

Jessica Mendoza is an ESPN Major League Baseball analyst on Sunday Night Baseball—*the exclusive national game of the week. Mendoza is the first female analyst to regularly call nationally televised MLB games.*

AUTHOR'S NOTE

Major-league records, for our purposes, begin with the 1876 National League. They include the Federal League (1914–1915), the Players' League (1890), the Union Association (1884), and American Association (1882–1891), as well as the usual AL and NL data. Team names are per baseball-reference.com.

CHAPTER 1

TURNING AN UNASSISTED TRIPLE PLAY

Number of Times Accomplished: 15 (or is it 16?).

First Instance: Good question. Either Paul Hines, Providence Grays, May 8, 1878, or Neal Ball, Cleveland Naps, July 19, 1909.

Most Recent Instance: Eric Bruntlett, Philadelphia Phillies, August 23, 2009.

Likely Achievers: The extremely unusual nature of the play renders it a matter of almost complete chance. Troy Tulowitzki (five-time All-Star, approaching 1,500 hits and 250 career homers) and George Burns (2,018 career hits, 1926 AL MVP) are probably the most famous players of the triple play turners.

Surprises: Plenty of guys in this group were fringe players. For instance, Ernie Padgett had 838 big-league at-bats and was a regular for only one season. Bruntlett amassed 789 career at-bats, with no more than 212 in any season.

Likelihood of Additional Occurrences: Other than a span of 65 years with only one unassisted triple play (from June 1927 to September 1992—broken only by Ron Hansen in 1968), the unassisted triple play happens every few years or so. When and where will always be unexpected, but it likely will keep happening.

It is the play that produces the biggest momentum swing in baseball. Take a promising inning—at least two runners on, maybe the bases loaded, with nobody out. Have the next hitter smack a hard-hit line drive, enough to draw those runners on toward their other bases. And then the elation turns to defeat. An agile fielder makes a tough catch, steps on a base, tags a runner, and all by himself, he has destroyed the promising inning.

More than almost any feat in this book, the unassisted triple play is a fluke of timing. It requires a very specific setup, runners sent in motion, a sharp line drive, and a good jump, usually by a middle infielder. The peculiar combination of required elements is why it happens only an average of about once a decade. Unlike so many baseball accomplishments that are the product of tremendous buildup, the unassisted triple play happens so quickly that a literal blink can almost miss it. But it still has its own internal drama, and although the setup of the play is always pretty similar, the variety of ways that the players find themselves dropped into the lap of baseball history always keeps the story fresh.

The first unassisted triple play *might* have happened in 1878. Yes, might have—most official records call Neal Ball's 1909 play the first. But it's far from a sure thing.

Providence led Boston 3–1 in the eighth inning of their game on May 8, 1878. Boston had Jack Manning on third base and Ezra Sutton on second with no outs in the bottom of the frame. Batter Jack Burdock laced a ball over the shortstop for an apparent hit, and Manning and Sutton dashed off to try to tie the score. Providence center fielder Paul Hines was playing shallow, and he raced in, making a shoestring catch of the ball, and heading toward third base. Manning was well down the third base line—indeed he apparently had crossed home plate—and many sources believe Sutton had passed third. Hines easily won the noncompetitive footrace with Manning to the third base bag. Then—in a moment of confusion—Hines threw the ball to second baseman Charlie Sweasy, who touched second base as well—and the triple play was complete. So did Hines turn an unassisted triple play, or an unassisted double play, with an assist to Sweasy for the third out? Excellent question.

The central issue in the inquiry is whether Sutton, on the move from second base, had indeed passed third base when Hines tagged it after his catch. Under the rules of the time, if Sutton had passed third when Hines tagged it, not only was Manning out for failing to return to third, but Sutton was also out. To say that the sources are unclear and contradictory would be an understatement. John Thorn, the official historian of Major League Baseball, made the case ably for the play being unassisted in his 2015 blog post on the official MLB blog. This position has promptly been rebutted by historian Richard Hershberger in SABR's *Baseball Research Journal*. Both sides draw on multiple sources who convincingly indicate that Sutton had passed third and the play was unassisted or that Sutton had not passed third and the play was not unassisted. In spite of Thorn's position, MLB does not list Hines's play as an unassisted triple play.

Either way, it is clear that Paul Hines made a phenomenal play—one account called it "one of the most brilliant of the few triple plays yet chronicled" and another recalled Hines "completing a brilliant triple play amid the wildest shouts and demonstrations of delight imaginable." The *Providence Journal* continued, "The members of the [Providence] nine expressed their delight at the play by sundry slaps and demonstrations of pleasure, all of which Paul received with becoming modesty. It was a long time before the crowd became sufficiently composed to resume their attention on the game."

Whether he did or didn't make the first unassisted triple play, Hines did have a fine 1878 season. In fact, in 1969, when Macmillan published the first edition of its *Baseball Encyclopedia*, Hines was posthumously credited with another honor that he indisputably deserved, as baseball's first Triple Crown winner, with a .358 batting average, four home runs, and 50 RBI.

If Paul Hines didn't turn the first unassisted triple play, then Neal Ball did. On July 19, 1909, Ball's Cleveland Naps held a 1–0 lead in the second inning. Boston shortstop Heinie Wagner singled to center, and then first baseman Jake Stahl beat out a bunt. With a 3-2 count on second baseman Amby McConnell, the runners both took off on pitcher Cy Young's delivery. McConnell lined the ball back up the middle, and Ball, a 5'7" shortstop purchased from the New York Highlanders on May 18, made a leaping catch. By the time Ball made his catch, Wagner was around third base, and so he was easily retired when Ball tagged second base. Stahl, who was running from first, was most of the way to second, and two or three strides allowed Ball to tag him (Ball recalling later that Stahl "ran right into my hands") and easily complete the triple play.

So sudden and surprising was the play that when Ball threw down his glove and headed off the field, Cy Young, surprised, asked him, "Where are you going, Neal?" Ball replied that there were three outs. When the spectators caught up with the play, they gave Ball a rousing ovation—and a 20-minute delay was needed to clear all of the hats thrown onto the playing surface.

In case that wasn't enough, Ball led off the bottom of the inning and slashed an inside-the-park home run over Tris Speaker. Neal hit only four career home runs in 1,613 big-league at-bats, so that play was almost as rare as the triple play.

Ball was a career .250 hitter, and his career ended in 1913 with the Red Sox. The following year, he found himself coaching the Baltimore Orioles, where he was assigned to work with a particularly raw young signee, Babe Ruth. Ball later recalled of his young prodigy, "He had baseball sense. You'd only have to tell him something once." And while the Babe's 714 home runs would outstrip Ball's career total by 710, Neal Ball finished up with a 1–0 advantage on unassisted triple plays—an advantage that has kept the glove he used to complete his masterpiece on display at the Baseball Hall of Fame more than a century later.

Of course, one of the many ways of making any play particularly memorable is to make it at an opportune moment. Consider, for instance, Bill Wambsganss, a solid, if unremarkable second baseman of the 1910s and 1920s. Wamby was a career .259 hitter and hit a career total of seven home runs in the Dead Ball Era. In his one and only World Series, in 1920, Wamby was 4-for-26 at the plate. But in Game 5, with his Indians trying to control the Series, and the Brooklyn Robins looking to rally back from a 7–0 deficit, Wamby had his moment of glory.

Pete Kilduff singled and Otto Miller followed suit. Indians pitcher Jim Bagby faced opposing pitcher Clarence Mitchell, who despite his position was no weak link with the bat, as a career .252 hitter. Mitchell lined the ball up the middle with a hit-and-run on, and Wambsganss made "a leaping one-hand catch," which Damon Runyon termed "a great catch under any circumstances." But under the instant circumstances, Wamby tagged second, retiring Kilduff, who was most of the way to third base, and quickly turned and ran down Miller, a catcher, between first and second base. "The crowd is fairly stunned for a moment," wrote Runyon in the next day's *Washington Herald*, "and then realizing the play, sets up a clamor."

Most of the following day's headlines were stolen by Elmer Smith's first-inning grand slam, which was the first such play in Series history. Ultimately, though, 18 Series slams have followed since Smith's blast, but Wamby is still alone in the baseball record book for not only the only unassisted triple play in World Series history, but the only triple play of any kind in the Fall Classic.

⌒

For some players, an unassisted triple play is not their shining moment of big-league fame, but instead, it's the confidence-building play on which a magnificent career begins. Such was the case for Colorado shortstop Troy Tulowitzki. Tulowitzki was a top prospect in the Colorado organization after they chose him in the first round of the 2005 MLB Draft, and after batting .240 in a September 2006 call-up, he was essentially handed the starting shortstop job in Colorado for 2007.

But the transition had not gone smoothly for the rookie in early 2007. On April 29, 2007, Tulo was hitting .203 and had struck out 21 times in 74 big-league at-bats. But that day, the Rockies took on the Braves, and Tulowitzki's career was about to begin an uptick.

In the seventh inning of a 5–5 game, Kelly Johnson and Edgar Renteria singled for the Braves. With a full count on All-Star third baseman Chipper Jones, Johnson and Renteria broke with the pitch from Colorado's Zach McClellan.

"As soon as I saw the runners take off, you think of a triple play, but it rarely happens," admitted Tulowitzki later that evening. But a liner from Jones was caught by the shortstop, who stepped on the base to double up Johnson, and then tagged Renteria, who froze about two steps shy of second base, to complete the unassisted triple play. So sudden and befuddling was the play that Tulowitzki, perhaps echoing Paul Hines long ago, went back and tagged second again and threw to Colorado first baseman Todd Helton. Asked after the game why he made the throw, Tulo joked, "I just wanted to be sure. I was trying to be the first person ever to get about five outs."

Tulo's unassisted triple play was the 13th in big-league history. "It kind of just fell into my lap," he said after the game. "But I'll take it."

Tulo also scored the tying run in the game's ninth inning, and had tripled in two runs earlier in the game. A contemporary account of the game mentioned Tulowitzki's offensive struggles, but also his impressive defensive skills. His offensive skills soon caught up. After his unforgettable game at the end of April, Tulowitzki hit .303 in May, and hit .289 with six home runs in June. He finished the season at .291, with 24 home runs and 99 RBIs—good enough to earn him second place in the NL Rookie of the Year balloting behind Ryan Braun.

Since those early struggles, Tulowitzki has been an All-Star five times, finished in the top eight in MVP voting three times, and won a pair of Gold Gloves. He was traded to the Toronto Blue Jays, and continues his career in the American League, where he could end up as the first unassisted-triple-play fielder to play his way into the Baseball Hall of Fame.

―⁓―

While an unassisted triple play jump-started Tulowitzki's career, it essentially capped the career of veteran Eric Bruntlett. Bruntlett was a utility player who played every position except pitcher and catcher at some point in his seven seasons. He hit .231 with 11 home runs in his career, and saw most of his time as a defensive replacement. Bruntlett had won a World Series ring with the Phillies in 2008, and played in 120 games. But in 2009, his luck had gone south. Bruntlett was batting just .128 on August 23rd, when the Phillies visited the New York Mets.

Bruntlett broke out of his season-long slump with three hits at the plate, but he went from being a possible hero to a possible goat in the ninth inning. The Phillies led 9–6, but after the first batter of the inning reached base, Bruntlett (playing second base that day) bobbled a ground-ball by Luis Castillo for an error that brought the tying run to the plate and cut the lead to 9–7. The next batter, Daniel Murphy, hit a groundball up the middle that Bruntlett again fumbled. It wasn't scored an error, but it represented another uncharacteristic fielding miscue from Bruntlett, who had just turned in his fourth error of the year.

Up stepped Met cleanup hitter Jeff Francoeur, and on a 2-2 count, both runners took off. Bruntlett ran to cover second base, just in time for Francoeur to line the pitch right at him as he reached the bag. He caught the ball with his foot on second base, and turned to Murphy, who briefly attempted to dodge a tag, but was quickly reached for the final out of the inning and the game.

Bruntlett had gone from hero to zero and back again in the time it took Francoeur to line a fastball up the middle. It was only the second game-ending unassisted triple play (following Johnny Neun in 1927), and it allowed the veteran a moment to wax philosophic.

"It really is true that when you think you've seen it all, you see something like this," he said after the game. "It was huge, especially because I was part of the reason we got into such a bad spot there in the ninth. So it feels extra special that it happened there to finish off the game."

It also virtually finished Bruntlett's career. Not completely so—he did play 38 more innings with the Phillies, even collecting four more hits. But what could he possibly do as an encore? After spending the 2010 season in the minor leagues, Bruntlett retired to be a stay-at-home dad. A stay-at-home dad who can tell the story of his unassisted triple play might be the rarest sort ever known.

CHAPTER 2

PITCHING AN IMMACULATE INNING

Number of Times Accomplished: 89.

First Instance: John Clarkson, Boston Beaneaters, June 4, 1889.

Most Recent Instance: Rick Porcello, Boston Red Sox, August 9, 2017.

Likely Achievers: While pitchers from literally all walks of baseball have been among the immaculate hurlers, it is interesting that all four of the men who have pitched multiple immaculate innings are Hall of Famers—Sandy Koufax (three immaculate innings), Lefty Grove, Nolan Ryan, and Randy Johnson (two innings each).

Surprises: Among the many unlikely names on the list are Carlos Contreras (0 MLB wins or saves, 47⅓ career innings pitched) and Juan Perez (two MLB victories, 59⅓ career innings pitched).

Likelihood of Additional Occurrences: Given that 2017 featured eight immaculate innings, the question is not whether there will be more immaculate innings, but rather who, when, and where.

The perfect game is one of the most celebrated accomplishments in baseball history, primarily because of the difficulty of mowing down 27 consecutive big-league hitters without a flaw. Of course, no hurler achieves a perfect game solely because of his own flawless pitching. Sometimes outfielders have preserved perfect games with diving catches, sometimes hitters chase poor pitches with a three-ball count, and almost without fail, there is an element of luck in the perfect game.

A purer feat—although admittedly a much briefer one (and thus almost four times more common) is the immaculate inning. An immaculate inning happens so quickly that its simplicity makes it seem not only plausible, but fairly normal. A trio of strikeouts, each on three pitches—that is to say, no balls, no pitches put into play. The immaculate inning is true pitching perfection, and if it might require a broad strike zone or an undisciplined hitter, it still stands as an achievement of stark exactness.

Not only does the pitcher set down three hitters, but he does it without wasting a single pitch. *That* is perfect.

As is so often the case with many baseball firsts, the first immaculate inning wasn't recognized by that name. Indeed, until John Clarkson had an immaculate sixth inning on June 4, 1889, it's unclear that anyone would have contemplated such an accomplishment. But if you had to invent a pitcher to accomplish such a far-flung feat, Clarkson was probably the man for the job in the 19th century.

Throughout the 1880s, baseball consistently tweaked its rules trying to align the dynamic between hitter and pitcher (i.e., the gradual shift from seven balls required for a walk in 1882 down to the sacrosanct number of four in 1889). But under whatever rules he faced, Clarkson was a dominant pitcher. When the National League allowed overhand pitching in 1884, Clarkson flourished. Noted for control and tough breaking pitches, Clarkson won 53 games in 1885, beginning a five-year run in which he won at least 33 games each season.

Like most 19th-century hurlers, his arm eventually wore down—Clarkson won just 24 games after the 1892 season, during which he turned 31 years old. Still, he won 328 total games, and was inducted into the Hall of Fame posthumously in 1963. He also led the league in strikeouts three times, although in that era, strikeouts were a luxury most hitters could not allow. For instance, in 1889, Clarkson led the National League in strikeouts with 284—which sounds amazing until the fact that he pitched 620 innings is noticed. At 4.1 strikeouts per nine innings, Clarkson's K rate was hardly blazing the way for Nolan Ryan.

Still, on June 4, 1889, for his Boston Beaneaters against the Philadelphia Quakers, Clarkson blazed through three hitters in just nine pitches, and was described by the *Boston Globe* as having "a full head of steam." The three hitters who Clarkson dispatched—Jim Fogarty, Sam Thompson, and Sid Farrar—respectively hit .259, .296, and .268 that season, so he wasn't exactly getting easy pickings. But after Farrar "was . . . made to knock three big holes in the air," the immaculate inning was born.

If Clarkson's feat was under the radar, the same would not be said of the third man to throw an immaculate inning. Pat Ragan, in the last game of the Brooklyn Robins' 1914 season, made his effort at history—and there was nothing understated about it.

When Ragan began the eighth inning of a Brooklyn matchup with the Boston Braves on October 5, 1914, by throwing a called strike to Possum Whitted (a career .269 hitter), he apparently threw his cap into the air as if acknowledging cheers from fans up the third base line. When he threw strike two, he repeated the performance, but toward first base. After a third strike past Whitted, he acknowledged applause from fans behind the plate—which had slowly started to increase during this act of showmanship.

He repeated the performance as he threw three more called strikes past Butch Schmidt (career .272 hitter). With the crowd getting into this performance, Red Smith (career .278 hitter) decided he wasn't going to look at three called strikes. Instead, he swung and missed three times, as Ragan continued his hijinks to the delight of the crowd.

Despite Ragan's big inning, the game quickly humbled him. Brooklyn had trailed 4–1 when Ragan had his memorable inning—but the Dodgers rallied to claim a 5–4 lead. In the ninth inning, though, Boston laughed last, as Possum Whitted got his revenge on Ragan with a grand slam that staked the Braves to the 9–5 victory. The *Pittsburgh Press* noted Ragan's feat, but commented that "he exploded in the ninth."

Ragan was a career 77-104 pitcher, but for one inning, he was a superstar—and a wildly entertaining star at that. But alas, his fame went stale even faster than his mound act.

The king of the immaculate inning was Sandy Koufax, who is the only MLB pitcher to throw three such innings. He also managed to throw them in three consecutive years, but none were more memorable than his first immaculate inning.

After a decidedly up-and-down early career, Koufax was coming into his own in the summer of 1962. This neatly coincided with the National League's expansion, and the newly minted New York Mets were Koufax's victims on June 30, 1962. The Amazin' Mets were 20-52 coming into that game, and were well on their way to finishing deeply in the National League basement in their inaugural campaign.

Koufax opened the game with an immaculate inning, striking out Richie Ashburn, Rod Kanehl, and Felix Mantilla each on three pitches. He left the mound after the first half-inning of the game to a standing ovation from the Dodger Stadium crowd. Mets third base coach Solly Hemus asked Koufax, "It isn't really that easy, is it?" Koufax answered, "No, it surely isn't," although the rest of the game would raise the question. Koufax's first immaculate inning was the first inning of his first career no-hitter, as he held New York hitless while striking out 10 more hitters in addition to his perfect opening frame.

Koufax afterward admitted, "In essence, every pitcher takes the mound trying to pitch a no-hitter. The main idea is to keep the batter from getting a base-hit, isn't it? But you have to be lucky to keep 27 batters from dunking one in or hitting one on the nose."

Lucky or perhaps just immaculate.

As in so many areas of his career, Koufax stands alone or nearly alone. He pitched two more immaculate innings, and three more no-hitters during his career. But never again did he—or anyone else, for that matter—manage to pitch an immaculate inning as part of a no-hitter. It was an inning to remember that opened an evening to remember, in a five-year span of pitching glory that could scarcely be imagined.

Unfortunately, every pitcher of an immaculate inning isn't paving his way to Cooperstown with one moment in a career of highlights like Koufax. Carlos Contreras is a young Dominican reliever whose career stats, as they stand, will not earn his way to Cooperstown. He was 0–1 with a 5.51 ERA in 47⅓ major-league innings with the Reds in 2014 and 2015. But one of those innings was immaculate.

Contreras was a hard-throwing reliever who represented the Reds at the 2013 MLB Futures Game. After pitching well in High-A ball and Double-A that season, he pitched productively for the Double-A Pensacola Blue Wahoos until the Reds called him up in June 2014. Contreras had a strong arm, and an ability to avoid contact—but unfortunately, he also struggled to keep the ball in the strike zone.

He had pitched a grand total of 4⅓ major-league innings on July 11th, when the Pirates played the Reds, and Contreras found himself in the crosshairs of history. Contreras entered with the Reds trailing 4–1 in the sixth inning. He gave up a run while setting the Pirates down in the sixth, and then returned to the mound for the seventh inning.

Pittsburgh's Jordy Mercer went down swinging on three pitches. Opposing pitcher Jeff Locke then watched a called third strike—on the third pitch. Finally, Gregory Polanco struck out on three more pitches, and Cincinnati fans had witnessed an immaculate inning—only the third in the team's illustrious history.

The Reds rallied to win the game 6–5, but it was after Contreras left the mound. He walked 17 batters in 19⅓ innings with the Reds in 2014. He worked his way back in 2015, but walked 20 batters in 28 more innings—and just like that, his career was likely over.

Contreras was released by Cincinnati in the spring of 2016, and he has since been a Laredo Lemur and a Texas Air Hawk. His most recent stop was with the Vaqueros Union Laguna of the Mexican Baseball League. The dream of returning to the major leagues is not dead for Contreras, but it is definitely on life support. No doubt the memory of that one magical inning, when the Pittsburgh Pirates were at his mercy, has kept him grinding and dreaming.

A conversation with Bob Gibson at age nine set Drew Storen down the path to his immaculate inning. He loved Gibson's focus and his attitude, and that same "take no prisoners" mentality would inspire Storen to add his own name to baseball history. For the many feats Gibson accomplished during his Hall of Fame career, he never pitched an immaculate inning. But he inspired (at least) one.

It was a long path to that inning for Storen. He hailed from small Brownsburg, Indiana, and grew up as something of a Reds fan—one who would don giant sports goggles and pose as third baseman Chris Sabo at Halloween. Storen shone at Stanford University and was drafted 10th overall by the Washington Nationals in 2009.

Twice, Storen was anointed as the Nats' closer—in 2011, he saved 43 games and in 2015, he saved 29 more. In between, he bounced between roles, and had one amazing season as a setup man in 2014, posting a 1.12 ERA. But for all the ups, there were downs. After the 2015 season, Washington traded him to Toronto. After pitching 33⅓ innings, with an ERA of 6.18, he was then dealt to Seattle. He finished the season there, but was granted free agency after 2016, and signed a one-year deal, coming nearly all the way back home to pitch for the Reds. "It's a lot of full circle stuff," Storen said of his move to Cincinnati.

He pitched well for the Reds, earning a win and a save in his first six appearances, but in his seventh time out, he joined the Cincinnati record book. Taking a mop-up ninth inning against Baltimore with the Reds ahead 9–3, Storen wasted no time or pitches showing his new teammates what he could do.

Jonathan Schoop of Baltimore watched a strike and then flailed at two breaking pitches for the inning's first out. J. J. Hardy watched strike one, swung over top of strike two, and then watched a nasty knee-high fastball end his at-bat. "I got the second strikeout, and I was like, 'I've got to do this!'" recalled Storen. Suddenly, Hyun Soo Kim was the only man between Storen and an immaculate performance.

Strikes one and two split the plate and strike three burrowed in on Kim as he chopped at it hopelessly. In nine pitches, not only had Storen struck out the side, but he had avoided *any* contact—even using the same ball to complete the entire inning. "It's a rarity for me to use the same ball for a whole inning," admitted Storen.

While there are no statistics on such information, the vast majority of immaculate innings appear to include a foul ball or two. Of the eight immaculate frames recorded in 2017, only Yankee Dellin Betances also managed to avoid any contact.

Storen was the first of eight pitchers to work immaculate innings in 2017. As time has gone on, it has transitioned from being a starting pitcher's feat to being a goal for relievers, as five of the eight pitchers who fired immaculate innings in 2017 did so from the bullpen.

"Being a . . . career reliever, it's about as good as it's going to get when you're working with one inning," said Storen. "I had no idea before how rare it was, I just wanted to do it because it was pretty cool."

For Storen, the immaculate inning was in many ways the completion of a circle. Pitching for his fourth organization in a year and a half, he found himself playing for what could loosely be called his hometown team, making history while pitching to catcher Tucker Barnhart—who was actually his high school teammate.

"Throwing to your high school catcher, and having him call that inning, that's something you can't script," remembered Storen.

CHAPTER 3

STRIKING OUT 20 BATTERS
IN A SINGLE GAME

Number of Times Accomplished: Six.

First Instance: Tom Cheney, Washington Senators,
September 12, 1962.

Most Recent Instance: Max Scherzer, Washington Nationals,
May 11, 2016.

Likely Achievers: In Randy Johnson (4,875 strikeouts) and Roger
Clemens (4,672), this group has two of the most prolific strikeout
artists ever.

Surprises: Cheney struck out only 345 batters in his career, so he is
kind of the odd man out. Injuries shortened Kerry Wood's career and
drove him from starter to reliever, but he still totaled over 1,500 career
strikeouts.

Likelihood of Additional Occurrences: Given the lack of contact hitting
in today's game, if a pitcher like Scherzer can withstand a high pitch
count, another 20-strikeout game seems entirely plausible.

It is one of the most glamorous accomplishments in all of sports. To see a
flame-throwing pitcher blowing fastballs past hitters again and again, to
watch the strikeouts climb, the fans improvising "K" signs out of someone's T-shirt, the ballpark starting to buzz as the total reaches double
figures and just keeps growing—it is a level of excitement all its own. If
it isn't thrilling for the hitters, it definitely is for the five men who on six
different occasions (yes, one of them did this twice) struck out 20 batters in a single major-league game. Like the pitchers themselves, each
of these historic games has its own story—and each slice of the record
comes from its own unusual place.

In the case of Washington Senator Tom Cheney, striking out 20 batters was simply an exercise in stubbornness. Cheney actually whiffed 21 hitters, which makes him the only pitcher to have done so. He took 16 grueling innings to compile those strikeouts.

Cheney was a journeyman pitcher. At age 27, the Senators were his third major-league team when he pitched his history-making game. He had only eight prior major-league wins, but pitched well for the Senators in 1962, and made his scheduled start on September 12th at Baltimore. Only 4,098 fans were on hand in Memorial Stadium, and probably fewer still were left when Cheney made history.

Cheney struck out 13 Orioles in nine innings. Catcher Ken Retzer would later recall, "That curveball of his looked like it was falling off the table. Tom was getting a lot of the hitters out with screwballs, too, and he came in with his knuckler now and then and was getting *it* over." Brooks Robinson of the Orioles called Cheney's stuff "the greatest stuff I've seen from any pitcher." But after nine innings, Cheney had a 1–1 tie. So he did what any bull headed young pitcher would do—he kept going.

In the 10th, he struck out Robinson and Jim Gentile. The following inning, he fanned Marv Breeding and pitcher Dick Hall. At one point, recalled later by Cheney to be around the 12th inning, Washington manager Mickey Vernon asked him if he wanted to come out of the game. Cheney recalled, "I told him, 'Hell no.' I was gonna win it or lose it." He also was going to make history.

The 12th and 13th innings went by without any additional strikeouts, but while Oriole hitters tired, Cheney kept firing bullets. In the 14th inning, he again struck out Breeding and Hall, with the latter strikeout setting a new "modern" record of 19. Still, the game continued.

In the 15th inning, Russ Snyder became Cheney's 20th victim. And after a home run from Washington outfielder Bud Zipfel in the top of the 16th inning, Cheney finished the game strong, striking out pinch-hitter Dick Williams to end the game. The last pitch was his 228th.

"Back in those days," Cheney later reflected, "You finished what you started."

Unfortunately, Cheney's career was soon finished. He built off the momentum of his big game with an excellent start to 1963, winning eight early games before throwing a pitch on July 11th when, as he recalled, "it felt like someone had a knife and ripped me down the forearm." Cheney was ultimately diagnosed with epicondylitis, better known as tennis elbow. He won one more game in his major-league career.

The next pitcher to strike out 20 batters in a game came from a troubled background. His parents split before he was a year old, he lost a stepfather to a heart attack at age eight, and so, the lanky young Texan grew up idolizing his older brother. The big brother taught the young pitcher a lesson: "Either you're a winner or you're a failure." That lesson would both haunt and define the checkered career of Roger Clemens.

Clemens would not be a failure on the mound. He starred in college, he starred in the minor leagues, and he arrived in the big leagues with the Boston Red Sox in 1984. Clemens won nine games in '84 and seven more in 1985. He was still establishing himself on the evening of April 29, 1986, when the Red Sox took on the Seattle Mariners in Fenway Park. It was time to show the world exactly what a winner he could be.

Clemens was 3-0 on the young season, and was showcasing the repertoire of pitches that would make him a legend. Mariner outfielder Phil Bradley later called Clemens "a power control pitcher." Bradley admitted, "He had velocity, he had four pitches and he could truly throw all four for strikes. . . . [H]is out pitch was basically any pitch he wanted to throw you."

On April 29th, Clemens had many out pitches. He opened the game with a fastball strike to shortstop Spike Owen. On the next pitch, a fastball got away and broke high, as Owen hit the dirt. The eighth pitch of the at-bat was a swing and a miss at strike three. Phil Bradley swung and missed at strike three and so did Ken Phelps. Clemens was on fire.

Two more strikeouts came in the second inning, one in the third, and then all three Mariners in the fourth, with all three going down swinging, one after a lucky break for Clemens's strikeout totals when first baseman Don Baylor dropped an easy foul popup. Jim Presley, who led off the fifth inning, became Clemens's 10th strikeout, and was followed by Iván Calderón and Danny Tartabull. Clemens made it eight in a row by striking out the first two batters of the sixth inning. Even after Spike Owen somehow made contact—which happened on a fair ball only ten times all game long—Clemens had 14 strikeouts in six innings.

Two more strikeouts in the seventh, two more strikeouts in the eighth—onward marched Clemens in pounding the Mariners into a record level of futility. Staked to a 3–1 lead, Clemens, despite having thrown 124 pitches, returned to the mound for the ninth inning in search of baseball history.

His fifth pitch to the leadoff man, Spike Owen, was another rising fastball, and Owen hacked wildly and missed for the 19th strikeout of the game. Phil Bradley came up next, and after getting ahead in the count 2-0, watched the next three pitches slice through the plate and into history. Clemens had reached 20 strikeouts. The game ended with an anticlimax, as Ken Phelps grounded to short.

Clemens finished the game without allowing a walk, and without even reaching three balls to a batter after the fourth inning. He had been masterful. In the afterglow of the performance, the Associated Press noted, "If setting the [nine-inning] record for strikeouts in a game is any measure of a career, Roger Clemens is heading for the Hall of Fame."

It would prove to be much more complicated. Clemens was a brilliant pitcher—even striking out 20 batters in a game *again* in 1996, and again without walking a single opposing batter. His pitching excellence is compromised by the controversy surrounding his alleged use of performance-enhancing drugs, and the perjury charges he faced over his testimony regarding the same. Ultimately, his own hubris clouds the issue of Clemens's legacy.

For Cubs rookie Kerry Wood, his greatest game wasn't so much making a statement about being the best as just making a statement about being a major-league pitcher. The 6'5" Texan had been the fourth overall pick of the 1995 MLB Draft, and had progressed through the minors, but always struggled with wildness. His jumping fastball and hopping breaking pitches gave batters fits, but also tended to elude the strike zone. In four major-league starts, Wood had twice been knocked out before he could complete five innings—including a 1⅔-inning, seven-run nightmare on April 24th. In another game, he could only go five innings, because he needed 102 pitches to complete that much of the game. He had a 5.89 ERA and had walked 12 batters in 18⅓ big-league innings.

On May 6th, he faced the first-place Houston Astros at Wrigley Field. Astros reliever C. J. Nitkowski later remembered talking with an excited Cub fan before the game, who told him he had made 16 "K" signs for Wood strikeouts, and he wondered if it would be enough. Nitkowski told the fan it would be more than enough. Against a lineup that included future Hall of Famers Craig Biggio and Jeff Bagwell, All-Star Moises Alou, and outfielder Derek Bell, who was hitting almost .400, that was a smart bet. However, it was a losing bet.

Wood himself didn't see his big game coming, later commenting, "I know I warmed up bad and didn't feel very good at all, and didn't throw too many strikes." Indeed, he began the game auspiciously, with a first-pitch fastball that overran catcher Sandy Martínez and drilled home-plate umpire Jerry Meals in the mask. But that was almost the last mistake he made in the game.

In the top of the first, Wood struck out Biggio, Bell, and Bagwell. Two Hall of Famers and a guy flirting with .400 all looked completely clueless. It would be that kind of day. In the second inning, Jack Howell and Alou struck out, making five in a row before Dave Clark flied out. The only hit of the Astros' day was a shaky infield single by Ricky Gutiérrez to lead off the third inning. It could have been an error (by third baseman Kevin Orie) and probably should have been an out. In any case, it was one of exactly two baserunners Houston would manage. Wood struck out one more Astro in the third, giving him six for the game.

He got stronger, whiffing two in the fourth inning and fanning the side in the fifth frame. He managed his 12th strikeout in the sixth inning and hit Craig Biggio in the elbow for the Astros' last baserunner of the day.

Bagwell, Howell, and Alou all went down swinging in the seventh inning, looking foolish on curveballs and tardy on fastballs. Wood needed only 13 pitches to strike out the side again in the eighth inning, which gave him 18 strikeouts.

In the ninth inning, shortstop Bill Spiers led off by swinging and missing at a 1-2 breaking ball for Wood's 19th strikeout. After a groundball from Biggio, a final two-strike slider to Derek Bell became the 20th whiff of the day. Wood had tied the nine-inning record and became the third 20-strikeout pitcher—in his fifth career start. He also set the major-league record for strikeouts by a rookie.

The praise was immediate and effusive. Astros manager Larry Dierker commented, "He reminded me of the first time I saw Ryan. . . . He's going to pitch a no-hitter and maybe a few no-hitters. His stuff is the real item." Cubs manager Jim Riggleman admitted, "That game was one for the memory banks. The best I've ever seen pitched by anybody."

That performance started a memorable run for Wood that culminated in striking out 233 hitters over 166⅔ innings and winning the 1998 NL Rookie of the Year, but it was a peak he could not hold. He would later admit that he felt a twinge in his elbow on the final slider of his 20-strikeout game, his 122nd pitch. Seven more times in that rookie season, Wood remained on the mound for more than 120 pitches. Wood missed a month of the regular season, and then his elbow gave out in the spring of 1999. He missed the entire season.

Wood rebounded to strike out over 200 batters in four of his next five seasons, winning 14 games and leading the NL in strikeouts in 2003 with 266. But he started his last game in 2006, when he was limited to

19⅔ innings for the year. Wood hung around as a reliever, becoming an All-Star closer for the 2008 Cubs, but he retired in 2012, winning 86 games in the major leagues and a World Series with the 2010 Yankees.

For his part, Wood accepted his demise, telling an interviewer years later that the damage he felt in his elbow that May day was "worth it." A decade after Wood's game, manager Riggleman wondered, "Did we take advantage of having this great guy and pitch him too much? Who knows? It certainly was not anybody's intent. . . . If I had to do it over, I'd have done some things different. I only lost one diamond, but it was the Hope diamond, you know?"

Astros catcher Brad Ausmus also weighed in, saying of Wood's game, "It set the bar too high."

Indeed, Wood's masterpiece moved the bar enough that the wild rookie trying to prove that he belonged left the mound as the Hope Diamond—one of the few pitchers who managed to amass 20 strikeouts.

Since Wood, two more 20-strikeout pitchers have emerged. Arizona lefty Randy Johnson struck out 20 Reds in 2001, but like poor Tom Cheney, didn't get the nine-inning decision. The game went 11 innings, but Johnson left after the ninth, having thrown 124 pitches to strike out 20 batters. Because the game went extra innings, Johnson's masterpiece isn't classified with those of Clemens, Wood, or the other pitcher to since strike out 20.

In 2016, right-hander Max Scherzer of the Washington Nationals joined the group in an interleague game against his old team, the Detroit Tigers. Scherzer had 18 strikeouts in eight innings, and fanned two batters in the ninth to reach the mark. He did give up a home run that trimmed his lead to 3–2 in the process, but after another hit, induced a groundout to end the game. For his part, Scherzer enjoyed the moment, telling reporters, "Tonight . . . was a special night. Because, I mean, the strikeouts are sexy. And to be able to punch out 20—it's sexy."

It is sexy—although it is also an exercise in stubbornness, a statement about being a winner, and a means of establishing oneself as more of a diamond than a wild kid just up from the minor leagues. High pitch counts aside, generations of young pitchers will take aim at the 20-strikeout club. Pity the hitters who will flail and miss.

CHAPTER 4

TWO GRAND SLAMS IN ONE GAME

Number of Times Accomplished: 13.

First Instance: Tony Lazzeri, New York Yankees, May 24, 1936.

Most Recent Instance: Josh Willingham, Florida Marlins, July 27, 2009.

Likely Suspects: Frank Robinson is the big name on this list, but although he hit 586 career home runs, he hit only eight grand slams. Robin Ventura, who had 294 career home runs and 18 grand slams, is the second most prolific slugger of the group.

Surprises: Tony Cloninger hit 11 career home runs—but two were grand slams, and they both came in the same game. Most of the players on this list were guys with reasonable power.

Likelihood of Additional Occurrences: Between 1970 and 1995, there was a 25-year gap between two-slam games, but that aside, there is generally a pretty consistent record of hitters dropping a double-slam game.

In many ways, the grand slam is the perfect fulfillment of skill and opportunity. Even the greatest hitter alive can't load the bases in front of himself in order to tee off on a four-run blast . . . and at the same time, the bases being loaded generally makes a pitcher even more reluctant to make a mistake. Barry Bonds's 762 home runs included only 11 grand slams. Rudy York, however, managed a dozen slams without ever topping 35 homers in a season, and ended his career with a relatively modest total of 277 homers.

So if there's a component of luck (and of skill) in hitting a grand slam, what about hitting two in the same game? Well, a double shot of both skill (two *homers* in a game is no small thing) and luck (having six teammates on base ahead of a hitter in two at-bats isn't exactly typical) are in order. The two-slam sluggers below had measures of both in order to make their own bids at history.

Tony Lazzeri is a Hall of Famer largely because of being part of the greatest dynasty in baseball history. As a second-year player, Lazzeri batted sixth and played second base for the 1927 New York Yankees, perhaps the greatest team of all time. Hitting behind Hall of Famers Earle Combs, Babe Ruth, and Lou Gehrig, Lazzeri had plenty of chances to drive in runs. Indeed, he knocked in over 100 runs seven times between 1926 and 1936. A career .292 hitter, Lazzeri never eclipsed 18 home runs in a single season.

In 1936, Lazzeri was 33 years old and in the waning days of his prime. *The Sporting News* reported, "Before the season, it was generally believed that this might prove to be Lazzeri's final season in the majors." They weren't far off. He would play in only 207 big-league games after the season, and frequently batted eighth in '36. But he knocked in 109 runs, and the Yankees eventually won another World Series. Ruth was retired, but young Joe DiMaggio joined the lineup, and future Hall of Fame catcher Bill Dickey hit fifth. And on May 25, 1936, the guy known as "Poosh 'Em Up" Tony had one incredible game.

Against the lowly Philadelphia A's, in the second inning, Lazzeri came up with Dickey, Ben Chapman, and George Selkirk on base ahead of him. He cracked George Turbeville's pitch deep into the bleachers at Shibe Park for a grand slam. The Yankees had trailed 2–0 when Lazzeri struck the first blast in what became a 25–2 thumping.

In the fifth inning, with the score 10–2, Dickey tripled, and Chapman and Selkirk walked. Against reliever Herman Fink, Lazzeri struck again with a blast to left field for a second grand slam. Lazzeri added a third homer, a solo shot, in the seventh inning, and tripled in two more runs in the eighth inning—the *New York Times* noting that he "missed a fourth [home run] by a matter of inches."

There was tremendous enthusiasm over Lazzeri's feat. "It will be many a day before another player will twice in the same game hit a home run with the bases filled," opined the *Brooklyn Daily Eagle*. While Lazzeri would never hit another grand slam in the major leagues, there would be others who joined the double-slam group sooner rather than later.

⁓

The most unforeseeable of double-slam sluggers is doubtlessly Braves pitcher Tony Cloninger. Yes, pitcher. Cloninger was a hard-throwing six-foot right-hander from North Carolina who won 113 games between 1961 and 1972. And yes, in one game in 1966, he hit two grand slams.

Cloninger was a mainstay on the mid-60s Braves. He won 19 games in 1964, and the following season, went 24-11 with a 3.29 ERA. In 1966, the Braves moved to Atlanta and Cloninger, while not as sharp as the previous two seasons, was on his way to winning 14 games when he ended up making history at the plate.

Cloninger was a decent hitting pitcher, boasting a career .192 average in 621 at-bats. He did manage 11 career home runs, but he also struck out 161 times on his way to a career line of .192/.205/.277. On July 3, 1966, Cloninger was hitting .200 for the season, but those who studied the tea leaves might have noticed a two-home-run game on June 16th against the Mets.

On the mound, Cloninger was 8-7, with a 4.35 ERA. The Braves were taking on the Giants in Candlestick Park on July 3rd. The Giants started lefty Joe Gibbon, but Gibbon was already gone by the time Cloninger first came to bat. At that point, the score was 3–0, and Frank Bolling, Woody Woodward, and Denis Menke were on base. On a 3-2 pitch from reliever Bob Priddy, Cloninger connected with a high drive to center field, which cleared the 410 sign in Candlestick Park for the pitcher's first career grand slam.

He wasn't finished, because in the fourth inning, with a 9–0 lead, he came up again with the bases loaded, again with Bolling, Woodward, and Menke. He drove an 0-1 pitch from reliever Ray Sadecki out to right field for his second grand slam of his career—and of the last four innings.

Cloninger singled in another run in the eighth inning, and his final line for the day included a complete-game, seven-hit, three-run performance on the pitching mound, and a 3-for-5 day with nine RBIs at the plate.

After the game, Cloninger soaked up his big day. "I always told [Braves manager] Bobby [Bragan] I could hit," he told reporters after the game. He admitted, "It was a thrill to hit the first grand slam. But the second was unbelievable."

He recalled that Braves teammate Joe Torre had asked him afterward if he remembered touching the bases, and Tony confessed, "I didn't remember a single one."

Cloninger's big game improved his season's batting average by 36 points and his slugging percentage by a margin of .133. He ended the year hitting .234 with five home runs and 23 RBIs—good enough work that he was called on to pinch-hit seven times during the season. His season OPS of .675 outreached starting second baseman Woodward's .650 mark.

Years after his double-slam game, Cloninger looked back and joked, "Funny thing, nobody asked me about my pitching."

In case hitting two grand slams in a single game wasn't difficult enough, how about dividing the opportunity by nine innings? Only once in the imposing history of Major League Baseball has a player hit two grand slams in a single inning. Suffice it to say that Fernando Tatís had a third inning to remember on April 23, 1999.

Tatís was a 24-year-old third baseman from the Dominican Republic, obtained by the St. Louis Cardinals in a trade from the Texas Rangers the previous summer. He was a highly touted prospect who was brought in to protect St. Louis slugger Mark McGwire. As McGwire set the single-season home-run record in 1998, Tatís had a solid couple of months quietly hitting behind him.

In early 1999, Tatís was having a solid start to his first full season as a Cardinal, hitting .250 with four home runs in the first couple weeks of the season. On April 23rd, the Cardinals were in Los Angeles, facing the Dodgers and pitcher Chan Ho Park. Tatís had 23 career home runs and had never hit a grand slam. How quickly that changed.

The Dodgers led 2–0 after two innings, but in the top of the third, Darren Bragg singled, Edgar Rentería was hit by a pitch, and McGwire hit a single to load the bases. On a 2-0 pitch from Park, Tatís blasted a drive not only over the left field wall, but beyond the left field bullpen at Dodger Stadium for a no-doubt grand slam. Dodger left fielder Gary Sheffield never even moved.

As the Cardinals continued to batter Park, Tatís came to bat again in the third inning, this time with the score at 7–2 and the bases once again loaded. On a 3-2 pitch, Park hung a slider, and Tatís crushed a line drive into left-center field and the history books, with his second grand slam of his career. And of the third inning. Tatís not only became the first single-inning double-slammer, but in so doing, he set a record for most RBIs in an inning with eight. While Tatís was 0-for-3 the rest of the way, the damage was done in St. Louis's 12–5 victory.

"I just want to enjoy the moment," Tatís told reporters after the game. "I can't believe it. I know this will probably never happen for me again."

He retraced his amazing inning, admitting, "I didn't think the second ball would go out. I still can't believe I did it."

For his part, Cardinals manager Tony La Russa expressed his own awe at the moment. "It's a thrill to witness big league history," said La Russa. "I don't care if you're a fan or sitting in the dugout or whatever. What have they got, 100 years of baseball and this is the first time it's ever been done? Wow."

Tatís hit .298 with 34 home runs and 107 RBI in 1999. He began struggling with injuries the following year, and never surpassed 18 home runs or 400 at-bats in a season again. In nearly 20 years since his historic inning, Tatís is still the sole player to hit two grand slams in one inning. For the player who was traded to support one of the most powerful sluggers in history, it was appropriate that in his moment of glory, he far outshone McGwire . . . and everybody else who ever played Major League Baseball.

⌒

The last player to have a double-slam game was well-traveled outfielder Josh Willingham. A strong Alabama native, Willingham did one thing especially well—hit for power. He didn't hit for an especially high average (career mark of .253), he was something of a defensive liability, and he didn't become a full-time big leaguer until he was 27 years old. Accordingly, Willingham bounced around—three full years with the Florida Marlins, two with the Nationals, one with the A's, two and a half with the Twins, and the end of his career with the Kansas City Royals. But wherever he played, Willingham hit home runs—195 of them, to be exact, averaging 28 per 162 games over his career.

On July 27, 2009, Willingham and his last-place Washington Nationals were in Milwaukee to play the Brewers. Willingham hit sixth and played right field that night. His game was uneventful early. He doubled in the second inning, and grounded back to the pitcher in the fourth.

In the fifth inning, the Nationals trailed 2–0, but had rallied to tie the game when Willingham came to bat. Cristian Guzmán, Ryan Zimmerman, and Adam Dunn were on base, and on starter Jeff Suppan's first pitch, Willingham cracked a flyball to left field that carried well over the outfield wall for a grand slam.

In case anyone missed the moment, Willingham provided an encore performance in the very next inning. The Brewers trimmed the lead to 6–5, but Washington had already answered with three runs when Willingham came to bat again. Zimmerman, Dunn, and Nick Johnson were aboard the bases, and Willingham cranked the second pitch from reliever Mark DiFelice out a few feet to the right of his first blast, for his second grand slam in consecutive innings.

The Nationals rolled from there, winning 14–6, but most of the discussion after the game centered on Willingham. He told reporters, "[W]hen I was coming up to the plate the second time, I knew I had a chance to do it. Obviously, I wasn't thinking about doing it; I wasn't trying to do it. But when the game is over and you look back on it—for years to come, when I look back on it—it's going to be something that will be very special."

Willingham went on to comment, "That's the beautiful thing about baseball. You never know what can happen."

As if an extra illustration of the same principle was needed, that same evening, Fernando Tatís hit a grand slam for the New York Mets in their game—the last of his big-league career.

Some day soon, another player—given the opportunity to hit twice with the bases loaded—will demonstrate baseball's uncertainty yet again.

CHAPTER 5

FOUR STRIKEOUTS IN AN INNING

Number of Times Accomplished: 87.

First Instance: Bobby Mathews, Philadelphia Athletics, September 30, 1885.

Most Recent Instance: Zack Godley, Arizona Diamondbacks, August 13, 2017.

Likely Suspects: Four Hall of Famers are on the list—Walter Johnson, Don Drysdale, Bob Gibson, and Phil Niekro.

Surprises: 1990s reliever Derek Wallace pitched just 33 big-league innings and had 20 strikeouts, but had four in one inning.

Likelihood of Additional Occurrences: With four instances in 2017, this group will likely grow to a triple-digit count soon. One intriguing question is whether anyone will equal Chuck Finley's record of three four-K innings.

It sounds like some sort of bizarre science-fiction fantasy. How do you strike out four batters in an inning? The answer lies in Rule 5.05(a)(2), which provides that if a third strike is not caught, and first base is either unoccupied, or is occupied with two out, then the batter can run for first base. If that discussion doesn't work, ask any surviving Brooklyn Dodger fan about Mickey Owen, and be regaled with the story of his dropping a third strike in the 1941 World Series. With a dropped (or just plain missed) third strike from a catcher, a fourth strikeout is now possible. Even a fifth is possible, although that hasn't happened yet.

So what kind of pitcher gets four strikeouts in an inning? Many, many different kinds, but the common thread is having good enough stuff to strike out four batters—and to elude his own catcher on a strike-out. Beyond that, every one of the 87 four-strikeout innings has its own peculiar story.

The first four-strikeout inning came from the right arm of Bobby Mathews, a 5'5" bundle of fire who won 30 games (exactly 30) three straight seasons from 1883 to 1885. Mathews was one of the first pitchers to throw a curveball and master a spitball, and he used his entire repertoire to win 297 big-league games. While the records are far from clear, perhaps a particularly sharp spitter or curve was to credit/blame for a missed third strike, allowing the first four-strikeout inning.

On September 30, 1885, Mathews took the mound against the American Association's Pittsburgh Alleghenys. Not much is known of the game. The *Philadelphia Inquirer* reported that the game "was dull and stupid, devoid of any commendable feature, barring a good throw by Stovey to the plate." The *Pittsburgh Post-Gazette* concurred, saying the game was "dull, uninteresting, and poorly-played." Apparently baseball history did not avoid the stigma of dull stupidity. The game was a seven-inning game, and Mathews somehow allowed both Pittsburgh runs during his four-strikeout inning. The *Inquirer* notes that a triple was hit by Pittsburgh's Pop Smith and that there were "bad throws of missed third strikes by Milligan." Note the plural—two of Mathews's four strikeouts were missed third strikes, so he theoretically could have had a five-strikeout inning. Another source indicates Charlie Eden, Art Whitney, Fred Mann, and Frank Ringo were the strikeout victims, with Whitney and Ringo both reaching first by a missed third strike.

However it happened, Mathews struck out four Pittsburgh batters in the seventh inning. This was no small feat for a pitcher whose career totals reflect 1,528 strikeouts—in 4,956 innings. Mathews was on his last legs when he accomplished his apparently not-so-memorable inning. He won only 16 more games before he was out of the big leagues. Mathews spent a few seasons as an umpire, but was rapidly declining due to failing health, and passed away in 1898.

In sharp contrast to the unappreciated season-ending game when Mathews picked up a four-strikeout inning, in the 1908 World Series

Chicago Cubs pitcher Orval Overall had a four-strikeout inning on baseball's greatest possible stage. Overall is a forgotten part of the Cubs' dynasty of the end of the first decade of the 20th century. Overall, a 6'2", California-bred right-hander, was traded by the Cincinnati Reds to the Cubs in mid-1906, and he promptly settled in behind Mordecai Brown as a Cub mainstay. Known for a wicked curveball and noted by one biographer to have had "a reputation as a 'money pitcher,'" Overall shone in postseason play.

The Cubs lost the 1906 World Series, but Overall allowed just two runs in 12 innings of relief. In 1907, he pitched two complete games against the Tigers. The Cubs won as he allowed two earned runs in his 18 innings that fall. But in 1908, once the Cubs had overcome the Giants in a one-game playoff for the NL pennant, Overall was at his best.

After a brief and ineffective relief appearance in World Series Game 1, Overall held the Tigers to four hits and one run in a complete-game performance in the Series' second game. With the Cubs up 3–1, Overall got the start in Game 5.

In the bottom of the first inning, Overall opened the game by walking Matty McIntyre. He struck out Charley O'Leary before allowing a single to Sam Crawford. With runners at first and second and one out, the Tigers brought Ty Cobb to the plate. Overall bore down—and made history. He struck out Cobb, who the next day's *Chicago Tribune* noted was "reaching for his fast drop." Overall then struck out Detroit's Claude Rossman, although the third strike was a wild pitch that allowed Rossman to reach first and thus loaded the bases. The *Tribune* called the third strike "a drop so sharp and pronounced that it struck the ground and shot past Kling to the stand." Next was Germany Schaefer, who also fell victim to the curveball, and when Overall struck him out, he had the only four-strikeout inning in World Series history—then or since. "Not often does a pitcher get a chance to strike out four men in one inning," wrote the *Tribune*.

The Tigers were finished. They got only two more hits off Overall, and no runs, as the righty struck out 10 for the game. The Cubs won

2–0, and claimed what turned out to be their last World Series title for 108 years.

Overall improved his record from 15-11 in the 1908 season to 20-11 the following year, but the Cubs could not catch Pittsburgh in the National League pennant race. Overall won only 16 more major-league games thereafter, finishing his career 108-71, with a sparkling 2.26 ERA. After baseball, Overall ended up as a bank executive back in his native California.

~

Not every baseball feat is enveloped in a cocoon of memorable brilliance. While most of the feats considered in this book are the sort that players want to sit around and reconjure after their playing days are over, sometimes it's really quite the other way around. Take the story of Charlie Hough, for instance. Once a promising young pitcher in the Dodger organization, Hough hurt his arm in the late 60s. He simply didn't tell anybody, and learned to throw the knuckleball, which kept him in the major leagues from 1970 until 1994.

Over his career, Hough saw pretty much everything. He was an ace reliever (saving 18 and 22 games for the 1976 and 1977 Dodgers), an All-Star as a starting pitcher (1986, when he went 17-10 with the Texas Rangers), and mostly a survivor. His career record? 216 wins, 216 losses. But one thing that Hough likely doesn't spend much time remembering is his four-strikeout inning.

It was July 4, 1988. In his last start, Hough had pitched 11 shut-out innings to beat the Seattle Mariners, throwing 163 pitches. He had pitched eight consecutive scoreless innings before that game, for a streak of 19 in a row. But as anyone who has seen a knuckleball can attest, consistency is not the pitch's strong suit.

On July 4th, Hough's knuckleball was everywhere. He lasted just 2⅔ innings, surrendering eight runs with six walks. It took him 101 pitches to labor through that sub-three-inning start. And he struck out six batters, four of them in the first inning.

Hough opened the game by walking the Yankees' Rickey Henderson. He struck out Claudell Washington, who nonetheless reached first base on a passed ball. On a 3-2 pitch, Don Mattingly crushed a three-run homer to right field off Hough. Hough then struck out Jack Clark looking, Dave Winfield swinging, and Mike Pagliarulo looking. He gave up three runs and threw 40 pitches in the inning, but he also struck out four batters.

Hough was blasted for three runs in the second and had allowed another in the third before he was pulled (an inherited runner also scored). The Yankees won the game, 13–2. Hough saw little to be pleased with after the game.

"That's the worst command of the knuckler I've had all season," he told the media. "I wasn't throwing it right. I was trying to find my release point and the pitch was all over the place."

Funnily enough, the assessment was not necessarily shared by the Yankees. Mattingly, who homered and grounded out against Hough, told reporters after the game that he found the knuckleball hard to hit.

"I thought he had a nasty one," he said. "When he's throwing like that, you just hope to get one that doesn't move too much."

So not only is the knuckleball unpredictable, but sometimes, the hitter and pitcher can't agree on whether it's working. Hough struck out 2,362 batters in his career, but he never managed four in an inning at any other time. Fortunately, the career included many memorable moments, such as becoming the first pitcher to take the mound in the history of the Florida Marlins in 1993 at the ripe age of 45. Hough won the game that day, so he probably remembers it a bit better than his four-strikeout nightmare.

The king of the four-strikeout inning, the man who performed the feat three times before anyone else performed it twice (three players have since had two such innings), was amazing before he started striking out scads of batters—simply by virtue of his presence on the field. Not so long before he was making baseball history, Chuck Finley had nearly walked away from the game.

Finley was a skinny, wild, left-handed pitching prospect out of high school from West Monroe, Louisiana, when he almost gave up on the game. He played a season of college baseball at Louisiana Tech, and walked 33 batters in 26⅔ innings. He was tired of baseball, tired of school, tired of being away from home. He quit. His father decided to make the decision to quit a little harder—mostly by employing Chuck in their family's 200-acre tree nursery, planting trees and lawns for 10-hour days at pay of $4.75 per hour. Chuck got the message. He walked on at Northeast Louisiana (which later became Louisiana-Monroe), and improved in a hurry—harnessing his fastball, learning a quality curveball, and managing to get drafted by the California Angels. The old phobia resurfaced for Finley, who recalled, "I was really happy [at Northeast]. . . . I thought the biggest adjustment for me if I was drafted would be leaving home." Indeed, his parents had to counsel him to give professional baseball a shot, to see more of the country while he was still young.

Finley would soon see lots of parts of the country. After just 41 innings of minor-league baseball, the big leagues beckoned. Finley never looked back. He took his early lumps, but in 1989, his fourth season in the big leagues, he went 16-9 and earned a spot on the American League All-Star team. Finley followed that performance by winning 18 games in both 1990 and 1991. He was quickly established as one of the best left-handed pitchers in baseball. And as Finley added a forkball (alternatively referred to as a split-finger fastball) to his repertoire, he also gained a reputation for throwing singularly nasty stuff—apparently sometimes almost as hard to catch as to hit.

It wasn't until 1999 when Finley had a four-strikeout inning. On May 12th, he and the Angels traveled to Yankee Stadium to face a talented New York squad. In the game's third inning, Finley gave up a single to Shane Spencer. He then struck out Scott Brosius on three pitches. The next batter, Joe Girardi, reached base on an error. With Chuck Knoblauch at bat, Finley wild-pitched Spencer and Girardi up to second and third. He then struck out Knoblauch on a pitch in the dirt. The next batter was Derek Jeter, who swung and missed at another third strike in the dirt, which eluded catcher Charlie O'Brien enough that Jeter scampered to first, although the other runners held. Finley then worked out of the bases-loaded jam by striking out Paul O'Neill on a split-finger fastball for his fourth strikeout of the inning. After that, what else could the Yankees do? They lost to Finley 1–0, as he gave up three hits and struck out 11 in eight innings.

Paul O'Neill told reporters after the game, "When he's on like that, it is a tough game to play, no doubt about it."

Angels manager Terry Collins was more effusive, noting, "That was the best forkball and the best location of his fastball that I've seen." The manager continued, "When I need a big game from a pitcher, this guy has come through."

On August 15, 1999, just three months after his first four-strikeout inning, Finley struck again. In Detroit against the Tigers, he wasted little time. After the Angels erupted for four runs in the top of the first inning, in the bottom of the frame, Detroit leadoff batter Kimera Bartee singled up the middle. Second hitter Deivi Cruz struck out, although Bartee moved up on a wild pitch (Cruz was still out). Juan Encarnación then struck out. Dean Palmer whiffed on a 1-2 pitch, but it eluded catcher Bengie Molina for a wild pitch that allowed Palmer to take first, with Bartee moving up to third base. Tony Clark then whiffed at a 1-2 pitch for Finley's fourth strikeout of the first inning.

Finley worked 6⅔ innings in the game, before departing due to a blister on his middle finger, allowing two runs and striking out a dozen batters in a 10–2 Angels win. Finley had struggled over the month before the trade deadline, and was relieved to pitch well again.

Asked about becoming the first pitcher to repeat a four-strikeout inning, Finley quipped, "Maybe that will end up in one of those video trivia machines in some bar somewhere. It's one of those freaky things."

Freakier still was a third four-K frame. After the season, Finley became a Cleveland Indian. In his third Cleveland start, on April 16, 2000, Finley had another big inning at home against the Texas Rangers. It looked like that inning might lose him the game, though.

In the third inning of a scoreless tie, Finley allowed a single to Luis Alicea. Tom Evans then struck out swinging, and Royce Clayton followed suit. With two out, Alicea stole second, and then went to third on a passed ball from a curveball that had struck out Ranger Chad Curtis. Alicea was then driven in on a single from Iván Rodríguez, before Rafael Palmeiro struck out looking for the fourth strikeout of the inning.

That 1–0 lead held until the bottom of the ninth, when the Indians put up a pair of runs to get Finley his first Cleveland victory. He had pitched nine innings, allowing five hits and one unearned run with 13 strikeouts to his credit.

"I was throwing everything today," an excited Finley said after the game. "I think I surprised them. I had a freaking buffet going for me, today."

He also had baseball history. Finley won a total of 200 big-league games, amassed 2,610 strikeouts, and is still the only three-time four-strikeout pitcher. That's pretty impressive for the small-town kid from Louisiana who almost gave up before he got started.

Chapter 6

POSITION PLAYERS PITCHING

Number of Times Accomplished: Around 500, although it is impossible to be exact because the lines between pitchers and position players were sometimes blurred in old-time baseball. It has happened slightly over 200 times since World War II, which is a bit more precise.

First Instance: So many position players pitched and vice versa in 1876 that it would be difficult to even guess who was first—or whether they were legitimately regarded as a pitcher or not.

Most Recent Instance: J. D. Davis, Houston Astros, September 9, 2017 (⅔ IP, 1 H, 0 R, 1 BB, 2 K).

Biggest Names: People like Ted Williams, Stan Musial, and Wade Boggs have gotten their shot on the mound. Sometimes, it's guys with big arms who get a try like outfielders Rocky Colavito or Jeff Francoeur.

Surprises: Who isn't a surprise as a position-player pitcher? Twins catcher Chris Gimenez is one surprise—based off the fact that he's pitched nine times since 2014. Hard to say why—Gimenez has allowed 11 hits and eight earned runs in his nine innings.

Likelihood of Additional Occurrences: Wherever there's a blowout or a bizarrely long game, there'll be another position player pitching.

Inside the hearts of most baseball fans, there lurks a fantasy of taking the pitching mound for their favorite team, surprising the crowd with their secretly brilliant pitches, and hurling their team toward glory. The surprising thing is that apparently, many major-league position players hold that dream too. Few of them fare much better than fans would.

In the early days of baseball, players routinely transitioned from the mound to the field and back again. Early Hall of Famers like John Montgomery Ward and Babe Ruth were among the many who switched fairly seamlessly from one side of baseball to the other.

But as baseball eras have come and gone and pitching has become increasingly specialized, position players tend to take the mound in only one of two scenarios—either their team trails by a massive gap and a manager protects his depleted pitching staff by asking a fielder to pitch for an inning or two, or else a game extends to a high number of innings, and the same concerns about wearing down the pitchers lead to a position player on the mound despite a competitive situation. The first scenario is more common than the second, but in either situation, the few fans who brave a blowout or a late, late night are generally rewarded with some interesting baseball memories. Indeed, that seems to be the one consistent thread about position players pitching—it makes for a great story.

Once upon a time, the Cardinals had a young left-handed pitching prospect from Donora, Pennsylvania. He worked his way up through the minor leagues, battling control troubles. In 1940, the prospect was 18-5 with a 2.62 ERA in the Florida State League, but late in the season, playing the outfield, young Stan Musial attempted a diving catch and injured his shoulder, which finished his career as a pitcher. Well, it almost finished his career as a pitcher.

Of course, Musial fulfilled his Hall of Fame destiny as an outfielder instead of as a pitcher, winning seven batting titles on his way to 3,630 hits. But in 1952, as Musial tracked his sixth hitting crown, he would get a minor assist—from Musial the pitcher.

Honestly, the ploy was more about publicity and less about baseball. Musial's Cardinals weren't in the running for the NL pennant, but Stan the Man held a decent lead on Cubs outfielder Frankie Baumholtz for the batting race. Cardinal manager Eddie Stanky, hoping to boost the sagging box office receipts for the season finale against the Cubs, announced that not only would Musial win the title, he would do it by shutting down Baumholtz with his pitching.

Musial entered the game at 193 for 575 (.3357). Baumholtz was 132 for 405 (.3259). Stanky was better with publicity than with math. The only way that Baumholtz could win the title was to go 5-for-5 (or better) while Musial simultaneously went 0-for-5 (or worse).

But in the game's opening inning, starting pitcher Harvey Haddix walked the first batter, which brought up Baumholtz. Stanky was true to his word, bringing in Musial from center field and shifting Haddix to the outfield. Musial took only a few warmup pitches, and despite having an arsenal that included a curve and a knuckleball, he kept his plan simple. Baumholtz, who was a left-handed hitter, countered the absurdity of the situation by batting right-handed. Musial threw a first-pitch fastball and Baumholtz hit it to third base, where Solly Hemus bobbled the ball for an error. Haddix returned to the mound, Musial went back to right field, and with the batting title now decided, the pitching ruse was over. Incidentally, Musial went 1-for-3 and Baumholtz went 1-for-4.

For his part, Musial later told *St. Louis Post-Dispatch* writer Bob Boerg that he regretted being involved in the whole publicity stunt. He admitted in 2002, "I wanted to get it over with."

Musial's experience aside, other Hall of Fame hitters couldn't wait to get on the mound. Another legendary hitter with five batting crowns and 3,010 hits to his credit, Boggs had perfected a knuckleball in his down time, and always wanted the opportunity to pitch. Years of persistence paid off on August 19, 1997, when Boggs talked Joe Torre into giving him an inning on the mound. The Yankees trailed the Angels 12–4 when Boggs took the mound.

Boggs told reporters after the game, "It's something that I've always wanted to do in my career, and I just never really had the opportunity." He also recalled that reliever Jeff Nelson told him, "We're second in the league in pitching. Don't screw it up."

Boggs didn't. Relying exclusively on the knuckleball, he quickly got ahead of Luis Alicea 0-2 before he walked him. Boggs then got Tim Salmon to ground into a force play to shortstop. He got another out when Garret Anderson grounded softly to second base. With two out and a runner on second, Boggs completed his dream inning by whiffing

Todd Greene to draw a loud ovation from the Angels fans and some good-humored laughter from the Yankee dugout.

Salmon gave Boggs credit, admitting, "All of a sudden, you get 0-2 and say, 'OK, this isn't so much fun anymore.'"

It was enough fun for Boggs that he got another relief outing in 1999, three days after he collected his 3,000th career hit. On August 10th, he worked another inning and a third, allowing three hits and a run, but adding another strikeout, this time Oriole Delino DeShields.

It won't match Boggs's lifetime batting average of .328, but his career ERA of 3.86 is nothing to sneeze at.

Position players pitching isn't all publicity stunts and Hall of Famers begging into a blowout. Sometimes, the position player is stuck trying to win the game. Such was the life of José Oquendo, who had one of the more Herculean outings of a position player on May 14, 1988.

Oquendo was a utility player for the Cardinals in the truest sense of the word. He literally played every position in the 1988 season, and in his 148 games played, it seemed like he rarely played the same spot twice. Oquendo began the May 14th game against the Atlanta Braves on the bench, and he entered in the ninth inning, playing first base. The game was 5–5, and as it moved into extra innings, Cardinals manager Whitey Herzog was burning through his bullpen.

Closer Todd Worrell pitched the 9th, 10th, and 11th innings, and the game was still tied. Bob Forsch entered for the 12th inning and worked three innings before being removed for a pinch-hitter. The game was still tied. Reliever Randy O'Neal pitched the 15th inning, but when the team went out for the 16th frame, Herzog made a move.

"I don't think [Herzog] thought that I could pitch," Oquendo later remembered. "But I was kind of durable, a guy who liked playing different positions, and we ran out of pitchers. I was the guy to waste."

Oquendo had pitched an inning in 1987, and allowed three runs then. But here he was in the 16th inning of a tie game, facing the middle of the Braves lineup. Ken Griffey doubled, and after Oquendo intentionally walked Gerald Perry, Ozzie Virgil singled to right field. Fortunately for Oquendo, right fielder Tom Brunansky threw Griffey out at the plate as he tried to score the lead run. Oquendo then got a pair of flyouts, and the game continued in a 5–5 tie.

The Cardinals did not score, so Oquendo returned to the mound. He allowed a single in the 17th, but otherwise emerged unscathed, helped by pitcher José DeLeón, who caught a flyball in left field. With the score still tied, Oquendo worked a third inning, and after getting two quick outs, he walked two batters. He ended the inning getting Ron Gant to line out to third base.

The Cardinals blew a bases-loaded, one-out opportunity in the 18th inning, and poor Oquendo returned to the mound once more.

His fourth inning was not a good one, as Ken Griffey doubled home two runs off Oquendo, and the Cardinals went down in order in the bottom of the 19th inning. Oquendo took the loss, working four innings, allowing four hits and a pair of runs. He walked six batters against one strikeout. Oquendo looked back and acknowledged the choppy nature of his outing.

"I got in a lot of trouble. I walked a lot of guys. It would be a big situation and . . . I'd throw a lot of split fingers and [get out of it]," he recalled.

The Braves gave Oquendo credit. Dale Murphy told reporters, "The guy had good stuff. He threw me some great forkballs." But Murphy admitted, "But if he had beaten us, I wouldn't have known what to say."

One thing Oquendo didn't say after the game was "No." The next day, Cardinal center fielder Willie McGee was a bit under the weather and Herzog asked Oquendo to play center field.

"We know our roles," Oquendo told the *St. Louis Post-Dispatch* a quarter-century after that game, "We can't say much in those situations."

Oquendo played on, though he told the paper later that "I was hurt from head to toe."

Oquendo pitched another inning in 1991. His final career pitching totals: 0-1 record, six innings, 10 hits, eight runs, nine walks, two strikeouts.

When the *Post-Dispatch* asked him in 2013 how long it took his arm to bounce back from his 65-pitch outing in 1988, Oquendo deadpanned, "It hasn't come back. That's why I don't throw [batting practice]."

⌒

If position players pitching in lost causes have a patron saint, it might be Doug Dascenzo. A 5'7" outfielder who spent most of his career with the Chicago Cubs, Dascenzo was notable for defensive excellence (he once went 241 games without an error) and good baserunning. Eventually, he became known for pitching.

Dascenzo said that he met most of the requirements for being drafted to pitch—he had pitched some in college, he was on the bench, and ultimately, he was willing. On June 12, 1990, with the Cubs trailing the Mets 19–6, Dascenzo got the call to pitch the ninth inning. The Mets had scored off the Cubs in every inning but one, but to the delight of the Wrigley Field partisans, Dascenzo quickly worked through an eight-pitch scoreless inning. Throwing a fastball that reached the low 80s, as well as a decent curveball and occasional changeup, Dascenzo got Howard Johnson to line out to center field. After he allowed a single to Dave Magadan, he got Tim Teufel to bounce into a 6-4-3 double play to end the inning and draw the applause of his home fans.

The Cubs knew when they were onto a good thing, because Dascenzo took the mound three more times in a month in 1991. First, he worked two hitless innings against the Dodgers on June 10th. Next, he added a scoreless inning against the Cardinals on June 28th (he walked José Oquendo, for whatever it's worth). His last outing was another scoreless inning on July 2nd, against the Pirates team that went on to win the NL East division. That game included Dascenzo's personal pitching highlight, when he found himself facing Barry Bonds.

"I couldn't get the first two pitches over the plate, which happened to be little spinning curveballs," said Dascenzo. "I had thrown change-ups in high school. . . . And so, I threw him a change-up. It was *perfect*. It was high enough. He swung right through it and fell down, and he started laughing and I started laughing."

Highlights aside, Dascenzo's big-league pitching days were soon over. His career record: five innings, three hits, no runs, two walks, two strikeouts.

"That's a pretty good line," Dascenzo admits with a chuckle. Still, his approach was based in a very fundamental modesty.

"You want to throw the ball over the plate," he said of his pitching experience. "My second biggest thought was that I didn't want to hurt anybody or I didn't want to get hurt. . . . If you can do that, you did your job."

These days, Dascenzo is a minor-league outfield and baserunning instructor for the Cubs. He was a career .234 hitter in 1,225 career at-bats. When asked if he minds being remembered for his pitching exploits, Dascenzo doesn't think twice. "Anything that happened at the major league level, it's cool," he admits. "You're very lucky to be fortunate to have the opportunity to play there . . . to play against the best players in the world." If that spirit isn't what makes position players pitching fun, then what is?

The trend still lives on. Well over a dozen position players pitched in 2017. Among the crowd, Cubs outfielder Jon Jay made his claim on Dascenzo's throne, working a scoreless inning despite throwing a 46-mile-per-hour changeup off a 58-mile-per-hour fastball. As long as there are one-sided games and managers who don't want to burn out pitchers, there will be a spot for position players pitching. It will continue to be good, clean fun—except to the hitters who make outs.

CHAPTER 7

HITTING FOR THE CYCLE

Number of Times Accomplished: 319.

First Instance: Curry Foley, Buffalo Bisons, May 25, 1882 (probably, although some other sources believe George Hall hit for the cycle in 1876).

Most Recent Instance: José Abreu, Chicago White Sox, September 9, 2017.

Likely Suspects: Plenty of Hall of Famers are on the list of hitters who had cycles, including Tris Speaker, Honus Wagner, Lou Gehrig (twice), Joe DiMaggio (twice), Ted Williams, Jackie Robinson, Stan Musial, George Brett (twice), and Cal Ripken Jr.

Surprises: Frankly, there are many average players on the list, but perhaps the biggest surprise is that none of the four players who are the all-time leaders in cycle games (with three) is a Hall of Famer (yet). Not sure that John Reilly, Bob Meusel, Babe Herman, or Adrian Beltre qualify as surprises, but they might not be the first guesses of players with the most cycle games.

Likelihood of Additional Occurrences: You have to go back to 1983 to find the last season that didn't include at least one player hitting for the cycle. Seven did in 2017.

The cycle is a completely illogical construct. Dave Kingman told reporters in 1972, after he hit for the cycle, that he had returned to the dugout and been told of his accomplishment, but admitted, "I didn't know what it meant. I had never done it, and I had never even heard of it." Unlike hitting four home runs in a game, there's no real particular benefit in hitting a single, double, triple, and home run in the same game—apart from the fact that it constitutes hitting for the cycle. Even in great games, the cycle can be easily frustrated. A player may need a double to hit for the cycle, but then wallop a second home run instead. So aside from the fact that it requires four hits in a game, and that by their nature, one or more have to be hit pretty well, there's a very fair amount of luck involved in hitting for the cycle. That said, luck can't explain the natural cycle (when the single, double, triple, and home run fall in that order) or the same player notching his two career cycle games 11 days apart. The cycle has a life of its own.

~

The first acknowledged big-league cycle was on May 25, 1882. There were no glowing tributes to the occurrence—for one thing, the first public acknowledgment of hitting for the cycle was still about 50 years away. For another, attention focused on Curry Foley's first at-bat, when he walloped a grand slam that actually cleared the left field fence at Riverside Grounds in Buffalo.

Foley was an Irish immigrant, a lefty, and a solid player as both a pitcher and an outfielder. Foley was 27-27 as a big-league pitcher, working most of his innings during his first years in the big leagues, 1879 and 1880. Even as his time on the mound became rare, he continued to be a productive player, batting .286 for his career.

On May 25, 1882, Foley's Buffalo Bisons took on the Cleveland Blues. Foley unwittingly became a part of history in an absolute thumping of a game. It was scoreless in the bottom of the first inning, when Foley came to bat with the bases loaded and two out. He blasted his grand slam off Cleveland pitcher George Washington Bradley, and the tone was set for the day. To this day, only nine players have hit for the cycle with their home run being a grand slam.

Foley tripled in an eight-run second inning, with all the runs coming with two outs in the inning. By the fifth inning, Buffalo led 14–0, and Foley's double played a role in adding yet another run. With one hit remaining, Foley singled during a five-run seventh inning, padding Buffalo's lead to 20–0. The final score was 20–1. Most of the postgame coverage from the *Buffalo Commercial* consisted of ragging pitcher Bradley, who the paper concluded "should no longer lay claim to the title of 'Professional Pitcher.'"

Poor Foley is barely mentioned in the account of what had to be his greatest individual game. He had only six career home runs, but hit .305 in 1882. Unfortunately, his success was fleeting, as he missed almost the entire 1883 season due to what subsequent biographers have concluded was "a particularly virulent form of rheumatoid arthritis." He played 23 games that season, and was finished in the major leagues.

To the extent that Foley is remembered, it is less for his cycle-hitting game than for his precedent as an injured player. The Buffalo team apparently felt that his injury was a ploy to jump to another team, so he was kept on their "reserve list," which restricted him from signing with another team. A few years later, when John Montgomery Ward attempted to unionize baseball, the "shameful" treatment of Curry Foley was one example he held up to baseball ownership of their misuses of the reserve system.

Foley dabbled in sportswriting in the later years of his life, but multiple sources indicate that he either could not walk or could barely walk by the end of the 1880s. Foley died in 1898 at the age of 42, memorialized more as a labor casualty than a great hitter—although before he was the former, he clearly also was the latter.

Cycles came and went through the late 19th and early 20th century—still unacknowledged, but piling up in old box scores waiting for someone to find them. Sometimes, a cycle took on an unusual form, as in the case of Lon Knight on July 30, 1883. Nobody told Knight at the time, but not only did he hit for the cycle that day for the Philadelphia Athletics against Pittsburgh, but he hit for what is now credited to be the first-ever natural cycle in baseball history.

Knight was an outfielder/pitcher whose biggest claim to fame is probably throwing the first pitch in the history of the National League. Knight was 10-22 as a pitcher in 1876, and went just 16-28 for his career. As a hitter, Knight was not particularly exceptional. After playing in the National League in 1876, he was out of the major leagues for three seasons.

In 1883, Knight was playing outfield for Philadelphia. On July 30th, the Athletics put a beating on Pittsburgh, winning the game 17–4 and racking up 23 hits in the process. Knight himself managed five of the hits. As a contemporary account noted, "the heavy batting of the home club really demoralized the visitors."

In the first inning, he hit an RBI single to center field. In the third inning, Knight hit a double and later came around to score, as the A's had a 6–1 lead after three innings. His third at-bat was unsuccessful as Knight popped out.

In the sixth inning, he returned to form with an RBI triple to center field. This left only the home run to complete the natural cycle. This was no small thing—Knight hit just three career homers in 2,288 major-league at-bats, and didn't yet have one in 1883.

But in the eighth inning, with a man on base, Knight lined a ball up the left-center field alley and legged out an inside-the-park home run to complete his natural cycle. To put an exclamation point on his great game, Knight doubled in two more runs in the ninth inning. Total damage: five hits, four runs scored, six runs batted in, and a dozen total bases.

Knight lasted in the big leagues only through 1885, and he retired as a career .243 hitter, passing away in 1932. The natural cycle, of course, has outlived its inventor. Fourteen other natural cycles have been recorded since Knight's, with the last coming from Texas Rangers outfielder Gary Matthews Jr. in 2006.

⌐⌐

Some of the greatest stars in baseball history either never hit for the cycle, or did so only after a career of persistence. Ty Cobb and Joe Jackson never hit for the cycle. Honus Wagner did, but only after he was the oldest player in the National League. Jimmie Foxx reached mid-career before his cycle—and incidentally, that 1933 cycle was the first time when media referenced the feat by its name. Pete Rose or Hank Aaron never hit for the cycle. That's right—Hank Aaron never hit for the cycle, but Aaron Hill did twice—in 11 days.

"There's no way to explain it," admitted Hill with a laugh.

Hill was a right-handed second baseman. He played for five teams, but spent the majority of his career with the Toronto Blue Jays and Arizona Diamondbacks. Hill was a solid player, a career .266 hitter with 162 home runs. He had two explosive seasons in his career, one as a Blue Jay (2009) and one as a Diamondback (2012), and he won a Silver Slugger award in each of those seasons.

Hill was in the middle of his eighth major-league season before he ever hit for the cycle. On June 5, 2012, he needed a double for a cycle, but popped out in his last at-bat. But less than two weeks later, on June 18th, he completed the job. His Diamondbacks hosted the Seattle Mariners that evening. Hill batted second, and singled to left field in the first inning off Seattle starter Héctor Noesí. With Arizona ahead 3–0, Hill led off the third inning with a triple to left-center field, and later scored. In the fifth, with Noesí still on the mound, Hill lined a double into the left field corner.

The Diamondbacks held a 6–1 lead in the seventh inning, when Hill came up to bat again. The game was all but over, and the only question remaining was whether Hill would homer to complete the cycle.

"It's human nature to think about what you're doing," said Hill. "I caught myself on-deck, and was laughing, thinking, 'Come on, man, you've had a great day. When have I ever tried to hit a homer and done it?'"

This time, he drove an 0-1 pitch from Shawn Kelley around a dozen rows over the left field wall to complete the cycle. Hill recalled third base coach Matt Williams doffing his cap to him when he rounded the bases, a memory that he said "to this day, gives me chills."

Just 11 days later, on June 29th, the Diamondbacks were in Milwaukee to face the Brewers. In the top of the first inning, Hill, hitting second as usual, pulled a long drive to left field that took a hop and jumped over the wall for a ground-rule double. In the third inning, with the score 1–1, he broke his bat on a flare that dropped behind second baseman Rickie Weeks for a single, as part of a five-run inning that put the game away.

He followed with a two-run homer to left field in the fourth inning, leaving himself five innings to hit a triple.

"I remember not even having that thought in my head," says Hill. "Because I'd went through it already. I just kind of went up there and said, 'You're having a great game, you're winning . . . and no matter what happens, it's been a great day.'"

Hill only needed two innings to make more history. In the sixth, he ripped a 2-0 pitch into the right-center field gap. "I hit it to right-center and I remember thinking, 'I've got to go!'. . . . If he catches this, hey, I hit it good. But if he doesn't catch it, I'm going to end up at third, or I'm going to get thrown out trying."

Hill legged out a triple, tying the record for most cycle games in a season. Not since 1887, when Tip O'Neill hit for two cycles in eight days, had anyone managed to space two such career games so close together.

"Baseball is so weird," said Hill. "Sometimes it works out, sometimes it doesn't, but I think it helped me to realize . . . if you get a chance for a cycle, you're having a great day. Worst case scenario, you end up with three hits."

Few before and none since have had things work out quite like Aaron Hill, who spent 13 seasons in the major leagues, and dropped two cycle games in a fortnight.

Readers may get the idea that the cycle exists only as a cherry on top of lopsided games. Admittedly, it often takes some significant team success to get a player enough chances at bat to complete the cycle. But sometimes, the cycle can take a backseat to the game itself. Consider June 18, 2017, when Nolan Arenado hit for the cycle in completely electrifying fashion.

Arenado, a slugging 6'2" third baseman for the Colorado Rockies, led the National League in home runs and RBI in 2015 and 2016. As the surging Rockies became competitive in 2017, Arenado was a significant part of that transition.

The Rockies had won three straight games from the San Francisco Giants and were trying to complete the first four-game sweep of the Giants in franchise history on June 18th. Arenado batted in the bottom of the first inning and lined a Ty Blach pitch into the right field corner. It took a funny hop, and Arenado legged out a triple. The game remained scoreless, and in the fourth inning, Arenado added a single to right field.

The Giants led 2–0 in the sixth, when Arenado next batted and cracked an RBI double to left-center field to get the Rockies on the scoreboard. The Rockies went on to grab a 3–2 lead, despite Arenado striking out in the seventh inning.

But the Giants struck for three runs in the top of the ninth inning, and heading into Colorado's last at-bat, the 5–3 deficit was more important than a shot at the cycle for Arenado. Lo and behold, after a groundout, a trio of singles made the score 5–4 and brought Arenado to the plate with runners at first and third. On the first pitch from closer Mark Melancon, Nolan lifted a high flyball to deep left field that drifted and drifted and fell into the first row of the stands for a walkoff, cycle-completing home run. The blast set off an ecstatic celebration at home plate, where Arenado was doused with bottled water and pounded with congratulatory hugs and thumps.

Afterword, the moment was not lost on the young slugger.

"It crossed my mind," he said of the cycle possibility before his home run.

His teammates played some part in that, as Arenado recalled with a chuckle, "Parra was telling me, 'If you hit a single, just run home.'"

For his part, Arenado claimed that he wasn't aiming for a home run, instead trying to hit a flyball to the outfield to tie the game.

He admitted, "It's probably one of the best moments of my career. I've hit some big homers but by far the best, obviously, for the cycle."

He went on to say, "I've never done it. I feel like I've been kind of close but I've always needed a triple and I ain't getting that. Today is a great day."

Chapter 8

HITTING FOUR HOME RUNS IN A GAME

Number of Times Accomplished: 18.

First Instance: Bobby Lowe, Boston Beaneaters, May 30, 1894.

Most Recent Instance: J. D. Martinez, Arizona Diamondbacks, September 4, 2017.

Likely Achievers: Five Hall of Famers are in this group, including legendary sluggers like Willie Mays (660 career homers), Mike Schmidt (548), and Lou Gehrig (493).

Surprises: Lowe and Ed Delahanty reached this mark in the Dead Ball Era, which was surprising in and of itself. Pat Seerey (86 career homers), Mark Whiten (105), and the active Gennett (62 going into 2018) would also qualify as longshots.

Likelihood of Additional Occurrences: It's already happened six times in the 21st century, so it's almost certain to be replicated in the near future.

Since Babe Ruth exploded the Roaring Twenties into a love affair with the home run, there has been a special corner of history for the men who somehow hit four home runs in a single game. It's an accomplishment that takes both some offensive excellence from the hitter, and a stubborn failure to acknowledge reality by an opposing pitching staff. Fool me once, shame on you, fool me four times, well, you earn a spot in the record book. Despite the Herculean nature of the task, mere mortals occasionally play their way into the longball record book.

⌛

The four-home-run club was brought into being in 1894. A fire at the Boston Beaneaters' usual South End Grounds moved their games to Congress Street, where a short left field has been estimated at about 250 feet from home plate. Playing the second game of a doubleheader, Bobby

Lowe, a 5'10" outfielder who was not especially known as a power hitter, made an out in the first inning on May 30, 1894, which he blamed on a huge fish dinner (complete with apple pie à la mode) he had enjoyed with his wife between the day's games.

But in the third inning, he hit not one, but two home runs over the short left field wall. Lowe recalled Cincinnati left fielder Bug Holliday standing with his back against the left field wall in the fifth and sixth innings, but Lowe clouted pitches over his head both times. The Boston crowd excitedly threw money onto the field, which the Beaneaters collected for Lowe, who enjoyed an unexpected $160 payday. Unbelievably, Cincinnati pitcher Elton "Ice Box" Chamberlain pitched a complete game, so he allowed all four homers to Lowe.

Lowe apparently returned to the same restaurant and enjoyed another fish dinner after the late game, but he never replicated his feat of power, although *The Sporting News* notes, "[H]e got so tired of fish, apple pie, and ice cream that he could no longer bear the sight of them." Lowe lived until 1951, when he passed away at the age of 83, so presumably he had a long time to rue his menu choices.

⌁

Two years later, Ed Delahanty hit four homers in a game, although three were inside-the-park shots at Chicago's West Side Grounds. Then, after a gap of 36 years, which included the introduction of the cork-centered "rabbit" baseball, Lou Gehrig became the third major leaguer to hit four homers in a single game.

Gehrig, playing in Philadelphia's Shibe Park on June 3, 1932, homered to left-center field in the first inning, pulled a blast to right field in the fourth, went back to left-center in the fifth inning for his third homer, and ripped another right field shot in the seventh inning to join the record book. Incidentally, of all the four-homer sluggers, Gehrig was closest to claiming a fifth homer. In his final at-bat of the day, he hit a drive to deep center field, near the deepest part of Shibe Park, which measured 468 feet from home plate. It would have easily been a home run in most fields, but ended up being a long out, as Al Simmons flagged it down near the wall.

One of the unexpected delights of Gehrig's feat is that the Yankees soon played at Detroit. Bobby Lowe, then 63 years old, read about Gehrig's feat in the paper. Lowe put on his old-time uniform and came to Navin Field, where he was introduced to Gehrig and the two were photographed together, Lowe trim and wiry, Gehrig towering a head taller and much thicker than his fellow home-run king. Lowe told reporters, "I had hoped that somebody would tie or break the record before I died and I am glad it was Gehrig, for he is a good hitter and a nice, clean fellow." Indeed, the talk of mortality seems surprising in retrospect, because Lowe outlived Gehrig by over a decade, and indeed lived to see three other players hit four home runs in a game.

But back in 1932, while enjoying the attention of the day, the venerable Lowe held forth on home-run technique, telling the media, "It doesn't necessarily take big fellows to hit home runs, although Ruth and Gehrig are big enough. It depends on how you meet the ball."

For Mark Whiten, trying to meet the ball was a sufficient goal when his historic game began. On September 7, 1993, the outfielder had a rough first game of a doubleheader between his Cardinals and the Cincinnati Reds. Whiten was 0-for-4, and mishandled a critical play in right field as the Reds notched a comeback 14–13 win. Whiten at that point had gone 80 at-bats without a home run. When asked about ever going to bat trying to hit home runs, Whiten admitted, "I talked to some guys who did try, and I'm like, 'I can't do that, man. I'd make an out every time.'"

So when Whiten stepped up to bat in the evening nightcap with the bases loaded in the first inning, he recalled, "I was just trying to get a run home." Instead, he got four runs home, with a grand slam to left-center field off starting pitcher Larry Luebbers.

Still, when Whiten popped out to third baseman Chris Sabo in the fourth inning, it certainly didn't look like he was on his way to history. A nice game, maybe, but not anything historic.

It was 5–2 in the sixth inning when Whiten came up against reliever Mike Anderson. Anderson had walked the first two batters of the inning, and so when he threw Whiten a strike on his first pitch, Whiten jumped on it, driving the ball to right-center field for a second home run, and his seventh run batted in of the game.

From there, Whiten only poured it on. He came up with two runners on in the seventh against Anderson, and on a 2-1 count, ripped a fastball out of the park for his third home run and his 10th RBI of the game.

In the eighth inning, the Reds brought in reliever Rob Dibble, on the back end of a career in which he was one of the "Nasty Boys" who pitched the Reds to a 1990 championship. Dibble still possessed a fearsome fastball, and was hardly the type of pitcher to either work around Whiten or concede him any ground, multi-homer game or not.

For his part, Whiten remembers the bat boy asking him if he was going to try to hit another home run. He recalled telling him, "I didn't try to hit the other three, so why should I try to hit another one?"

Dibble fell behind in the count and challenged Whiten with a fastball, and he promptly blasted his fourth home run well over the center field wall. "It was like when Michael Jordan was in a zone," recalled Whiten. "You really don't know you're in a zone until after the game. I think my teammates knew it before I did. But it didn't matter where the ball was."

Indeed, with four home runs, 12 runs batted in, and a historic game, Whiten had certainly atoned for his horrible performance in the first game of the doubleheader. No one went away from Riverfront Stadium remembering the poor first game.

While Whiten had an up-and-down doubleheader, to say that fellow slugger Josh Hamilton had an up-and-down *career* would be an understatement. The top pick in the 1999 MLB Draft, Hamilton had a 97-mile-per-hour fastball and a penchant for blasting gargantuan home runs. He also ended up experiencing an almost unending string of severe injuries and developing life-threatening addictions to alcohol and drugs. Hamilton played in 72 minor-league games in 1999 and 96 more in 2000, and admittedly, showed many of the tools that caused talent scouts to drool over his power. But between injuries (knee, shoulder, and elbow) and suspensions for drugs, he played in just 96 games between 2001 and 2006.

By the time Hamilton made the major leagues in 2007, he had been taken by the Cubs in the Rule 5 Draft and sold to the Reds for the waiver wire fee plus $50,000. Hamilton was a Red for one season, hitting .292 with 19 home runs in 90 games before he was traded to the Texas Rangers.

His life under control with a reliance on his wife and born-again Christian faith, Hamilton attacked the baseball as a Texas Ranger. He was an All-Star all five seasons from 2008 to 2012. While Hamilton struggled some with durability, he did rip 142 home runs in those five seasons. On May 8, 2012, Hamilton delivered the ultimate signal of his turnaround from prospect to suspect to star.

In the first inning, against then-Oriole Jake Arrieta, Hamilton, who had homered in his last at-bat the night before, hit a two-run blast to center field. In the third inning, he faced Arrieta again, and tattooed a sinker into the left field stands. Arrieta must have figured Hamilton out, because he held him to a mere double into the right-center field gap in the fifth inning.

In the seventh inning, the Orioles brought on lefty Zach Phillips to pitch to the left-handed Hamilton. The second pitch of the at-bat became a third home run, this one to center field. The eighth inning brought Hamilton up again, this time against former teammate Darren O'Day.

Hamilton denied thinking about a fourth home run. "I prepared like any other at-bat," he said after the game. "If I don't hit another it's still a great night."

O'Day got ahead in an 0-2 count, and then threw Hamilton a sinker, which he deposited just over the center field wall, to an impressive ovation from the home crowd in Baltimore.

Hamilton admitted he had trouble processing the game right away. "When I get away from it and have time to think about it, it will sink in," he said. "But all I can think about now is, what a blessing."

Hamilton ended up with 43 home runs and 128 RBI in 2012. He parlayed his seasons into a lucrative contract with the Angels, but then his career fell apart again.

Hamilton was healthy but unproductive in 2013 (.250, 21 home runs), and was injured again in 2014. He had a relapse in his drug addiction early in 2015, and Angels ownership was so furious that the team essentially ate the majority of his contract and gave him away to the Texas Rangers. The guy who Anaheim couldn't wait to throw $125 million at had become the guy they were now willing to pay much of that cash *not* to play for them.

Hamilton did not find a time machine back in Arlington. He was solid with Texas, but didn't look like his old self. The injury cycle flared up again, and Hamilton played 50 games and hit eight home runs in his second stint in Texas. While he's only 36 at the time of writing, it appears that he will never play another MLB game. Still, the up-and-down career of Josh Hamilton had a very memorable up in Baltimore one night in 2012.

For another member of the four-home-run club, his big game was a triumphant homecoming. Scooter Gennett, who grew up in Cincinnati, was a 16th-round draft pick of the Milwaukee Brewers as a slightly undersized infielder. Gennett made his way to Milwaukee in 2013, and played solid baseball as a punchy second baseman. In 2016, Gennett hit .263 with 14 home runs.

Gennett was slated to earn $2.5 million in 2017, but Milwaukee wanted to hand the second base job to Jonathan Villar. Gennett offered to try to learn to play the outfield, and Milwaukee considered sending him to the minor leagues. But at the end of spring training, the Brewers instead waived Gennett, and he was claimed by the hometown Cincinnati Reds.

"It was bittersweet," remembered Gennett. "I had to say goodbye to some friends and guys that I consider family. But at the same time, my childhood dream came true, I got picked up by the Reds, and I came back home. It was definitely a weird day of emotions, but I couldn't think of another team I'd want to play for, other than the Reds."

And so two months later, on June 6, 2017, Gennett found himself living out something beyond a dream when he made history against the Cardinals. Gennett had never topped his 14 home runs from 2016 in any previous season. He was hitting .270 with three home runs just over two months into the 2017 season. But all of that changed on June 6th.

Gennett began the game with a bloop single in his first at-bat against Adam Wainwright, which brought in a run. It was still 1–0 in the third inning when he faced Wainwright again with the bases loaded. On a full-count pitch, Gennett drilled a fastball well over the right-center field wall for a grand slam.

In the very next inning, the Cardinals brought in reliever John Gant to face Gennett, who countered with a long home run to center field, giving him seven RBIs in four innings. The little lefty was just getting started.

Gant was still in the game in the sixth inning, and left a 3-1 fastball high to Gennett, who poked it to left field, just inside the foul pole for his third homer of the day. It was then that the moment dawned on Gennett. "It was a pitch that was borderline," he recalls. "I knew something was going on. I just think that God was working that night, and for some reason, He picked me."

After a walk in the eighth inning, Gennett got one more at-bat, this time against John Brebbia.

"I just tried to relax . . . tried to get a good pitch to hit and put a good swing on it," remembered Gennett.

Unlike the other three blasts, each of which came with three balls, Brebbia got ahead of Gennett in an 0-2 count. The third pitch was a fastball, and Gennett pounced on it, lining the ball just over the right field wall, and into history.

"I never expected to do something like that," said Gennett. "I remember watching [on television] Josh Hamilton do it and thinking, 'Wow, that has to be the greatest feeling in the world. But it never was a goal . . . to be able to do four, it's just unreal.'"

Like the unlikely Bobby Lowe who began the four-home-run club, perhaps there was a digestive element to Gennett's feat?

"I ate a burger before the game," Gennett reported with a laugh. "I like burgers, so I'm going to keep eating those. I'm not too superstitious in terms of doing the same things over and over and expecting four home runs every night."

Near the end of the 2017 season, the four-homer club added a new member with Arizona Diamondbacks outfielder J. D. Martinez. A mid-season trade acquisition from the Detroit Tigers, Martinez added substantial punch to the Arizona attack—never more than on September 4, when he ripped four homers against the L.A. Dodgers.

Martinez relied on a late explosion to reach the mark, homering in the fourth inning but then adding a home run in each the seventh, eighth, and ninth innings of his team's 13–0 victory. This made him the 11th player in MLB history to homer in three consecutive innings.

Martinez drew upon his experience from a 2015 game when he hit three home runs and had a chance at a fourth, but flied out. When the ninth inning brought him another chance at history, he was ready.

"This at-bat, I came up and I was like, just go up here and try to have a good at-bat," Martinez told the media after his historic homer. "You know what, if it's meant to be, it's meant to be."

On a 1-0 slider from Dodger reliever Wilmer Font, Martinez drove the ball high and well into the left-field bleachers. None of his home runs provided much doubt, as each reached the stands by a solid ten feet or more.

The four homers gave Martinez 18 home runs in 144 at-bats with Arizona, as the Diamondbacks mounted their climb to an NL Wild Card playoff spot. Still, even at a pace like the torrid one Martinez displayed, four home runs was something special.

"It's . . . one of those things where you're kind of laughing about it," said Martinez.

CHAPTER 9

SIX WALKS IN A GAME

Number of Times Accomplished: Five.

First Instance: Walt Wilmot, Chicago Colts, August 22, 1891.

Most Recent Instance: Bryce Harper, Washington Nationals, May 8, 2016.

Likely Suspects: Jimmie Foxx and Jeff Bagwell are both Hall of Famers, and it's early in his career, but it will be a surprise if Bryce Harper doesn't join them.

Surprises: Walt Wilmot was a .276 hitter with 58 career home runs.

Likelihood of Additional Occurrences: Given the shift in intentional walk rules, teams don't even have to throw four wide lobs to give a hitter first base. Wherever there's an uneven lineup balance and an extra-inning game, walking history could occur.

The chestnut delivered on every Little League diamond goes that a walk is as good as a hit. But is that true, or is that something that kids are told to work around the horrific wildness of most young pitchers? Only five hitters have ever drawn six walks in a game, and three of the group needed extra innings (two of them needed 16 innings, to be more specific). So were these guys just selective hitters, or were the opposing teams determined to pitch around them and test the next hitter? And did it work? Not surprisingly, the answers are varied.

~

Walt Wilmot would be hard to mark as a king of walks. A good hitter with relatively significant power for his time (he led the National League in 1890 with 13 home runs), Wilmot, as was typical for his era, made contact frequently. In almost 4,000 career at-bats, he totaled only 350 walks and 233 strikeouts. But the switch-hitting left fielder must have been downright selective back on August 22, 1891, against Cleveland.

Wilmot batted second for the Colts that day, hitting ahead of second baseman Bill Dahlen and superstar first baseman Cap Anson. Wilmot batted .275 with 11 home runs in 1891, but the men hitting behind him weren't exactly slouches. Dahlen batted .260 with nine home runs, and Anson hit .291 and knocked in 120 runs. And yet somehow, on all six plate appearances that day, Wilmot drew a walk.

Cleveland pitchers Lee Viau and Cy Young allowed only four walks in the game to hitters other than Wilmot. It would be hard to expect that the Cleveland hurlers pitched around Wilmot, because Chicago's other hitters were quite productive in a 10–4 victory, albeit with help from nine Cleveland errors. The *Chicago Tribune* jokingly attributed Wilmot's game to rheumatism, noting "[T]here are more pleasant things to con-template than swinging a forty ounce club at a flying ball with rheumatic pains playing hide and seek in one's joints." The paper concedes that rheumatism aside, the six walks "may have been the exercising in him of rare discrimination in discerning . . . that the ball was not cavorting across the centermost portion of home plate." The paper went on to note that the six walks "establishes a record that is likely to stand for years, if not for all time." The *Cincinnati Enquirer* credited Wilmot's feat to "the poor pitching of both Viau and Young."

In any case, Wilmot drew only 49 walks over the entire rest of his season. He remained in the major leagues until 1898, and his biggest non-walk-related claim to celebrity was either stealing eight bases over back-to-back games in August 1894 or getting hit with the ball twice while running the bases in a game in 1890. Unfortunately, none of this information clarifies whether Wilmot was pitched around or was just the recipient of flukish wildness on August 22, 1891.

There is absolutely no mystery as to how Jimmie Foxx drew six walks in a game, particularly in 1938. Foxx was one of the most formidable power hitters in the history of the game, leading the American League in homers four times, including hitting 58 round-trippers in 1932.

In 1938, he didn't lead the league in home runs (he hit "only" 50), but he did lead it with 175 RBIs. The St. Louis Browns apparently determined on June 16th that they wouldn't allow Foxx to hit a home run, or knock in a run, because they put him on first all six times that he batted. Only one of Foxx's walks was apparently classified as intentional, although the fact that he drew six walks while the entire rest of the Red Sox team drew just two combined seems instructive.

Before just over 1,000 fans at Sportsman's Park in St. Louis, fans watched Foxx walk again. And again. The strategy didn't pay off for the Browns, as Foxx was indeed held homerless and without an RBI, but fifth hitter Joe Cronin, who hit behind Foxx, picked up the slack. Cronin had four hits and four RBIs in the game, as Foxx scored two runs on the basis of his six walks.

For his part, the big slugger apparently didn't appreciate the gesture. *The Sporting News* quotes him as saying (allegedly during the game, so this is very possibly apocryphal), "What good is a record like that as compared to making a hit with one of your own men out there on base waiting to be driven home?"

⌁

Andre Thornton might not have seemed a likely candidate to tie Wilmot and Foxx for the walk record, but on May 2, 1984, he did just that. Thornton, a 6'3" designated hitter and first baseman with the Cleveland Indians, did have a history of hitting for power—he had two prior 30-home-run seasons. But coming into play on May 2nd, he was hitting .217 with three home runs. Thornton had received 10 walks over the first month of the season, but suddenly added six more in a single game.

If the issue wasn't Thornton's production, it wasn't a lack thereof from the hitters behind him. Pat Tabler (who hit behind Thornton) was

1-for-4 with a double, and six-hole hitter Brook Jacoby had two hits, including a three-run homer.

Perhaps as much as anything, the problem was that Baltimore Oriole pitchers simply couldn't throw a strike. They had plenty of innings to try, as the marathon game that day went on for 16 innings, clocking in at just past five hours. Thornton drew a walk from Scott McGregor to lead off the second inning. With two out and none on in the fourth, he again walked, later scoring on an error.

He batted again with two out and none on in the sixth inning, and again drew a walk. In the eighth inning, with a runner on base, he flied out to right field for one of his two official at-bats of the game. With Julio Franco on second and two outs in the ninth inning and the score tied at 7, Thornton took his fourth walk of the game, this one intentional.

In the 11th inning, with a runner at third and two out, he was again walked intentionally, this time to face reserve first baseman Mike Hargrove, who made an out to end the inning. Thornton led off the 14th against Oriole Jim Palmer, who was pitching in his next-to-final major-league game in a disastrous attempt to become a reliever. Palmer walked five batters in three innings, the first of whom was Thornton, who thus tied the single-game walk record.

Unlike the other hitters who reached six walks, Thornton had an opportunity to break that record. He batted in the 16th inning with runners at first and second and no outs. He flied out to deep center field, allowing both runners to advance. Those runners subsequently scored, as Cleveland won the game 9–7 in 16 innings.

Though Thornton slumped early in the 1984 season, he picked up his play in the warmer months, making his second All-Star Game appearance, and ultimately hitting .271 with 33 home runs and 99 RBI. Perhaps the biggest surprise of Thornton's six-walk performance was that he was alive and on a baseball field to make history. After the 1977 season, Thornton, his wife Gertrude, and their two children were involved in a horrific auto accident that took the lives of Gertrude and Theresa Thornton. Thornton was fortunate to survive the accident, and he credited his Christian faith for helping him through the difficult time. He battled injuries throughout his big league career, finishing as a .254 career hitter with 253 lifetime home runs.

The next six-walk game looked like a perfect storm. Take an incredibly wild opposing pitching staff, and let them pitch 16 innings. Then add a batter who is both highly respected (in the midst of a season that included 124 runs scored, 42 home runs and 126 RBI), but then also let that hitter be incredibly patient (drawing 149 walks in that 1999 season). That was Jeff Bagwell on August 20, 1999.

Bagwell and the Astros did go 16 innings against the Marlins, whose pitchers—led by starter Ryan Dempster, who walked seven batters in 3⅓ innings—managed to somehow deal out 17 walks, only two shy of the all-time MLB team record. Six of those walks were intentional, including two of Bagwell's total. On a night when the Marlins staff totaled 310 pitches, 143 of those pitches were balls.

For Bagwell's part, in a year when the slugger managed to lead the National League in runs scored and walks, he willingly accepted the inability of his opponent to throw him a strike. The hitters behind Bagwell flourished, with cleanup man Carl Everett delivering two hits and two RBIs (as well as taking three walks himself), and fifth hitter Ken Caminiti adding two hits and three RBIs.

Bagwell flied out to right field in the first inning, for one of only two official at-bats in 16 innings. He walked on five pitches in the third, walked to load the bases in the fourth (at which time Dempster left the game), and drew a five-pitch walk with two out and none on in the sixth. He grounded to second base in the eighth inning, and in a typical nine-inning game, his total of three walks wouldn't have even been unusual. But the game was tied at 4–4, and would stay that way until the 16th inning.

Bagwell drew a five-pitch walk with one out and no one on in the 11th inning. In the 13th inning, with the lead run at second base and one out, he was walked intentionally. With a runner at second and two out in the 15th inning, he was again passed intentionally, and a Carl Everett grounder then kept the game tied.

Bagwell was on deck once the Astros scored two runs in the 16th inning, but he didn't get a chance at a seventh walk. Soon thereafter, a strikeout ended the 6–4 Astros win a few minutes before 1 a.m. While the majority of Bagwell's walks appear to have been more of a happenstance than a strategy, the game was a peculiar one. While Florida pitchers handed out 17 walks, they also totaled 21 strikeouts. The Astros left 20 runners on base in the game.

For his part, Bagwell took the moment with the modesty one might expect from a player known for hitting, but reduced to walking. "Not really the record I'm looking for," he said after the game. "It was a crazy game. But it's nice to play 16 when you win."

Unsuccessful starter Ryan Dempster's verdict was more succinct: "Walks are a pain in the butt."

⁓

None of those first four opposing teams that walked a hitter six times won the game—which suggests that ultimately, to the extent that a six-walk game is strategy more than coincidence, it's flawed strategy. But just when baseball seems to have shown viewers everything, something else happens.

Maybe the Chicago Cubs' Joe Maddon is a better manager than the four walk-happy skippers who walked and lost. Or maybe he was just lucky. But on May 8, 2016, Maddon had clearly decided that he did not want to let Bryce Harper of the Washington Nationals beat his Chicago Cubs. And Harper didn't.

The 6'3" left-handed power machine was being his usual self when the Nationals came to Wrigley Field in May. Harper had 10 home runs in the season's first 30 games. But Harper couldn't homer if he couldn't swing. And it turned out that the Nationals couldn't drive him in enough to make Maddon and the Cubs pay.

In the first inning of that day's matchup, reigning Cy Young Award winner Jake Arrieta not only walked Harper, but he walked him on four pitches. In the third inning, Arrieta walked Harper on five pitches. Harper was doubled home by cleanup hitter Ryan Zimmerman, but that was the only time all day that Harper scored a run.

In the fourth inning, Harper came up with the Nats holding a 2–0 lead, and runners at second and third. He was intentionally walked, and Arrieta then struck out Zimmerman to end the inning. Arrieta departed after five innings, and reliever Trevor Cahill broke the cycle when he hit Harper with the first pitch of his sixth inning at-bat. Cahill was still on in the eighth inning, with the score tied 3–3, when he walked Harper on five pitches with two out and no one on base.

The game moved into extra innings, and Maddon doubled down on his strategy. When Harper came to bat with runners at first and second and two out in the 10th inning, he was intentionally walked. Reliever Adam Warren then coaxed Zimmerman to line out and end the inning. In the 12th inning, the same situation presented itself with reliever Justin Grimm on the mound. Again, Harper was intentionally walked, again without first base open. And again, Zimmerman could not drive him (or the runners in front of him) in.

In the bottom of the 13th inning, the Cubs won the game on a walkoff home run by Javier Baez. In seven plate appearances, Harper was hit once and walked six times, three acknowledged as intentionally, but the other three times with more or less the same intent. Cumulatively, he saw 27 pitches in the game. One hit him, two were strikes, and 24 were balls. But because Zimmerman couldn't protect him, the strategy paid off.

Incidentally, the entire series clearly featured the same gameplan. In the four-game set (with the May 8th game being the last game of the four), Harper was 1-for-4 with 13 walks and scored only three times. The Cubs swept all four games.

So, unlike every previous player to walk six times, Harper didn't have the last laugh. He was predictably frustrated by the turn of events. He told reporters after the game, "They had a plan. They stuck with their plan. Unfortunately, it worked."

And because it worked, we'll probably see it again.

CHAPTER 10

KNOCKING IN 10 RUNS IN A GAME

Number of Times Accomplished: 15.

First Instance: Wilbert Robinson, Baltimore Orioles, June 10, 1892.

Most Recent Instance: Scooter Gennett, Cincinnati Reds, June 6, 2017.

Likely Suspects: Alex Rodriguez and Reggie Jackson are among the bigger names on this list, four of whom are in the Hall of Fame.

Surprises: Norm Zauchin (159 career RBIs) and Phil Weintraub (207) aren't among the more notable sluggers of their day . . . although, coming into 2017, neither was Gennett (160 RBI in first three and a half seasons in MLB).

Likelihood of Additional Occurrences: Two 10-RBI games in 2017 suggest that this small group will continue to grow, perhaps rapidly.

The idea seems absurd—for a team to score 10 runs generally equates to a powerful offensive performance, with lots of hits scattered throughout the lineup. But for one player to knock in 10 runs? It takes both an extraordinary hitting performance and a fair bit of luck. A hitter can go 6-for-6 and not approach 10 RBIs—for that matter, 11 players in the post–World War II era have gotten six hits in a game without a single RBI. Or consider Mike Cameron, who hit four home runs in a game in 2002, but all four were solo shots. He came up six RBIs short of 10. The 10-RBI club, then, is a superb hitting performance plus an assist from teammates. And there's always a story.

⌒

The first 10-RBI game was Wilbert Robinson of the Baltimore Orioles on June 10, 1892 (see chapter 12). Unlike Robinson's seven hits in that game—which hasn't been eclipsed in a nine-inning contest—his total of 11 RBIs wouldn't last as baseball's all-time record. And "Uncle Robbie" would have a front-row seat for the demolition of that piece of baseball history.

—

"Sunny Jim" Bottomley was a six-foot lefty first baseman from rural Illinois who became the second 10-RBI man in baseball history. Bottomley turned to baseball to escape from the coal mines, which claimed his only brother's life. He told an interviewer, "When I went into baseball, it was a choice of making good at that or returning to the mines. So it hardly was any choice at all." Bottomley was nicknamed for his sunny disposition, presumably attributable to successfully escaping a mining career. Late in his life, he noted, "I don't have a regret in the world. If I had to do it all over again, I wouldn't change a thing." One thing Bottomley certainly wouldn't change was September 16, 1924.

Bottomley and the St. Louis Cardinals were on the road, taking on the Brooklyn Robins, who happened to be named for and managed by one Wilbert Robinson. Bottomley had finished 10th in the NL in RBI with 94 in 1923, and was in the midst of a more successful second season. He had 92 RBIs with a dozen games still to play, and a 100-RBI season didn't look out of the question. In fact, he would break it that afternoon.

Bottomley came to bat in the first inning with the bases loaded, and his single to center field plated two runs off Brooklyn starter Rube Ehrhardt, who never got an out in the game. In the second inning, he added an RBI double down the left field line to stretch St. Louis's lead to 5–0. But his day truly got interesting in the fourth inning, when with the bases full after an intentional walk to Rogers Hornsby, Bottomley unleashed a grand slam to right field off reliever Art Decatur, giving him seven RBIs in four innings.

In the sixth inning, Bottomley got Decatur again and he homered again, this time a two-run blast, which was his 14th of the season. In the seventh inning, Bottomley added a two-run single to right field to tie Robinson's mark with 11 RBIs.

Bottomley singled in Rogers Hornsby in the ninth inning for the final run of the 17–3 beating. It marked his 12th RBI of the day, a record that was tied by Mark Whiten in his four-home-run game in 1993 (see chapter 8), but has never been broken.

Robinson may not have held a grudge against Bottomley, but he couldn't avoid some good-natured busting of Sunny Jim's chops. *The Sporting News* recounted that the following day, Bottomley stopped by the Dodger bench for some chewing tobacco from Robinson, as was apparently common between the two of them. Robinson told him, "You'll get no more chews from me. Do you know what you did yesterday? You chased me right out of the record book. Now get outta here."

He may not have had another chew from Uncle Robbie, but Bottomley had an excellent career, hitting .310, twice leading the National League in RBIs, and winning the MVP award in 1928, when his 31 home runs and 136 RBIs helped the Cardinals to a pennant. Bottomley died of a heart attack in late 1959, but ultimately joined "Uncle Robbie" in the Baseball Hall of Fame after his posthumous induction in 1974.

The next National League player after Bottomley to manage 10 RBIs in a game had very similar stats—batting average over .300, well over 200 career home runs. But while Bottomley is immortalized in Cooperstown at the Baseball Hall of Fame for his major-league production, Phil Weintraub would be remembered best in the cities where he put up his sterling stats—Waco, Danville, Tyler, Dubuque, Terre Haute, Dayton, Nashville, Rochester, Columbus, and so on: minor-league cities. The biggest mystery of Weintraub is why a hitter with a career .295 big-league batting average and capable power (.440 slugging percentage) could never get more than 361 at-bats in a big-league season—or top 1,382 career at-bats.

It certainly wasn't struggles at the minor-league level. Weintraub's minor-league stats are incomplete, but his records from the highest minor leagues indicate a .322 batting average, 148 home runs in nine seasons, and a consistently high level of play.

One logical and disappointing conclusion is that perhaps Weintraub's heritage may have kept him out of more big-league exposure. One biographer cites anti-Semitic theories of the time, such as those advanced a generation earlier by sociologist Edward Ross—that Jews were small and weak, and incapable of physical activity. One could be forgiven for wishing Hank Greenberg could have spent some time hitting line drives at Ross's head.

But whatever the reason, Weintraub never stuck. In 1938, he finally got some playing time with the Phillies, hitting .311 with 45 RBIs in 351 at-bats. That Philly team hit .254 and had only two players who knocked in more runs than Weintraub. He was rewarded by being sent to the minor leagues for the next six years.

In 1944, when Weintraub resurfaced with the New York Giants, at the age of 36, he got his best chance to play. And he wasted no time making history in his ninth game as a Giant.

On April 30th, the Giants hosted the Dodgers at the Polo Grounds. Weintraub batted fifth and played first base, and in the first inning, his double scored Mel Ott and Joe Medwick. In the second inning, he drew a bases-loaded walk, which gave him a third RBI.

Batting with the bases loaded again in the third inning, Weintraub unleashed a bases-clearing triple, which extended the New York lead to 10–2. In the fourth inning, he doubled in two more runs, giving him eight RBIs in four innings.

Weintraub popped up to second in the sixth inning and led off the eighth inning with a walk. He came up again in the eighth, and this time ripped a three-run home run, also scoring Ott and Medwick. The lead was extended to 26–8, and Phil Weintraub had 11 RBIs in a single game.

Weintraub hit .316 for the Giants that year, knocking 13 home runs and knocking in 77 runs in just 361 at-bats. After one more season, his major-league career was over. Weintraub himself was either diplomatic, vague, or confused when asked about his career.

"I frankly don't how why I was [in the minors] for so long, but I suppose the final explanation is that is just baseball. It certainly is a strange game."

⌒

While some players never really get a chance to shine beyond a game, others have a magical season, or a few brilliant years. For Boston Red Sox rookie outfielder Fred Lynn, his magical season was 1975. For a title-starved Red Sox team, the athletic left-handed rookie seemed like a gift from heaven. Lynn could hit for average or power, run, throw, and made incredible catches as if he were turning Major League Baseball into his personal highlight film.

But perhaps the greatest moment of his 1975 season came on June 18th, when Lynn knocked in 10 runs in a game. Lynn was hitting .337 with 11 home runs going into the day's game. But Lynn's day got off to an inauspicious start. He had ended a 20-game hitting streak in the previous game, was unhappy with his performance, and found himself unable to get much sleep. "It probably shows how much of a rookie I was, walking the streets of Detroit at six in the morning," he recalled. He had an early breakfast, and used his extra time to take some batting practice.

Lynn hit cleanup that day, batting between future Hall of Famers Carl Yastrzemski and Jim Rice. Lynn hadn't faced Detroit starter Joe Coleman, and recalled being curious about what he would see.

"When you're a rookie, you haven't seen anything before, and everything is new. . . . So everything is for the first time," said Lynn. "Fortunately, I've always been pretty good at reading things, adjusting to things."

In his first at-bat, he blasted a two-run homer into Tiger Stadium's upper deck. Lynn did himself one better in the second inning, again crushing a long home run to right field, this one a three-run job off the façade of the upper deck. So much for the struggles of youth.

In the third inning, Lynn cranked a drive to left that nearly left the field, but instead ricocheted hard off the left field wall for a two-run triple. In three innings, he had 11 total bases and seven RBIs, as Boston led 11–1. He lined out to second in the fifth inning ("That would have been my double," he recalled, when asked about missing the cycle) and singled to open the eighth inning. In his final at-bat against reliever Tom Walker in the top of the ninth inning, Lynn tattooed another three-run homer into the upper deck in right field. He had three homers, 16 total bases, and 10 RBIs in the 15–1 victory.

Lynn's 1975 totals were astounding, as he helped Boston to the AL pennant. He hit .331 with 47 doubles, 21 home runs, and 105 RBIs. He was a Gold Glove outfielder, the AL Rookie of the Year, and the AL Most Valuable Player.

Unfortunately, while Lynn was an All-Star in every season from 1975 to 1983, he rarely approached his level of play from that astounding rookie season, mostly due to missing games. Much like Brooklyn's Pete Reiser from a generation before, Lynn was such a daring and talented outfielder that he could not avoid running himself into harm's way in search of great catches. Lynn recalled presenting an award to Reiser after the 1975 season, relating, "He was like me, always running into walls. But he was bald as a cue ball, so I thought, 'Damn, if that's what's going to happen if I run into walls, maybe I should rethink this.'" Intense play aside, Lynn also was sometimes just unlucky, like in 1980, when he fouled a pitch off his own foot and broke a toe.

Lynn ended his career as a .283 hitter with 306 home runs and four Gold Glove awards. Asked if he's bothered that injuries robbed him of more, Lynn answers, "People come up to me to this day, who admired the way I played. That's all I care about." Indeed, those who saw him at his best, like that June 1975 day in Detroit, remember him as one of the most talented players to ever grace a Red Sox uniform.

Another such player, who like Lynn earned the admiration of Sox fans but ultimately couldn't keep up a frenetic pace of productivity, was Nomar Garciaparra. "Nomah" was born in Whittier, California, the town that produced Richard Nixon. Garciaparra left Whittier, first for

Georgia Tech, and then for Boston, after the Red Sox made him their first-round draft pick in 1994. He was the AL Rookie of the Year in 1997, a skinny six-foot shortstop, who, like Lynn two decades before, was a true multi-tool player. In that rookie year, Nomar hit .306 with 30 home runs and 98 RBIs. He finished second in the AL MVP voting in '98 to Juan Gonzalez, and continued his assault on the record books with a 10-RBI game on May 10, 1999.

Garciaparra had hit .309 with a pair of homers and 14 RBIs in the first 30 games of the season. In the 31st, he topped that home-run mark and challenged the RBI total. Against unfortunate Mariners starting pitcher Brett Hinchliffe, who was on his way to an 0-5, 10.22 ERA career in the big leagues, Garciaparra hit a first-inning screamer to right field that became a grand slam. He hit a two-run shot off Hinchliffe, again to right field, in the third inning. In the eighth inning, he faced reliever Eric Weaver with the bases full. "I was probably going to swing at anything," Garciaparra later told reporters. He swung at a pitch up in the strike zone that promptly became his second grand slam, this one to left field. Three home runs and 10 RBIs belonged to Nomar in a 12–4 win.

The accomplishment left a beaming Garciaparra trying to explain his numerous feats afterward. He told reporters, "I've never hit three home runs in a game before—not in Little League, college, nowhere. I'm glad I waited until the big leagues to do it." Presumably, he hadn't knocked in 10 runs either.

Nomar led the AL in hitting that season (.357) and also in 2000 (.372). He missed almost the entire 2001 season with an injury, but was brilliant in '02 and '03. But near the end of the 2004 season, just after he turned 31, as the Red Sox were growing frustrated with the status quo, he was traded to the Chicago Cubs. Garciaparra thus just missed the end of the Boston curse, and to add insult to the matter, he was simply never the same player as he was in Boston.

He hit .323 with a .923 OPS in Boston. In a year and a half in Chicago, he was hurt often, and when he did play, he hit .289 with a .790 OPS. The Dodgers picked him up for three seasons, and he hit .289

with a .792 OPS. After a dismal final season in Oakland, Nomar retired. Much like Lynn, his career totals of 44.2 WAR and his .313 batting average with six seasons of at least 190 hits only wearily hint at the glory of those early Red Sox seasons. Like Lynn, he fought valiantly to bring Boston a title, only to come up short. And like Lynn, he left the memory of phenomenal games, like the 10-RBI performance, to inform those who missed his brief run of glory just how spectacular he really was.

The Reds' Scooter Gennett (see chapter 8) is the most recent 10-RBI man, and only time will tell whether his powerful 2017 season is the start of a new aspect of his career, or just a lucky season that will soon challenge the memories of hard-core Reds fans. As the careers above displayed, there's precedent in either direction—which is part of what makes the 10-RBI game interesting.

Chapter 11

HOMERING ON FIRST PITCH FACED IN THE MAJOR LEAGUES

Number of Times Accomplished: 30.

First Instance: So far as it is known, Walter Mueller, Pittsburgh Pirates, May 7, 1922.

Most Recent Instance: Willson Contreras, Chicago Cubs, June 19, 2016.

Likely Achievers: None of the players who homered in their first at-bat went on to Hall of Fame playing careers. The most homers by a member of the group belong to shortstop Jay Bell, who finished his career with 195 roundtrippers. Outfielder Marcus Thames (115 homers) is the only other player in the group who broke triple digits in his career home-run total.

Surprises: Too many to count. For one thing, of the 30 players, eight were pitchers. A dozen of the players failed to hit 10 career home runs, and seven failed to ever hit another home run.

Likelihood of Additional Occurrences: There's never a good way to project when this might happen, but there's no reason to suspect it will stop happening any time soon.

For most mere mortals, the dreams themselves are often the end of the road—dreams of playing in big-league stadiums, smashing home runs, hearing the cheers of the crowd. For a few, those dreams continue, to high school, to college, even to the minor leagues. And for the most talented, most fortunate subgroup, after decades of dreaming and years of baseball seasoning, the call comes, and they step into a big-league batter's box. Exactly 30 players have proceeded to use that heart-thumping first plate appearance to swing at the very first big-league pitch they see—and blast it for a home run. The struggle to get to that moment then transitions into the battle to form a career of real significance. None of it is easy, but those 30 players have assured themselves a great story to tell on the basis of that first pitch.

~

Walter Mueller was a 5'8" outfielder from near St. Louis who spent the late 1910s and early 1920s trying to earn his path to the big leagues. In the middle of that run, he enlisted in the Army, but the armistice kept him wandering the back woods of minor-league ball instead of the fields of France. Just when Mueller was set to finally earn his shot at the big leagues, disaster struck. He made a difficult catch of a flyball in spring training of 1922, but misjudged his landing and rolled head-over-heels down an 18-foot embankment. He played the rest of the game, but was eventually assessed with a fractured cervical vertebrae, a broken neck in layman's terms.

He eventually healed to the point where, on May 7, 1922, he was penciled into the starting lineup for the Pittsburgh Pirates, batting sixth and playing right field. They faced the Chicago Cubs, and legendary pitcher Grover Cleveland Alexander, who was destined for the Baseball Hall of Fame. And so Mueller's first at-bat in the big leagues came in the top of the first inning, with Pittsburgh already holding a 1–0 lead, two Pirates on base, and two outs. Mueller wasted no time swinging at Alexander's first pitch, and unleashing a line drive to deep center field in the friendly confines of Cubs Park, which would later be better known as Wrigley Field. The blast soared past Cubs center fielder Jigger Statz, and Mueller set off not on a stately trot around the bases, but on a speedy dash around them for an inside-the-park home run. As one account noted, "Home runs inside the rather limited ball yard at Chicago had not been plentiful and the smash of this hitherto unknown rookie caused quite a hullabaloo among the fans."

Mueller's good luck didn't hold. He reinjured his neck shortly after his big blast, and the market for diminutive 27-year-old rookies with neck injuries was not very strong. He managed 345 major-league at-bats, and hit a respectable .275 with two career home runs. He left the major leagues in 1926.

Mueller's lasting significance to baseball, other than his remarkable first-pitch homer, came in his offspring. The year after Mueller's major-league career ended, his son Donald Frederick Mueller was born. Don also was a baseball player, and he stuck in the major leagues from 1948 to 1959, hitting .296 with 65 home runs in his career, earning two All-Star selections. Mueller is probably best known for his ninth-inning slide into third base as a New York Giant in the decisive third game of the playoff for the 1951 NL pennant against the Brooklyn Dodgers. Whitey Lockman had doubled off Don Newcombe, cutting Brooklyn's lead to 4–2, and Mueller, sliding into third on the play, tore tendons in his left ankle. As Mueller departed for pinch-runner Clint Hartung, Brooklyn made a pitching change. The next batter, Bobby Thomson, hit the Shot Heard Round the World off Dodger reliever Ralph Branca. But if both members of the Mueller family had their 15 minutes of fame, the patriarch and his first-pitch blast came first.

Like Mueller, Bert Campaneris has a facet of his life that is more remembered than his first-pitch homer. But in Campy's case, it's not his progeny, but his versatility that sparks the memories of baseball fans. On most days, Campaneris played shortstop, where his speed and solid glove made him one of the more valuable players in the American League in the late 1960s and 1970s. His bat was generally an afterthought—but not in his first big-league at-bat.

In 1964, Campaneris was playing in Double-A Birmingham, where he hit .325 and made the Southern League All-Star team. On July 22nd, he was called up by Kansas City, after A's shortstop Wayne Causey injured his elbow. The following day, Campy found himself in Minneapolis, playing shortstop and batting second against Minnesota pitcher Jim Kaat. In the top of the first inning, Campy dug in for his first plate appearance, locked in on Kaat's first offering, and ripped a fastball over the left field wall. Not content with one homer, Campy hit another in the seventh inning off a Kaat curveball, leaving him 3-for-4 with three RBIs in Kansas City's 4–3 victory.

A jubilant Campy spoke of his happiness at his debut, and confessed when told that he was only the third rookie to hit two homers in his first game, "When I hear that, it makes me even happier." The skinny 5'10" shortstop hit only two more homers in the remainder of 1964—and save for a power surge in 1970 when he hit 22 homers, he otherwise never eclipsed eight in a season.

He did however eclipse eight positions played in a single game on September 8, 1965. With the A's holding up the rear of the American League, the team had a day for Campaneris at that night's matchup with the California Angels. Someone—likely the ever-enterprising A's owner Charlie O. Finley—came up with the idea of allowing Campaneris to play all nine positions that night.

Campy started the game at shortstop, played the second inning at second base, the third inning at third base, moved across the outfield from left to right in the fourth through sixth innings, played first base in the seventh inning, pitched in the eighth inning, and caught in the ninth inning. Campy was involved in a tough home-plate collision on a double steal that ended his night there, although the injury was not serious. He went 0-for-3 at the plate, had an error in right field, and allowed a run in his inning of pitching. Four players have since played all nine positions in one game (Minnesota's Cesar Tovar in 1968, Texas's Scott Sheldon in 2000, Detroit's Shane Halter in 2000, and fellow Tiger Andrew Romine in 2017), but Campy struck first. Just like he did at the plate.

⌐⌐

While a first-pitch home run can be a moment to launch a lengthy big-league career, it also can essentially *be* a big-league career. Such is the case with Houston Astros first baseman Mark Saccomanno. A 6'3", 210-pound first baseman from Houston, Saccomanno was a power hitter who launched 106 balls out of parks between 2004 and 2008. Unfortunately, 105 of them were hit in minor-league parks. Despite 22 homers at Triple-A Round Rock in 2007 and 27 more in 2008, Saccomanno initially did not get the September call-up from the Astros.

A week had gone by since the end of the AAA season, and Saccomanno recalled, "I actually went off and played around on the beach in Galveston for a few days with some buddies." He was doing laundry at his girlfriend's house near Austin when the phone rang on the afternoon of September 9, 2008. Houston third baseman Ty Wigginton had a minor injury and the Astros suddenly could use a power-hitting pinch-hitter. How soon could Saccomanno get to Houston?

After a pleading phone call to the Round Rock clubhouse manager, Saccomanno got into his old locker room to grab his equipment, jumped onto a flight to Houston, and made it to Minute Maid Park and into uniform just as the game began.

Saccomanno's former Round Rock manager Dave Clark was in the dugout as a coach for the Astros. The two had formed "a nice relationship," in Saccomanno's words, in several minor-league campaigns together, and Clark sat down by the nervous newcomer and told him that once the second inning began, he would toss some balls for a mini batting practice in the stadium tunnel.

Saccomanno was rusty, now recalling that he "hadn't touched a baseball in seven days, which is like dog years in baseball." Saccomanno asked if he would get in the game that night and told Clark that if he did get to bat, he would probably take a pitch. Clark, characterized by his former player as "a very aggressive guy," didn't agree with this approach. "Motherf—er, you better be ready," he told Saccomanno. "You get a fastball the first pitch, you better f—ing swing."

In the fifth inning, with two out and no one on base in a scoreless game, Houston manager Cecil Cooper called another pinch-hitter back to the dugout and sent up Saccomanno.

"Literally, not only was I cold, but I didn't get on deck to take any swings," remembered Saccomanno. "I had to walk straight from the dugout to the batter's box, trying to tell myself, 'Okay, left foot goes, then right foot goes.' I can't even feel my legs. I get in there, trying to act like I ... remember how to swing."

Pirates pitcher Ian Snell threw an outside fastball, just as Dave Clark had foreseen. Saccomanno was ready.

"There's a Malcolm Gladwell book where he talks about police officers in high-stress situations . . . and they said that it's like everything slows down and you are hypersensitive and your adrenaline is pumping so hard that the officer remembers seeing the bullet [that he fired] . . . clear as day," said Saccomanno. "When Ian Snell threw that pitch . . . I remember what it looked like, and I remember having to reach outside to get it."

Saccomanno thought he had flied out to right field, but the ball carried and flew over the wall for a memorable home run. In his hometown, in front of a large contingent of family and friends, the 28-year-old rookie had waited a long time for his debut, but he had made it a debut to remember—thanks to an assist from his minor-league manager.

"If Dave Clark never said that, I don't know if I would have swung," says Saccomanno. "I kind of figured that might be my 15 minutes. Going back and seeing a lot of people . . . it's amazing how many people say they were watching that game that had a nice experience watching that."

Saccomanno went 2-for-10 as a big-league hitter, but he certainly made his debut in style.

"He really made it big," said manager Cecil Cooper after the game.

Like many of the other first-pitch phenoms, Willson Contreras might have seemed like he came out of nowhere when he homered on the first big-league pitch he faced. But like most of those before him, he actually put in years of grinding, first to become a catcher, and second to become a major leaguer. After that, Contreras's next path appears to be the one to stardom.

To see Contreras catching for the Chicago Cubs is to see a player who looks like he was born to catch—take-charge attitude, machine-gun throwing arm, burgeoning leadership qualities. But in fact, he was a third baseman who was stuck in the minor leagues. In his fourth year of professional baseball, Contreras was frustrated with his role when one day at A-level Boise, he saw a vacant set of catching gear and put it on. He walked to the bullpen, where he encountered Oneri Fleita, who was the Cubs' vice president of player personnel. Fleita asked Contreras if he wanted to catch, and Willson answered in the affirmative.

Even once he became a catcher, Contreras languished in the minors until 2015, when he hit .333 at Double-A Tennessee. The Cubs appeared to be set behind the plate, but when veteran Miguel Montero struggled in early 2016, Contreras got the call from the parent club.

Cubs manager Joe Maddon brought Contreras along slowly, putting him in to catch the ninth inning of a 6–0 win over Pittsburgh on June 17th. After a day off for the rookie, Madden called on him to pinch-hit in the sixth inning of the game against Pittsburgh on the 19th. The Cubs held a 4–1 lead, and a runner was on base when Contreras stepped up to face reliever A. J. Schugel.

The Wrigley Field crowd knew about the promising newcomer, and greeted him to his first plate appearance with a standing ovation. ESPN was televising the game on *Sunday Night Baseball*. Pittsburgh pitching coach Ray Searage stopped the game to go to the mound and talk to Schugel. Or perhaps to ice Contreras, who smiled a slightly nervous grin as he waited. Whatever Searage said, it presumably wasn't to let Contreras murder the first pitch. The delay continued as Schugel threw to first base once, and then again. But Contreras had waited for more than seven years of minor-league baseball to get to his moment. He could spare a few seconds.

When Schugel finally pitched, he threw a breaking ball that hung in the middle of the plate. Contreras promptly crushed a high flyball that rode over the 400-foot sign in center field into the first few rows of the Wrigley Field bleachers. Contreras practically skipped around the bases, clenching his fist, thumping his chest, and later exchanging a round of elated high fives with virtually the entire Cubs dugout. He even briefly popped back up for a curtain call, as the Wrigley denizens burst into even louder applause.

Humility came quickly for Contreras. He recalled after the game, "After I hit the homer, they said, 'Hey, we're happy but you got to go to the bullpen.'" Contreras promptly did so, warming up pitchers in the late innings.

The Cubs won 10–5, and after the game, Contreras was still full of adrenaline. "I still feel like I'm in the high sky," he confessed to reporters.

The Cubs hadn't necessarily intended to carry a third catcher for the rest of the season, but after his quick start, Contreras was simply too good to send back down. He hit .282 with 12 home runs, and even found himself starting Game 7 of the World Series (he was 1-for-2 with an RBI double).

Contreras was even better in 2017, and looks poised to be one of the best catchers in baseball for the foreseeable future. Maybe he'll be the first Hall of Famer of the first-pitch phenoms. But even if not, he has a great story for his grandchildren someday.

CHAPTER 12

SIX HITS IN A GAME

Number of Times Accomplished: 114 times (in a nine-inning game).

First Instance: Davy Force, Philadelphia A's, June 27, 1876.

Most Recent Instance: Anthony Rendon, Washington Nationals, April 30, 2017.

Likely Achievers: While plenty of good hitters and Hall of Famers are in the club, only four players with 3,000 hits have gotten six hits in a game, and it took extra innings for Tony Gwynn to do so. Ty Cobb, Cal Ripken Jr., and Paul Waner are the only batters with 3,000 hits who knocked out six in a nine-inning game.

Surprises: Pitcher Guy Hecker (812 career hits) is the only pitcher on the list. Unbelievably, turn-of-the-20th-century outfielder Zaza Harvey had just 86 career hits—but managed six in one game in 1902. Jim Fridley was a .248 career hitter with 105 hits, but six came in a single 1952 game.

Likelihood of Additional Occurrences: With five games with six or more hits in the 2010s (eight players if extra-inning games are included), there should be many more players to join this group.

If the game of baseball can seem at times to be stacked against a hitter, it is certainly stacked against a hitter trying to put together a run of hits. Not only does he have to contend with quality pitching and athletes on defense, he must depend on the opposition to have a short enough memory to continue giving him a chance to amass base hits—and on his own team to get him enough times at bat to continue banging out hits. Six hits in a game accordingly stands as a feat of consistency, a bit of luck, and tremendous hitting.

"Wee" Davy Force would hardly seem a likely candidate to be the sport's first six-hit slugger. Standing a mere five feet four inches tall, and weighing as little as 130 pounds, Force looked more like a bat boy than a great hitter. Unfortunately, he often hit like the bat boy as well. Force was a career .249 hitter who managed a single home run in over 4,000 major-league at-bats. In the year that he wrote his name in baseball's record books, he batted .230—in fact, he batted .214 outside of the one game that made his mark.

On June 27, 1876, Force's Philadelphia Athletics visited the Chicago White Stockings. The game was a slugfest, as the *Chicago Tribune* noted that the game was won by "good batting and faulty umpiring." Another account criticized the teams' fielding performance and termed it "without doubt one of the worst, if not the worst" games of the year "except for batting."

It wasn't a bad day for Force, who opened the game with a bloop single to right field (actually, he opened the bottom of the first, as the visiting A's hit last, apparently due to winning a coin toss). Force was stranded that time, but had another hit in the third inning and came around to score. He managed another single in the fifth, and then added an RBI double in the sixth inning. Another Force single keyed a four-run inning in the eighth, and in the ninth inning, after Chicago had climbed ahead 13–10, Force had another single—his sixth hit of the day—but it looked like it would go for nothing after an apparent game-ending out. But the umpire subsequently ruled the ball to have been foul, and given a second life, the Athletics won the game, 14–13, with Force scoring the winning run. Despite the game being an offensive slugfest, Force stood very much alone. No other player eclipsed three hits.

Force was in the major leagues until 1886, but he never duplicated his great hitting feat. Probably the most interesting part of his life—other than his six-hit game—was being accosted as a murder suspect in a case of mistaken identity in 1897. A public statement from his employer assured the world that Force was no killer—just a pint-sized former shortstop who couldn't be gotten out one day in 1876.

Only twice in a nine-inning game has a player eclipsed six hits, and neither was exactly a foreseeable feat. Before he became a legendary manager, before he allegedly tried to catch a grapefruit dropped from an airplane, Wilbert Robinson was a catcher for the Baltimore Orioles. While his physique had not yet reached the rotund proportions that age would bring, a minor-league manager in 1885 described Robinson as looking like "a choice cut of sirloin." Later in his career, Robinson developed into a solid hitter—he batted .273 for his career. But in 1892, he had never hit above .271 in any season, and was coming off a .216 season the previous year. Robinson's mark as a player was as the good-humored catcher for the Baltimore mini-dynasty of the late 1890s. But he had quite a day on June 10, 1892.

The Orioles and St. Louis Browns were both near the bottom of the National League standings as the teams prepared for a doubleheader. In the opening game, St. Louis sent veteran Pretzels Getzein to the mound, and Baltimore greeted him roughly. Robinson singled in the first inning, but that was only a part of the five runs of damage inflicted by the Orioles. In the second inning, Robinson had another single, and the Orioles added five more runs. Two innings and 10 runs into his day, Getzein was pulled, trailing 10–1. It didn't get better for St. Louis, although it did for Robinson.

Reliever Joe Young followed Getzein to the mound for his only major-league appearance. It was his only appearance because he matched Getzein, allowing 10 more runs in just two innings, leaving the Browns trailing by a 20–1 count after four innings of play. Robinson continued his personal onslaught, singling in the third inning and doubling in the fourth. St. Louis turned to Ted Breitenstein to finish the game, but Robinson had his fifth hit in five innings when he singled off Breitenstein in the fifth frame.

Robinson singled in the seventh and again in the ninth, for his seventh hit of the game. He equaled the Browns' *team* hit total in the 25–4 rout, and also managed to knock in 11 runs, nearly 20 percent of his season's total. Robinson caught the second game as well, adding another pair of hits in that one—off poor Pretzels Getzein, who was battered for a 9–3 loss in the day's second game.

Contemporary accounts failed to appreciate the unusual nature of Robinson's feat. Multiple references mention seven hits as "the record of the season." There's no apparent recognition that he not only had set a nine-inning hit record that would stand for over eighty years, but a single-game RBI record that would last over 30 years. Indeed, multiple sources corroborate that it wasn't until the early to mid-1910s when Robinson's feat was confirmed and noted in the baseball record books.

But Robinson's mark in baseball would not come at the plate, but in the dugout. He coached under his old Baltimore teammate, John McGraw, and then managed the Brooklyn Dodgers for nearly two decades, winning NL pennants in 1916 and 1920. Robinson is remembered for feats like instituting a "Bonehead Club" in an effort to curb dumb plays, but then becoming the first and only member by utilizing the wrong lineup card. As mentioned above, in 1914, he tried to catch a baseball dropped from a plane—but instead, a grapefruit was dropped and the subsequent explosion horrified Robinson. The grapefruit substitution has erroneously been credited to one of Robinson's young Brooklyn players—an outfielder named Casey Stengel, who went on to a remarkable managing career of his own.

⁓

Robinson's big day aside, for most players, seven hits is an impossibility in a nine-inning game, based solely off the number of times at bat. To go above and beyond Robinson's total of seven hits would take extra innings—perhaps even nine of them. Cleveland shortstop Johnny Burnett used 18 innings—two full games of innings—to set the all-time record of nine hits in a single game on July 10, 1932.

Burnett was a solid, slap-hitting middle infielder, who wound up hitting .284 over nine big-league seasons—mostly as a part-time player. He was at .298 for the 1932 season when July 10th rolled around and found his Indians hosting the Philadelphia A's. The game may have been destined to be unusual. The A's were in the midst of a homestand, but Pennsylvania did not allow Sunday baseball, and so the A's and Indians traveled from Philadelphia to Cleveland for a single Sunday game. The game that day was termed "one of the most spectacular long-distance victories in baseball history" by Associated Press writer Gayle Talbot, who also called it "a game the likes of which won't be seen once in a blue moon." That was certainly true for Burnett.

Batting second, Burnett had an infield single in the first inning off Philadelphia starter Lew Krause. Krause allowed Burnett and two team-mates to score and was pulled after the first inning, with "reliever" Eddie Rommel pitching the ensuing 17 innings.

Burnett singled to left field in the second, and did so again in the fourth inning against Rommel. He had an RBI double to right field in the fifth inning for his fourth hit, which staked the Tribe to a 7–5 lead. He led off the seventh inning with a single to right field, and after the Indians had claimed a 14–13 lead in the inning, he finished the frame by proving human—striking out against Rommel.

With the Indians down to their last out in the ninth, Burnett delivered a sixth hit, singling home Willie Kamm to tie the game at 15 and send it to extra innings. He doubled to right field in the 11th for his seventh hit, but that inning ended with a double play, which extended the game.

In the 13th inning, Burnett singled to center for his eighth hit of the game, a mark that stands unequaled. In case that wasn't enough, he lined another single in the 16th inning for his ninth and final hit of the day. His teammates then rallied to tie the game at 17. A 17th-inning flyout ruined Burnett's bid for the only double-digit hit game in MLB history. Eric McNair doubled in Jimmie Foxx in the top of the 18th, and the A's won the game 18–17 in 18 innings.

Burnett's 9-for-11 day of work "might have established a major league record" per the Associated Press, which did reference Wilbert Robinson's big game. There were many offensive stars in a game with 58 total hits—with Cleveland's team total of 33 then an all-time mark. Earl

Averill and Ed Morgan each had five hits for Cleveland, while Foxx had six hits, including three home runs.

Burnett's average climbed 26 points to .323 after the game. He finished the season at .297 and was out of baseball after 1935. He never replicated his performance in the odd Pennsylvania blue law slugfest—but then, few teams have ever equaled the numbers put up that day.

Among the most unlikely of six-hit sluggers was a rookie outfielder for the Cleveland Indians named Jim Fridley. A former FBI employee and World War II veteran, Fridley went to college after the war and thus did not sign with the Indians until 1948, when he turned 24. He worked his way to the big leagues in 1952, and two weeks into the season, had the game of his brief career.

After a dozen games as a big leaguer, Fridley was hitting .216 and had amassed just eight hits. But on Tuesday, April 29th, he and the Indians played a night game at Shibe Park in Philadelphia that Fridley would never forget.

Facing Alex Kellner of the A's, Fridley batted sixth and singled in a run in the first inning. Cleveland added five more runs that inning, and blasted Kellner for three more in the second inning, including another single for Fridley.

With Cleveland's lead extending to 12–2 in the fourth, Fridley led off with an infield single and came around to score as Cleveland added two more runs in that frame. Fridley singled to left field in the fifth inning, for his fourth hit of the day.

In the eighth inning, Fridley batted second and hit another single to left field. The Indians batted around, and later that inning, he added another single to left for his sixth hit of the game, as Cleveland extended its lead to 21–6.

The Indians won 21–9, and because Fridley batted sixth, he found himself waiting "in the hole" when Dale Mitchell made the Indians' final out in the ninth inning. Still, the six singles earned him credit for tying "the modern record" for hits in a game, and raised his career batting average 110 points to .326. He wrote in a newspaper column that shortly after his big game, his wife had called and told him, "Well, it's about time." In the same article, Fridley speculated that he would stick with the Indians because outfielder Bob Kennedy had been activated by the US Marines.

But after getting six hits in one game, Fridley had only 10 hits in the entire month of May, as his average plummeted to .238. He finished the year at .251, but ended up collecting a career total of just 424 major-league at-bats for three teams. Aside from his six-hit game, Fridley's other historical footnote was being part of a 17-player trade between the Orioles and Yankees after the 1954 season that sent Don Larsen to New York. But on one great day in 1952, Fridley reached heights that most Hall of Fame hitters could only imagine.

On the day that Pittsburgh second baseman Rennie Stennett made baseball history, he didn't even expect to be in the lineup. It was September 16, 1975, and Stennett, a 24-year-old slap hitter who entered the game at .278 for the season, was playing hurt. "I got to the ballpark and I wasn't supposed to play that day," he recalled. "I had twisted my ankle and it was badly swollen." The Pirates were solidly ahead of the second-place Phillies and had all but clinched the NL East division title. Stennett could be forgiven had he chosen to sit out that afternoon's game at Wrigley Field. But he didn't, and he would be glad he didn't.

Leading off the game, Stennett doubled down the first base line off Cub starter Rick Reuschel. He later recalled, "[T]hat told me that day I was gonna do good because as a right-handed hitter, when I'm hitting the ball to the right side, I know I'm hitting good." So were the rest of the Pirates, who drove Reuschel from the game after just ⅓ of an inning. The team batted around and Stennett singled again as part of a nine-run first inning. With the game more or less immediately over, the question was how would Stennett fare.

He singled to center off Tom Dettore in the third, and doubled to left field to lead off the fifth. The Pirates batted around again in that inning, and Stennett singled in a run—making five hits in five innings with his second multi-hit inning. The Pirates stretched their lead to 18–0 after five innings.

Stennett's ankle was still balky, and he asked to come out of the game, but manager Danny Murtaugh, sensing history, told Stennett he would not pull him until he made an out. Stennett singled to center field to lead off the seventh, and with two out in the eighth, hit a triple to right field for his seventh hit of the day. Murtaugh then did oblige him, sending in pinch-runner Willie Randolph for Stennett. Murtaugh joked after the game that he had heard that Wilbert Robinson in his managing days would pull any hitter with six hits to protect his record. The Pirates won 22–0 and Stennett had his day in history.

Stennett was a career .274 hitter who left the big leagues at age 30 after signing a disastrous five-year $3 million contract with the San Francisco Giants prior to the 1980 season. But his greatest baseball legacy wasn't his seven-hit game—it was his role on September 1, 1971, when Stennett was part of the first all-black starting lineup in major-league history. Stennett led off and played second base in that game as well—joining future Hall of Famers Roberto Clemente and Willie Stargell in the historic lineup. Pittsburgh won that game 10–7 and manager Murtaugh (who was white—the managing color barrier would hold for another five years until Frank Robinson managed Cleveland) told reporters, "I put the best athletes out there. The best nine I put out there happened to be black. No big deal. Next question."

And so, four years after his first contribution to baseball history, Stennett had added a second achievement. And this time, nobody denied that it was a big deal.

On April 30, 2017, Washington Nationals third baseman Anthony Rendon became the newest member of the six-hit club. It was part of the up-and-down cycle that has already marked Rendon's brief career. In 2014, as a second-year player, Rendon exploded. He hit .287 with 21 home runs for the Nats, leading the league by scoring 111 runs. He finished fourth in the NL in WAR, and fifth in voting for the NL MVP award that fall.

The following year, Rendon slumped painfully. He hit .264, and his power disappeared, as his slugging percentage dropped from .473 to .363. In fact, his season was so awful that when he somewhat returned to form in 2016 (.270, 20 home runs), he was named NL Comeback Player of the Year.

April 2017 had not treated Rendon well. He was batting .226 with no home runs and five RBIs. On April 30th, facing Mets ace Noah Syndergaard, Rendon entered one of his "up" cycles of productivity. He grounded a single to left field in the first inning, knocking in two runs. In the third, against reliever Sean Gilmartin, he ripped a long home run to left field, his first of the season.

He faced Gilmartin again in the fourth, and blasted a three-run homer to left-center, giving him three hits, two home runs, and six RBIs as the Nats took a 10–5 lead. In the fifth inning, Fernando Salas took over for the Mets and he kept Rendon in the ballpark—barely—as his three-run double off the top of the wall in right-center field brought him to nine RBIs in the game.

Rendon lined a single to left field in the seventh, and finished his day in the bottom of the eighth with his third home run, another left field shot off backup catcher Kevin Plawecki. Six hits, three blasts, ten RBIs for Rendon—as suddenly, his April stats went from subpar to very solid, all on the strength of one game.

Only one other player—Reds catcher Walker Cooper in 1949—had six hits, three homers, and 10 RBIs in a single game. Rendon drew a large ovation when he took the field for the ninth inning, and admitted afterward of the history he had made, "I was aware of some of it."

Rendon was as mystified by the sudden hot streak as anyone, telling reporters after the game when asked if he had changed his approach, "No, I feel the same.... Your guess is as good as mine."

Guesses aside, Rendon rode his hot streak to his best season as a National, as he had already eclipsed his previous career highs for batting average (.301), home runs (25), and RBIs (100) in 2017.

CHAPTER 13

THE SUPER SLAM

Number of Times Accomplished: 28.

First Instance: Roger Connor, Troy Trojans, September 9, 1881.

Most Recent Instance: Rajai Davis, Detroit Tigers, June 30, 2014.

Likely Achievers: There are a few baseball immortals on the list—like Babe Ruth and Roberto Clemente.

Surprises: Early 1970s outfielder Ron Lolich—his cousin Mickey was the famous Detroit Tiger—hit just four career home runs, but he got his money's worth on at least one of them. Likewise for Pittsburgh first baseman Jack Phillips, whose career homer total was just nine.

Likelihood of Additional Occurrences: While there are some gaps in the history of this feat, there's no reason to think another addition to the group isn't right around the corner.

It's happened 28 times in the major leagues, but probably 28 million times in backyards and sandlots. What kid hasn't daydreamed it? It's a home game, the bottom of the ninth inning, the good guys down by three runs but the bases full. It's happened enough that it has a name—several of them actually. But whether you call it a super slam or an ultimate grand slam, every child who has fantasized about a baseball career has hit several—even if only in his or her own mind.

The men who hit super slams are a varied lot. There are a couple of stars, there are a few solid players who are known for something else in their careers, and there are a few more whose careers basically consisted of that single moment.

The man who hit the first super slam simply isn't as well-known as he should be. His super slam was disdained in press coverage, and his career of excellence was more or less forgotten for a half-century or so. But his story had a surprising last chapter that came decades after his death—and Roger Connor is a Hall of Famer, albeit still an underrated legend.

Connor was born in 1857 in Waterbury, Connecticut, and disregarded his parents' wishes in order to pursue a career in the disreputable art of baseball. In fact, Connor's father died when he was 14 years old, and as the oldest son in a family of 11 children, Connor worked in a brass foundry and a needle factory, among other jobs, to support his family.

At 6'3", and about 220 pounds, he was a giant for his era, and was a slugging left-handed first baseman—at least, after a rookie season as a left-handed third baseman who committed 60 errors. In his second season, playing for the National League Troy Trojans, Connor connected on his super slam.

On September 10, 1881, in Riverside Park at Albany, New York, the Worcester Brown Stockings held a 7–3 ninth-inning lead over Connor and his Troy teammates. The Trojans loaded the bases on a trio of hits, and after an out, pitcher Tim Keefe drew a bases-loaded walk to narrow the deficit to 7–4. But after leadoff hitter John Cassidy made the second out, the game was entirely up to Connor.

The big man did not disappoint. Connor slugged a blast that was contemporaneously described as "over the center fielder's head" and "a terrific drive to right." Wherever he hit the ball, it was a grand slam on the Trojans' potential last out of the game, and a 7–4 deficit became an 8–7 victory.

The super slam was hardly an overnight phenomenon in media circles. The *Troy Daily Times* referenced the game as being notable for errors, and the teams' play as "notable for its lack of life." The column went on to cite the Trojans winning the game only due to poor defense from Worcester's third baseman, poor pitching from Worcester's Lee Richmond, and "the accidental hit of the Megatherian Connor." In essence, Connor was rewarded for the first super slam by being called an elephant in his local newspaper.

Public perceptions aside, home-run heroics were not unusual for Connor. In 1886, he hit a ball out of the Polo Grounds, which impressed the crowd so much that when the hat was passed, accounts indicate that Connor took away about $500 for the blast.

In all, Connor hit 138 home runs in the major leagues, never topping 17 in any individual season and ending his big-league career in 1897. Today, Connor's home-run total doesn't sound especially impressive, but it was the career home-run record until it was broken by Babe Ruth in the 1920s.

Not only a great player, but also a devout family man, Connor was probably more remarkable as a man than a baseball player. He married the same month as he hit his super slam, and he and his wife, Angeline, had a daughter, Lulu, who was Connor's pride and joy. Tragically, she contracted dysentery and died just before her first birthday. A couple years later, Connor and his wife decided to adopt a child. They went to a local orphanage and asked for a blonde-haired girl, essentially a child in the image of the deceased Lulu. But Connor saw a dark-haired little girl in a rocking chair singing to her doll. Connor sat down and called to the little girl, who ran to him, snuggled into a hug, and didn't let go. And so the Connors adopted a dark-haired daughter, Cecilia.

Friends recalled Connor singing duets with young Cecilia in happy days, and later involving his wife and daughter in managing the local Waterbury minor-league squad, where he played for seven years after his big-league days. When the former player's finances dried up during the Depression, he and Angeline both lived out their days in Cecilia's house with her husband and children. Connor died in 1931, and given a general lack of money, was buried in an unmarked grave.

Fortunately, in the early 1970s, as Hank Aaron chased Babe Ruth's record, many wondered whose record Babe had broken. Given the uptick in interest, Connor was posthumously inducted into the Baseball Hall of Fame in 1976, and in 2001, the city of Waterbury, Connecticut, unveiled a suitable grave marker honoring the first great baseball slugger, the original super slammer himself, Roger Connor.

In the years since Connor's initial blast, only once has a slugger hit a super slam that culminated in a frantic dash for home plate rather than the leisurely lope of a victorious slugger. But on July 25, 1956, second-year Pirates slugger Roberto Clemente hit the only inside-the-park super slam in baseball history. It was one of the most electrifying ends to a game in memory.

Clemente wasn't the first Puerto Rican to play in the major leagues in the post-segregation era, but he was the first Puerto Rican superstar. That said, the 1956 version of Clemente was far from a finished product. He did bat .311 that season, and the *Pittsburgh Press* did note after Clemente's slam that "down in Puerto Rico, they're calling the Pirates the 'Clementes.'" This honor was for the young star "who's making a habit of winning games for the Buccos with his home runs." In fact, Clemente hit only seven homers in 1956, but he rapidly turned into a player who could win a game in every way possible.

But that metamorphosis was still ongoing on July 25th, when Clemente came to bat at Forbes Field in the bottom of the ninth inning with the bases loaded, no outs, and his team trailing the Cubs by an 8–5 count. Clemente faced Cub Jim Brosnan and turned on Brosnan's first pitch—apparently a hanging slider—and roped it deep into the left field corner. The ball overshot Cub left fielder Jim King and then hit the side wall, rolling along the warning track toward center field. The three runners ahead of Clemente—Hank Foiles, Bill Virdon, and Dick Cole—scored easily.

Clemente hustled into third where Pirate manager Bobby Bragan was coaching third base. With the score now tied and no outs, Bragan put up a stop sign, which Clemente promptly ran through. "I all but tackled him," Bragan admitted after the game, although he also stated that as Clemente beat the relay throw from Ernie Banks of the Cubs, he would waive the customary $25 fine for running through the stop.

Clemente, for his part, later told the Associated Press, "I say to Bobby: 'Get out of my way, and I score.' . . . I think we have nothing to lose . . . and [if] I score, the game—she is over and we don't have to play no more tonight."

Indeed, Clemente was safe at the plate, at which time "[h]is teammates mobbed him en route to the dugout and when they reached the clubhouse, they started in all over again."

The incident wasn't forgotten by Clemente or by some of his opponents. Before the 1960 World Series, Brosnan wrote of the play for *Life* magazine, chastising Clemente for "a Latin-American variety of showboating," going on to state that when Clemente "ran right over his manager" the play had "excited the fans, startled the manager, shocked me and disgusted my club."

More bizarre than Roger Connor's slam being reduced to an elephantine fluke, Clemente's consummate mixture of talent and hustle was somehow termed as showboating. Clemente and the Pirates won that 1960 World Series, and unlike Brosnan, Clemente is enshrined in the Baseball Hall of Fame on the basis of many of the skills that he showed in his historic slam.

⌒

The super slam isn't just a feat for Hall of Famers. And sometimes it's not just who hits the slam, it's the fact that the game ends up resting on one swing that is shocking. That was the case for Brooks Conrad on May 20, 2010. Conrad's entire career covers 460 major-league at-bats, in which he hit .200 with a total of 19 home runs. But more surprising than Conrad turning into Roy Hobbs of *The Natural* was that Conrad's memorable swing actually mattered.

Conrad was watching the game from the bench when his Atlanta Braves fell behind the Reds 8–0 in the second inning. The lead was 9–1 in the fifth inning, and with the game entering the bottom of the ninth inning, the Reds held a 9–3 advantage. The Braves' win expectancy had reached 0 percent in the eighth inning, and it still hung there as the ninth began.

Reliever Mike Lincoln had worked two scoreless innings and he was still in the game as the bottom of the ninth inning began. The Braves loaded the bases on a trio of singles from Troy Glaus, Eric Hinske, and Yuniel Escobar. When Nate McLouth singled in two runs and cut the lead to 9–5, Lincoln was pulled and reliever Nick Masset followed. Masset walked David Ross, bringing the tying run to the plate. He then induced Martín Prado to ground to third, but Red Miguel Cairo bobbled the ball, and the game was 9–6, with the bases still loaded. Reliever Arthur Rhodes got Jason Heyward to strike out, and with the pitcher's spot in the batting order due, manager Bobby Cox called for Conrad.

The significance of the moment was not lost on Conrad. Looking back seven years later, he recalled "being down eight runs early . . . and everybody just keeps battling and working some at-bats . . . and all of the sudden, it's 9–6 bases loaded, and we've got a shot."

Pinch-hit super slams are incredibly rare—only one had happened before Conrad's blast—but at least Conrad found himself with a chance to be a hero. The Reds countered with closer Francisco Cordero, who saved 40 games in 2010. Conrad worked a 2-2 count on Cordero, and the 5'10" switch hitter, who was hitting .222 with two home runs on the season, got his pitch.

Cordero threw a fastball and Conrad poked the ball to left field, high but seemingly within the grasp of Reds left fielder Lance Nix. Nix drifted back and farther back, timed his jump, and leaped. The ball hit his glove.

Watching near first base, Conrad told reporters after the game, "it looked like he brought it back." Indeed, Nix had a chance to catch the ball. Conrad thought he had done so. "I put my hands on my helmet and said . . . 'At least we got the sac fly.'" He turned toward the Braves dugout, certain that he was the inning's second out.

But Nix did not catch the ball. He only deflected it just behind him, over the left field wall of Turner Field and into comeback history. As shocked as the fans were, as shocked as his teammates were, no one was more surprised than Conrad. He admitted after the game, "I don't know if I want to watch [a replay]. I'm going to look like a dork out there, thinking he caught it."

A rejuvenated Conrad circled the bases, was mobbed by his teammates, got a congratulatory hug from his children in the clubhouse tunnel, and after apparently being congratulated/assaulted by his teammates with a bottle of sanitizer rub, he began that most 21st century of celebrations—returning missed messages and calls on his cell phone.

In the up-and-down nature of baseball, it is intriguing that Conrad's super slam was also a big moment for rookie reliever Craig Kimbrel, who notched his first major-league win courtesy of the ninth-inning comeback, after only his fourth big-league inning. Kimbrel remains a star who could approach the career saves record if he continues on his current path. Conrad played for five teams in parts of six big-league seasons, none of which saw him with over 156 at-bats. But his mark in history, even if he thought it was just a long out, is secure.

"That game was one of those games that you never know what's going to happen, so you have to play twenty-seven outs, every single game," recalled Conrad, who is now a coach in the Kansas City Royals organization. "It's what I teach now as a coach—you play every out *hard* until the last out is recorded."

If any of Conrad's young charges doubt his lesson, he may just pull out the video and show them his own unlikely moment of baseball glory.

The most recent super slam came from well-traveled outfielder Rajai Davis. Davis, who has played for six different teams, was a Detroit Tiger on June 30, 2014, when he became the 28th super slammer ever. The game occurred on a weekend when the Tigers were celebrating the 30th anniversary of their 1984 World Series championship team. Oddly enough, Detroit's last super slam had come in 2004, again on the weekend that the 1984 team was honored. The slam before that? Hit on June 21, 1994, by Lou Whitaker, who was a star on that 1984 team. Clearly, a

2024 Tiger super slam aligning with a promotional date for the 40th anniversary of the 1984 team is in the cards.

Davis's bases-loaded blast came off Oakland reliever Sean Doolittle, on a 1-0 hanging curveball that Davis popped over the left field fence, changing a 4–1 deficit into a 5–4 victory. Davis would hit other significant home runs—his eighth-inning blast to tie Game 7 of the 2016 World Series will likely remain his biggest—but his super slam was clearly a special moment.

"I can't even remember the last time I did that," Davis said of his super slam. "It must have been in my dreams, while I was sleeping."

All of us have had the dream. But only 28 players have made it a major-league reality.

CHAPTER 14

STEALING FOR THE CYCLE IN ONE INNING

Number of Times Accomplished: 51 (11 since World War II).

First Instance: John McGraw, Baltimore Orioles, July 4, 1899.

Most Recent Instance: Wil Myers, San Diego Padres, August 16, 2017.

Likely Achievers: In light of the fact that stealing home was essentially a staple of the dead ball game, but a rarity since then, this list makes sense—it includes Ty Cobb, Honus Wagner, Shoeless Joe Jackson, and Eddie Collins. Many of the game's legendary base stealers (Henderson, Brock, Coleman) are absent from this list.

Surprises: An aging Dusty Baker (stealing three of his four bases for the 1984 season in one trip) or scrappy infielder Chris Stynes (49 career steals) don't really fit the mental idea of guys who get to first and single-handedly steal a run. But they were.

Likelihood of Additional Occurrences: It had been more than six years since anyone had pulled off the thieving cycle before Wil Myers, but clearly it's still something that will pop up now and again.

While the old axiom is true and a baseball player can't steal first, once he avails himself of any one of the eight ways to reach first base, he can steal his way around the rest of the bases. Hitting for the cycle requires four separate feats, but since first can't be stolen, stealing for the cycle requires stealing second, third, and home. To make matters more interesting, consider the larcenous cycle in terms of a single inning—which will normally mean a single trip around the bases.

The feat is generally rooted in the Dead Ball Era, when baseball put a premium on manufacturing runs by any means possible. But that doesn't mean that stealing for the cycle died with the introduction of the rabbit ball. As long as baseball teams score runs, some speedy, lucky, or desperate runner will dash his own way into history, likely with a great story to accompany his feat.

Before he became baseball's dugout Little Napoleon, John J. McGraw was an outstanding third baseman. McGraw, who came up with the Baltimore Orioles, and moved with the Orioles from the American Association to the National League, was a pivotal part of the 1890s Baltimore dynasty. It was in this capacity, years before his fame as a manager overshadowed the glory of his playing days, that McGraw made an early entry into the baseball record books—by stealing his way around the basepaths.

McGraw the player displayed the same virtues that McGraw the manager would later press—smart, hard-nosed baseball with an emphasis on manufacturing runs. McGraw was 5'7", and even for the Dead Ball Era, wasn't a power hitter (13 career home runs in 17 big-league seasons). But as one author notes, he became "the NL's best leadoff hitter" based on an approach in which he "swung with a short, chopping motion that diminished his power, but he could place the ball anywhere he wanted."

How good was McGraw? Consider his .344 career batting average, 25th all-time—or better yet, for a small-ball advocate, consider his .466 on-base percentage, which is third all-time, behind only Ted Williams and Babe Ruth. Or weigh the testimony of a contemporary source, who wrote in the *Washington Evening Star* on July 5, 1899, "It is the consensus of opinion of base ball experts that it all depends upon McGraw whether the Baltimores finish in the first division or not. . . . Without McGraw, the team is very weak."

In fact, Baltimore slid to fourth place in the National League in 1899, although it can't be blamed on McGraw. At age 26, McGraw found himself managing for the first time. He also hit .391, third best in the NL, and was second in the league in stolen bases with 73. Each total was a career best for McGraw.

On July 4th, he rendered an especially impressive feat, when he stole his way around the bases in a single trip. It was especially amazing when considering that the sleep-deprived Orioles had traveled all night by train from St. Louis, arriving back in Baltimore around 7 a.m. before heading out to the ballpark to play a doubleheader against the Boston Nationals. In the first game of the twinbill, McGraw tried to steal home on a double steal, but was called out by the umpire. He launched himself into a rage, and was promptly ejected from the game. His aggressiveness on the basepaths would remain unchanged.

In the fourth inning of the second game, McGraw bunted for a hit, and then stole second base, and then third. With McGraw on third, outfielder Ducky Holmes drew a walk. McGraw immediately went for the double steal again, and this time he pulled it off, as a reporter explained, "while 'Ducky' was engaged in dodging up and down the base lines." McGraw's run ended up being pivotal—it stretched Baltimore's lead to 4–0, and they held on to win the game, 5–4.

McGraw would see other players steal for the cycle in one inning—twice when he was a manager, one of his Giants pulled off the feat (Bill O'Hara in 1909 and Art Fletcher in 1916), and twice, he watched as another player completed the feat against his team (Honus Wagner in 1907 and Greasy Neale in 1919). He remained a champion of small ball until he retired from the Giants in 1932. The game changed during McGraw's reign, but there were still other players trying to emulate his trick of stealing for the cycle.

McGraw was the first cycle-stealer, but the kings of the feat are two baseball legends who each accomplished it four times. Since it's only been done 11 times in total in the last 75 years, perspective provides an insight on just how dominant these two stars were as baserunners, although their success sprang from very different temperaments and techniques.

Ty Cobb was probably without parallel as a baserunner—if a scientist tried to construct his equal, it would require perhaps the speed and daring of Rickey Henderson in his prime, but combined with a burning and violent intensity that probably would have embarrassed John

McGraw. Always a star, often pilloried for being singularly difficult to get along with (though this confusion has been rebutted carefully and fairly conclusively), Cobb was a polarizing force who blazed a red-hot path through baseball.

Cobb used baserunning as psychological warfare. Fellow star Eddie Collins later recalled, "Cobb was always exerting pressure, always searching out a weak spot here and there to display his seemingly inexhaustible and tireless energy." Biographer Charles Leerhsen explains, "All the pretty slides and steals . . . all the crazy dancing off the bags and even crazier shouts to catcher that he was going on the next pitch . . . all that spoke to his core mission of, as he said many times, 'creating a mental hazard for my opponents.'"

Wagner, in contrast, was hardly imposing looking. Wagner didn't look like a superstar, and he didn't act like one either; he just was one. Cobb would punch you in the jaw and then steal his way around the bases; Wagner would inspire you to consider what a nice, funny-looking guy he was, and then do the same thing. Bill James wrote of Wagner, "He was a gentle, kind man, a storyteller, supportive of rookies, patient with fans, cheerful in hard times, careful of the example that he set for youth, a hard worker, a man who had no enemies and who never forgot his friends" before concluding that "there is no one who has ever played this game that I would be more anxious to have on a baseball team."

It is appropriate then that both men managed to steal for the cycle in an inning four different times. Cobb, in typical fashion, could make it an epic show. On July 12, 1911, for instance, he worked a walk in the first inning against Philadelphia pitcher Harry Krause. Not only did Cobb steal three bags on Krause—he did it on three consecutive pitches. He was insatiable as a baserunner, getting on and stealing second on his next time up. The *Detroit Free Press* noted that "he was about to move on third when Crawford very inconsiderately banged out a home run and thereby forced him to proceed around in the regular way."

While Cobb drew headlines, Wagner did the same, albeit in a less frantic manner. A month after McGraw was the first to steal for the cycle, Wagner replicated the feat in the fourth inning of a game between his Pittsburgh Pirates and the Louisville Colonels, stealing second, third, and then home "while Meekin was winding his arms around in the act of delivering the ball." Wagner's fourth cycle steal included a steal of home in which he "actually hit the plate before the ball left [Cubs pitcher Ed] Reulbach's hand." The *Chicago Tribune* observed, "It was the cleanest, most unquestioned steal home from third base ever yet accomplished."

Cobb and Wagner ended up constituting two-fifths of the first class ever inducted into the Baseball Hall of Fame in 1936. Some might say they stole their way there, one daring baserunning feat at a time.

Of course, stealing for the cycle isn't the exclusive domain of baseball legends. It isn't even the exclusive domain of the speediest players in baseball. Sometimes, stealing for the cycle looks more like desperation than genius. Consider rookie utility man Chris Stynes, who never stole more than 15 bases in a season (49 for his career). When Stynes and the offense-strapped Kansas City Royals faced Randy Johnson, it was time for a little outside-the-box thinking.

Stynes had been called up to the Royals only a few days prior, and had never stolen a base in his two brief periods of major-league service. But the Kansas City Royals were a bad offensive team. They went on to finish 1996 dead last in the American League in runs scored and next to last in home runs. They did, however, steal a lot of bases. On May 12th, they prepared to face Seattle and ace lefty Randy Johnson. Johnson hadn't lost a game since August 1, 1995, and the dominating lefty didn't figure to have a lot of trouble working through the Kansas City lineup. Accordingly, aggressiveness was the rule of the day, and it enabled Stynes to make history.

Batting second and playing left field, Stynes punched a single to right-center off Johnson in the top of the first inning. With a runner on base, Kansas City manager Bob Boone was quick to try to get to Johnson the only way he knew how—with the running game. With Bip Roberts next to bat, Stynes read Johnson's long move to home plate, and took off for second base on the second pitch. He beat catcher Dan Wilson's throw easily. Roberts flied out for the second out of the inning. With first baseman Joe Vitiello at the plate, Stynes took off on a 3-2 pitch from Johnson. It missed the strike zone, and Stynes stole third base standing up.

With Vitiello at first, the most difficult part of Stynes's feat awaited. On Johnson's second pitch to Craig Paquette, Vitiello took off for second. The instant Dan Wilson threw the ball to second base, Stynes broke for home plate on a delayed double steal. Mariner second baseman Joey Cora saw the play coming, took Wilson's throw on the move, and tried to catch Stynes. But Cora's return throw was wild up the third base line. Stynes was safe, and Vitiello went to third on the errant throw.

Stynes's run proved to be the only one the Royals could manufacture against Johnson, who won his 12th consecutive decision as Seattle took the game, 8–5. Stynes stole another base in the eighth inning, meaning that he reached nearly one-tenth of his career stolen base total in the game. Stynes was a career .275 hitter for six different major-league teams. He never made an All-Star Game or played in the postseason, but he did flummox a Hall of Fame pitcher in a memorable inning in 1996. More than two decades later, he's the last American League player to steal for the cycle in an inning.

～

Like Stynes, Jayson Werth would require a little bit of trickery to complete a cycle of stealing. At 6'5", 235 pounds, Werth did not look like a speedster. Fans who remember his later years will be especially surprised to find that he was a deceptively adept baserunner, stealing 132 bases and being caught just 23 times. In two seasons, he swiped 20 bases, and he was only caught four times between the two years.

In 2009, Werth was having one of the better years of his career with the Philadelphia Phillies. He made the All-Star team for the only time in his career, as he slugged 36 home runs and knocked in 99 runs—both marks setting career highs. And on May 12th, he swiped his way around the basepaths in the seventh inning against the Los Angeles Dodgers.

In the seventh inning of that night's home game with the Dodgers, Werth singled to left field with one out off Dodger reliever Will Ohman. Ryan Howard struck out for the inning's second out, but Werth then stole second on the second pitch to Jimmy Rollins. Rollins was then intentionally walked. On the 2-1 pitch to Raúl Ibañez, Werth and Rollins lit out on a successful double steal, which the Dodgers didn't bother to contest with a throw. Ibañez subsequently walked to load the bases, and the moment of truth had arrived for Werth's mad dash around the basepaths.

Reliever Ronald Belisario replaced Ohman, and with a right-handed reliever whose attention could be easily drawn at third, Werth seemed an unlikely candidate to steal home. He did notice, however, that Belisario was paying him almost no attention and catcher Russell Martin was lobbing return throws very slowly to Belisario. On a 2-1 pitch, Werth saw his opening. He worked down the line, took a huge secondary lead, and following a second strike to Pedro Feliz, the moment that Martin lazily tossed the ball back to Belisario, Werth lit out for the plate. Belisario hopped off the mound and fired the ball back to Martin, but too late to catch Werth, who had completed his cycle with a gutsy steal of home. It wasn't Ty Cobb or Jackie Robinson's steal of home, but it was a play that took a massive amount of moxie from Werth.

Werth said after the game that Phillies first base coach Davey Lopes deserved some credit for the play, because he had implored the Philadelphia runners to be more aggressive. "If they're not going to look at you . . . you have to take advantage," Werth told reporters.

For their part, the Dodgers were appropriately humbled.

"It was an embarrassing play," said catcher Martin. "That shouldn't happen. Yes, he timed it perfectly. But I should have been peeking."

Werth turned 38 during the 2017 season, which he spent with the Washington Nationals. He stole only four bases in 2017, but once upon a time, he was a great baseball daredevil. The next two players to successfully steal for the cycle in a single inning, Dee Gordon of the Marlins in 2011 and Wil Myers of the Padres in 2017, both completed the cycle with a delayed double-steal of home—an unusual play, but one lacking the theatrics of Werth's madcap dash. Perhaps the banner for stealing for the cycle should be carried by Werth, whose play has already emphasized that just when people fall asleep on the possibility, another base thief might be lurking.

CHAPTER 15

STEALING SIX BASES IN A SINGLE GAME

Number of Times Accomplished: Seven.

First Instance: George Gore, Chicago White Stockings, June 25, 1881.

Most Recent Instance: Carl Crawford, Tampa Bay Rays, May 3, 2009.

Likely Achievers: There are no flukes on the list—every player who stole six bases in a game was a legitimate big-time base stealer. That said, some of the expected names aren't on the list: Henderson, Brock, and Coleman, for instance.

Surprises: See above. Probably the biggest surprise on this list isn't an individual player, it's the fact that after almost 80 years of no one stealing six bases in a game, three players did so between 1991 and 2009.

Likelihood of Additional Occurrences: Since Carl Crawford's six-steal game in 2009, two players have swiped five bases in a game. This suggests, the general decline in the stolen base aside, that someone else will manage six.

Few players can frustrate opponents like a great base stealer. Fans who remember Maury Wills or Lou Brock or Rickey Henderson can recall those players dancing off the base, wordlessly taunting pitcher, catcher, and opposing manager alike, leaving entire ballparks wondering, "Will he go?" At different eras in baseball history, the cat-and-mouse game of the base stealer has occupied a central place in the drama of baseball. Sometimes, the base stealer controls the game, even when he doesn't run.

But other times, the base stealer does run—and he can stack up stolen bases one on top of the other until he drives the opponent crazy or his own fans into delirium. Six steals in a single game is the number that separates the great performances from the legendary ones. Stealing six bases requires timely hitting (either a batter has to steal home or reach base at least three times), incredible speed, and being lucky enough to not have the bases clogged in front of the would-be base stealer. In other words, like most baseball feats, it takes a perfect storm—and in this case, it also takes "A Perfect Storm." More on that in a few pages.

⌐

George Gore had a great nickname—"Piano Legs"—and the speed to run his way into baseball history, both as a base stealer and as the game's celebrated first salary holdout. Gore was a center fielder and key player on the Chicago White Stockings team that constituted perhaps the first National League dynasty, as they won their league six times in the NL's first 11 seasons. In a 1916 column, former Dead Ball player turned sportswriter Sam Crane named Gore and King Kelly as "the Ty Cobbs of their time and day."

Gore was a .301 hitter, a respected fielder, and—while the statistics of his era are incomplete—quite the threat on the basepaths. In 1881, Gore's third year with the White Stockings, he put together an unforgettable game.

On June 25th, the White Stockings faced the Providence Grays. Chicago, as it had so many times that season, came out on top, picking up a 12–8 win, as the *Chicago Tribune* noted "by virtue of superiority in every point of play, but notably so in base-running." The *Tribune* could have simply credited Gore. He was 3-for-4 in the game and also drew a walk. He reached base in all five plate appearances (it is unclear whether Gore reached on an error or a fielder's choice in the first inning), and on each of the five occasions, stole second base on Providence catcher Emil Gross. Gore is credited with stealing third base twice, apparently once in the sixth inning and once in the seventh inning. This is probably the point to indicate that a stolen base was construed very liberally in 1881. A runner who went from first to third on a single might be given a stolen base. If Gore's move from second to third in the seventh inning was indeed credited as a stolen base, the newspaper account ("Farrell . . . distinguished himself by a wild throw, which allowed Gore to get from second to third") suggests a play that modern scoring would not credit as a stolen base, but rather as advancing on an error. In any case, Gore was credited with seven stolen bases. The game was scored under the rules of its time, and if Gore's accomplishment is cheapened by the possibility that some of Providence's 10 errors may have helped his jaunts around the basepaths, well, that was baseball in the early 1880s.

Chicago won the league in 1881, and Gore's strong play continued, at least until the 1885 World Series, during which he was suspended for drunkenness. He left Chicago after 1886, and played out his big-league career in 1892. Gore's White Stockings teammate/manager Cap Anson reportedly said of him, "Women and wine brought about his downfall." But Gore lived until 1933, and is ultimately remembered less for his base stealing than for his negotiating skills.

Gore had played for New Bedford of the New England League in 1878, and was sold to Chicago after that season. White Stockings owner Albert Spalding offered Gore $1,200 (approximately $41,000 in modern money) to play for Chicago in 1879. Gore declined, asking for $2,500 (the equivalent of approximately $85,000 today). Gore recalled later in life: "I was stubborn. . . . [Spalding] was a little short of furious." The two met again, and for $1,900 (almost $65,000 today), Gore was signed. Few enough players won salary disputes with ownership in the 19th century that Gore's successful holdout probably was an even more rare feat than stealing seven bases in a game.

~

Of the seven occurrences of a player stealing six bases in a game, only one player has ever accomplished the feat twice. And he did it twice in 12 days. Eddie Collins didn't just a have a game to remember; he had a fortnight to remember within the overall context of a Hall of Fame career. But then Collins was almost always unusual.

Born to a railroad freight agent and his wife, Collins grew into a skinny young man who was an outstanding athlete, starring in football and baseball. Unlike most players of his generation, Collins matriculated into higher education, graduating from Columbia University in 1907. He put aside plans of a legal career to give baseball his best efforts.

Those best efforts were remarkable. Collins joined the Philadelphia Athletics in 1907, and became a regular fixture in their lineup in 1908. By 1911, Collins joined Home Run Baker, Stuffy McInnis, and Jack Barry to form the famous $100,000 Infield. Those Athletics teams won the World Series in 1910, 1911, and 1913.

In 1912, Philadelphia struggled to a third-place finish. The blame couldn't properly go to Collins, who hit .348 and led the American League in runs scored. He also stole 63 bases, and twice down the final stretch of the season, made base-stealing history.

On September 11th, the Athletics swiped 11 bases in beating Detroit 9–7. The game was a wild one, with the home-plate umpire getting hit in the face with a bottle thrown from the crowd after he called Ty Cobb out for leaving the batter's box while swatting an apparent run-scoring single. Collins totaled six of Philadelphia's steals, with two coming in the fourth inning, when he reached base on an error and promptly stole second and third. In the eighth inning, Collins had two more steals when he singled, stole second, went to third on a passed ball, and then stole home as the front end of a successful double steal. Collins had two more hits in the game, and stole second on each occasion. His six stolen bases were a once-in-a-lifetime achievement—for anyone except Collins, for whom it would be the gold standard for less than two weeks.

On September 22nd, Collins was back at it. In the first game of a doubleheader in St. Louis against the Browns, he stole second base in the first inning. He repeated that trick in the fifth inning. In the seventh, he singled, stole second, and later stole home on a double steal. In the eighth inning, Collins again singled, and this time, swiped second and third to again reach six steals in a single game. The A's won the game, 8–2, as Collins bashed out four hits to go with his stolen bases.

Collins continued to do great things in baseball, although he was sold for $50,000 to the Chicago White Sox after the 1914 season. He had the dubious honor of being the captain of the infamous "Black Sox" squad that threw the World Series. The college boy was squeaky clean, though, and the career .333 hitter with 741 stolen bases was elected to the Baseball Hall of Fame in 1939. It would be almost 80 years before anyone else would steal six bases in a game.

⌐

Before 1991, Otis Nixon lacked one crucial element necessary to steal six bases in a game—playing time. Nixon was a blazing speedster in the Rickey Henderson/Vince Coleman mold, but before 1991, he had never had more than 271 at-bats in any big-league season. Just before the beginning of the 1991 season, Nixon was traded by the Montreal Expos to the Atlanta Braves, who had been a last-place finisher in 1990.

"I was mad at them," Nixon admitted in a 2015 interview. "They traded me to the worst team. My family didn't want to go to the games." But Atlanta was in the midst of a worst-to-first turnaround, and Nixon now had playing time—and motivation.

The player who had not previously topped .263 in a season hit .297 in 1991, and also had 401 at-bats. Nixon stole 72 bases, finishing just four behind the NL leader, Marquis Grissom.

On June 16th, the Braves finished a three-game series in Montreal, Nixon's first return to his old team. He had a message to deliver. In the first inning, Nixon hit an infield single, and promptly stole second and third on Expo catcher Mike Fitzgerald. Nixon subsequently scored on a Ron Gant double. In the third inning, he singled again, and after watching the first pitch, he stole second and then third on the next two pitches, this time coming in to score on a Lonnie Smith single.

In the ninth inning, with the Braves down by a run, Nixon again singled. On a 1-1 pitch to Terry Pendleton, he took off for second, and just beat the throw on the only close play of his six steals. Two batters later, he swiped third base standing up, setting a new National League record with his sixth stolen base of the day. The Braves couldn't bring him home from third, and Montreal won the game, 7–6.

Nixon was enjoying his new career in 1991 when he tested positive for cocaine with three weeks left in the season. Nixon had previously been arrested on drug charges as a minor leaguer in 1987, and in his second run-in with MLB, he was suspended for 60 days. He thus missed playing in the 1991 World Series, although he rebounded to play in the 1992 Fall Classic and have several more strong seasons, en route to 620 career stolen bases.

Reflecting on his days in baseball recently, Nixon had lost none of his competitive edge. When asked about any threats to his mark of six steals in a game, Nixon expounded, "They [current players] can't steal six bases in a week—I give them one week to steal six bases—any guy out there right now. Not one game . . . a week. It's not bragging, but that's how dominant Rickey Henderson, Vince Coleman, Deion Sanders, Kenny Lofton were, that's what we thrived on."

Nixon's assessment of his own skills was accurate, but perhaps he was shorting his modern competition a bit.

Carl Crawford was "A Perfect Storm." No, that isn't a metaphor, it's just the nickname that Crawford was given—for his combination of contact hitting, power, speed, defensive skills, and baseball intangibles. At 6'2", 230 pounds, Crawford was built bigger than the type of speedsters who have usually dominated baseball's stolen base rankings. But in four of his first five full major-league seasons, Crawford eclipsed 50 stolen bases. Crawford had a decent power stroke, never topping 19 homers in a single season, but reaching double figures in eight of nine seasons. He also led the American League in triples four times, finishing with 136 for his career.

Crawford was candid about his inspiration as a player.

"I like to be like the old school guys," he said. "They played hard, man, and they played from the heart."

A four-time All-Star, Crawford made his mark on the single-game steals list on May 3, 2009. He and the Tampa Bay Rays hosted the Boston Red Sox. In the bottom of the first inning, Crawford walked and stole second, with Red Sox catcher Jason Varitek throwing the ball into center field on the play. In the third inning, he had an infield single, and again swiped second base, this time without a throw.

The pattern continued in the fifth inning. Crawford singled to right field and nabbed his third stolen base on the very next pitch. Two batters later, Crawford also stole third, again without a throw. In the seventh inning, he singled to left and stole second for the fourth time in the game, as Varitek juggled the ball and could not even complete a throw to contest the play. In the eighth inning, with the Rays clinging to a 4–3 lead, Crawford knocked in an insurance run with an infield single, and then tied the modern record by stealing second base, for his sixth swipe of the day.

The scariest part? Crawford didn't realize he had tied the ("modern") record.

"I wish I had known during the game," he admitted afterward. "I probably would have broken it if I knew. I'd have definitely tried."

All four of Crawford's All-Star seasons were in Tampa Bay, but he left the Rays after 2010. He subsequently struggled as a Boston Red Sox signee and then as an L.A. Dodger. Crawford finished his big-league career in 2016, collecting 1,931 hits, scoring 998 runs, and stealing 480 bases. "A Perfect Storm" had rolled his way into the baseball record books, and no one has equaled his feat since.

CHAPTER 16

GETTING ON BASE IN 17 CONSECUTIVE PLATE APPEARANCES

Number of Times Accomplished: Two.

First Instance: Piggy Ward, Baltimore Orioles/Cincinnati Reds, 1893.

Most Recent Instance: Earl Averill, Los Angeles Angels, 1962.

Likely Achievers: Neither really. Both players combined for fewer than 500 total major-league hits.

Surprises: The surprise is that none of the more decorated stars have reached this total. Ted Williams came close—close enough that he was erroneously credited with holding the record of 16 consecutive plate appearances reaching base. Frank Thomas managed 15 in the 1990s, but Ward and Averill carry the torch—even if only one of them gets credit.

Likelihood of Additional Occurrences: One thing is for sure! When and if another player reaches this mark, at least Ward and Averill will have the dignity of being acknowledged for holding the record! It hasn't always been that way.

Anonymity comes in many forms. Anonymity can be based around having a famous father—one whose career outshines your own. It can be having a nickname that nobody understands. It can be not being credited with holding a record that you actually hold—or share. It can be still being kept out of the official record book even once your record is discovered. All of these apply to Piggy Ward and/or Earl Averill.

What batter could get on base 17 times in a row? Surely it's Ty Cobb, the batting average champion of all time? No. DiMaggio, the hit streak king? Nope. Aaron or Ruth or Rogers Hornsby or Stan Musial? No again. The heroes who own this record fit the Everyman profile more than the Superstar profile. Indeed, they were so quiet about making history that nobody remembered that they made it.

Frank Ward was called "Piggy." Nobody seems to know why. Ward was born in Chambersburg, Pennsylvania, in 1867, and somehow made his first appearance in the major leagues at the age of 16 in 1883. He played in one game, went 0-for-5, and didn't make it back for six years. He played for five major-league teams, and totaled 780 career at-bats. Ward was a competent punch-and-judy hitter who had a career .286 batting average. He hit one career home run.

The only unusual thing about Ward's career was a streak he experienced in 1893. Ward got a little hot, a little lucky, and somehow, even while getting traded in the middle of the streak, he reached base in 17 consecutive times at bat.

On June 16, 1893, Ward was playing for the Baltimore Orioles, who were facing the Cincinnati Reds. He made an out in the game's first inning, but then singled in the fourth inning, tripled in the fifth, walked when he came up again in the fifth, and then drew a walk in the sixth inning. He thus ended the game getting on base in his last four plate appearances before the game was called due to rain in the sixth inning. It apparently didn't make much of an impression on the Orioles, who promptly traded him and $1,500 to the Reds for pitcher Tony Mullane.

Ward made his debut for the Reds on June 18th at Louisville. He walked in his first two at-bats, and eventually finished the day with two singles, five walks, and was once hit by a pitch. That made 12 consecutive plate appearances on base. On June 19th, the Reds again played Louisville, and Ward continued. He singled in the first, fifth, sixth, and seventh innings, and added in a walk in the second frame. All together now, Ward had gone 8-for-8, had drawn eight walks, and with a hit-by-pitch, he now totaled 17 consecutive plate appearances in which he reached base. Ward made an out in the first inning of the June 20th game with Louisville, and his streak came to an end.

His streak notwithstanding, Ward wasn't around the big leagues much longer, ending his career there in 1894. His best work of that season was probably after the season on November 30th, when Ward, who had returned to his home in Altoona, Pennsylvania, was drawn to the scene of a fire by the noise of a crowd. An African American barber named James Crocker had overturned a gas stove and was trapped in his shop. Ward ran into the burning building and dragged Crocker to safety, in spite of ferocious burns already inflicted on Crocker. Alas, Ward's efforts did not ultimately save Crocker's life, but in an era when the stark refusal of Cap Anson and others to play against African American opponents had led to the imposition of baseball's color barrier, it says something for Ward that he literally risked his own life to drag Crocker to safety.

He deserved better than to be forgotten. A news article from 1911, shortly before Ward's death, termed him to have been considered "one of the greatest second basemen in the game, being a speedy base runner and dangerous batter." But somehow, it would take 113 years for Ward's achievement to be recognized.

Howard Earl Averill was a .318 career hitter and was inducted into the Baseball Hall of Fame for his numerous and well-known accomplishments. His son, Earl Douglas Averill, was a baseball journeyman who had 1,031 career at-bats for five different major-league teams. He hit .242, with 249 career hits. And of course, the one of the two who also reached base in 17 consecutive plate appearances was Earl Douglas, not Howard Earl. Go figure.

Earl Averill (he preferred to avoid the "Junior" tag) had his best season in baseball in 1961, when he had a career-high 323 at-bats for the Angels and mashed 21 home runs during that period. Averill told a reporter in 2003, "I tried to follow in the footsteps of my dad, and that was a mistake because there was no following him. I guess the expectations were higher than any ambitions." Indeed, the constant media comparisons never helped, including left-handed compliments like a 1961 *Los Angeles Times* article that intended to praise Averill, but couldn't resist slipping in that "It never is fair to compare son with father . . . but there's a possibility that Earl might not look so bad." This was

Earl Averill's career—even the faint praise that a journeyman outfielder received was still damning.

Averill didn't have a great year in 1962, but he did make history. He was hitting .194 coming into play on June 3rd, but an eighth-inning pinch-hit double began his impressive streak. He didn't play in the next two games, but in the second game of a doubleheader on June 7th, he singled twice and drew a walk against the White Sox.

On June 8th against Kansas City, Averill reached base in the second inning on a force-out. This is the point at which the "official" MLB plate appearances by reaching base record leaves his realm of possibility. The official record is restricted to include only those methods of reaching base that improve a hitter's on-base percentage—hit, walk, or hit-by-pitch. But technically, Averill did reach base for the fifth consecutive plate appearance. He walked in the fourth inning, singled in the sixth, and walked in the seventh inning. By an unofficial count, he had now reached base in eight straight plate appearances.

On June 9th, Averill doubled and drew three walks, pushing his streak to a dozen consecutive times on base. In the first game of a June 10th doubleheader, Averill homered to left field in the second inning. He followed with a single in the third inning, and reached base on an error by pitcher Dan Pfister in the fourth. He then walked in the sixth inning and again in the eighth, making it 17 straight plate appearances in which he reached base.

In the second game of the doubleheader, Averill struck out in the second inning against Norm Bass, completely ending his feat. His batting average had soared to .311 during his streak, but he finished the season at .219, and was out of the major leagues after 1964. Averill passed away in 2015 in Tacoma, Washington, so at least he lived long enough to see his accomplishment recognized—somewhat.

~

Both Ward and Averill weren't even footnotes in the grand scheme of baseball records. Ted Williams compiled a 16-consecutive-plate-appearance streak in 1957, and was regarded as the holder of the official record by *The Sporting News* in its *Complete Baseball Record Book.*

In 1997, White Sox first baseman Frank Thomas reached base in 15 consecutive plate appearances, which raised the issue of whose record Thomas was pursuing. Williams was listed by *TSN*, but *Chicago Tribune* columnist Jerome Holtzman contacted Seymour Siwoff of the Elias Sports Bureau, which was baseball's official statistician, and was told, "We can't verify that." Siwoff told Holtzman that the "record" was not included in MLB's official record book because Elias had never been satisfied with the research.

And so began a new time of research. Trent McCotter of the Society of American Baseball Research dug and dug—and unearthed "Piggy" Ward, presenting his research to the public in a 2006 article for SABR's *Baseball Research Journal.* Interestingly, McCotter confined his research to the players whose streaks did not include force plays or errors, so he failed to unearth Earl Averill in his research (or more accurately, didn't consider Averill's streak within the range of his hunt).

So today, some record books list Ward, some list Ward and Averill, and some still don't consider the record at all. What a journey!

⌐⌐

The odds of another player equaling Ward and/or Averill are pretty solid. In a short run in the late 1990s, three players put together streaks of 15 plate appearances on base: Frank Thomas of the White Sox, John Olerud of the Mets, and Barry Bonds of the Giants. Ironically, whoever challenges the mark will lack one big advantage that both Ward and Averill enjoyed—neither of them had the pressure of a record bearing down on them. Sometimes, it's not so bad to be anonymous after all.

CHAPTER 17

GETTING A HIT IN 12 CONSECUTIVE AT-BATS

Number of Times Accomplished: Three.

First Instance: Johnny Kling, Chicago Cubs, 1902.

Most Recent Instance: Walt Dropo, Detroit Tigers, 1952.

Likely Achievers: None of the three hitters who reached this record are exactly household names. Pinky Higgins had a career .292 average and almost reached 2,000 career hits, which makes him the most likely suspect of the three.

Surprises: Kling and Dropo had similar resumes—both hit around .270 and had around 1,100 career hits. So if neither is shocking, it's still surprising that they succeeded where Cobb, Rose, Jackson, Hornsby, et al. failed.

Likelihood of Additional Occurrences: Dustin Pedroia came up one at-bat shy. For a 65-year-old mark, it's surprisingly vulnerable.

If a coin is flipped a dozen times, the odds that it will come up tails (or heads) all 12 times are 1 in 4,096. Getting a base hit is a much more unlikely proposition than tossing a coin—Ty Cobb's lifetime average of .366 is the gold standard, and that's barely above a 1 in 3 chance. For a .250 hitter, the odds of banging out 12 consecutive hits are around 1 in 16.8 million. But for three relatively average hitters (lifetime batting averages of .272, .292, and .270), the long odds paid off. So ultimately, the odds of getting 12 hits in a row are something like three in the history of baseball.

~

When the poets wrote of the early 20th-century Cubs dynasty, they honored Tinker, Evers, and Chance, and passed by steady catcher Johnny Kling. Kling was from Kansas City and worked his way onto the Orphans (later to become Cubs) roster in 1900. Two years later, he became the full-time catcher, and he batted .289 in 1902. It was a solid average by a solid player, but not the sort of thing that seemed likely to make baseball history. But when history came knocking, it was Kling and not Tinker, Evers, Chance, or leading hitter Jimmy Slagle who entered the record books.

On August 24, 1902, in the second game of a doubleheader against Brooklyn, Kling reached base on an error in his first at-bat. The next time up, he apparently hit an infield single to shortstop Bill Dahlen—the "apparent" is because some sources called the play an error. This mattered only because Kling then rifled base hits in his next 11 at-bats. But the consensus from the research of SABR scholar Trent McCotter was that the play was a hit. In his last three at-bats of the day, Kling tripled, singled, and doubled.

The next day, August 25th, the Orphans played Boston. Kling rapped out five hits in the game, doubling in his fourth at-bat to go with four singles. He began the next game with Pittsburgh on August 28th with a single, a triple, and finally, another triple to reach 12 consecutive hits. Kling did not get the hits cheaply—six singles, two doubles, and four triples. Indeed, his slugging percentage for his run was 1.833. Kling's streak ended in his next at-bat when he hit into a force play, although he did single again in his final appearance of the day.

Did Kling obtain fame for his performance? Not especially. *The Sporting Life* noted his good work, although they termed his "grand hitting" to be getting five hits in one game and four hits in each of three others. No real mention was made of a dozen hits in a row. Two other players would achieve the feat before anyone noticed Kling.

Kling's solid play with the Cubs was somewhat tarnished by his holdout for the entire 1909 season. At that time, it looked like the Cubs were a dynasty and Kling was signed for 1910, so it seemed that the team's failure to capture another championship (they won in 1907 and 1908) would not be especially significant. For over a century, Cubs fans rued that painful notion.

While Pinky Higgins's career was more colorful than that of Johnny Kling, he still was a long shot to get a dozen consecutive base hits. Higgins was a solid-hitting third baseman for the A's, Red Sox, and Tigers who made three All-Star teams in his career. He hit 20 home runs once and drove in 100 runs twice. As a hitter, Higgins's statistics are pretty close to those of another third baseman who toiled for both the Red Sox and A's—Carney Lansford, a good, but not great, player.

In 1938, his second season with the Red Sox, Higgins made history. It would be the final .300 season of his career, although his .303 average is not much different from his career .292 mark. Higgins was at .277 on June 19th, and he singled in the eighth inning, in his last at-bat of the first game of a doubleheader. In the second game of the doubleheader, Higgins beat out a bunt in the second inning. He doubled in the fourth, singled in the sixth, and was intentionally walked in the eighth inning.

After a day off, on June 21st, Boston played Detroit in a double-header, and Higgins picked up where he left off. He walked in his first at-bat, and then doubled in his next turn. He finished the game with three consecutive singles, which brought his hit streak to eight in a row. In the second game, Higgins singled to right in his first at-bat, singled to left the next time, and then singled to center the third time. That hit was erroneously believed to tie the all-time record of Tris Speaker in 1920 with 11 consecutive hits. In his last at-bat of the game, Higgins chopped a groundball just past Charlie Gehringer for another single, his 12th hit in a row.

Higgins opened his June 22nd game against Detroit by striking out against Vernon Kennedy, putting an end to his streak. Higgins told reporters after the game that he could just as easily go 0-for-12 now that his streak was behind him, and in fact, he did go zero for his next nine.

Higgins was in the big leagues until 1946, and he went on to manage the Red Sox from 1955 to 1962 (with an interruption in 1959–1960 when he was relieved of those duties). Higgins is most remembered for perhaps obstructing the glacial movement of the Red Sox toward integration with Pumpsie Green in 1959. Carl Yastrzemski commented that Higgins could have been racist, but noted, "He managed me for years and never said a word to me. I swear to God, he didn't know who I was."

Higgins would doubtlessly rather be remembered for his hot streak in June 1938 than for being distant or racist to his own players during a managing career that was much less successful than his playing days.

If Kling hated to be remembered as a holdout, or Higgins as a racist, Walt Dropo had his own issues with being the third man in history to hit in a dozen consecutive at-bats. Dropo had to deal with being remembered as a legend—which is to say that his rookie year was the best baseball he ever played. Like Herman Melville, Bob Dylan, or Herschel Walker, Dropo set the bar so high that whatever else he did would exist in the shadow of his former glory.

The big moose from Moosup, Connecticut, the 6'5" Dropo was an excellent college basketball player. When he finally made it to the major leagues with the Red Sox, he exploded. Dropo was the 1950 AL Rookie of the Year, as he hit .322 with 34 home runs and 144 RBIs, each figure representing a career high.

Within two years, he had struggled through a subpar season and been traded to the Detroit Tigers in June 1952. A month later, Dropo made history. On July 14th, Dropo went 5-for-5 against the Yankees in New York. All five hits were singles, and he knocked in two runs.

The next day, in a doubleheader at Washington, Dropo continued his tear. He again hit a batch of singles, four of them in a row in the first game. In the second game, things got truly interesting. In the first inning, Dropo slugged a triple to center field. In the third inning, he poked a single to center. In the fifth inning, he tied Higgins (and Kling) with a double to left field. Up in the seventh inning, with a chance to own the record all to himself, Dropo was overeager and fouled out to catcher

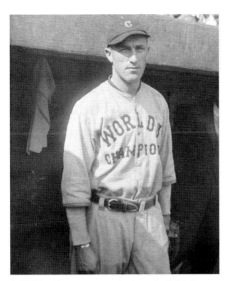

Bill Wambsganss made baseball history with his unassisted triple play in the 1920 World Series—still the only unassisted triple play in postseason MLB history. LIBRARY OF CONGRESS

John Clarkson, one of baseball's early pitching aces, won 328 games, was inducted into the Baseball Hall of Fame, and was the first known pitcher to throw an immaculate inning. LIBRARY OF CONGRESS

Troy Tulowitzki was a struggling rookie when he turned an unassisted triple play. He is shown here as an established veteran with the Colorado Rockies. KEITHALLISONPHOTO.COM

Now pitching for the Cincinnati Reds team he grew up rooting for, Drew Storen pitched an immaculate inning in early 2017 against the Baltimore Orioles. In fact, not only was Storen's inning immaculate, but no batter even made contact with a pitch. COURTESY OF THE CINCINNATI REDS

Shown here pitching in Fenway Park in his early years with the Boston Red Sox, Roger Clemens not only struck out 20 batters in a single game, but he did so twice. NATIONAL BASEBALL HALL OF FAME

Max Scherzer of the Washington Nationals became the most recent pitcher to strike out 20 batters in a game in 2016 against his former team, the Detroit Tigers. COURTESY OF THE WASHINGTON NATIONALS BASEBALL CLUB

As part of the Cubs' 1908 World Series title, pitcher Orval Overall recorded the only four-strikeout inning in World Series history. LIBRARY OF CONGRESS

Well-traveled slugger Josh Willingham is shown here with the Minnesota Twins. With the Florida Marlins in 2009, he became the 13th player to rip two grand slams in one game.
KEITHALLISONPHOTO.COM

Perhaps the patron saint of position player pitching—Doug Dascenzo, a reserve outfielder, also pitched five shutout innings for the Chicago Cubs. NATIONAL BASEBALL HALL OF FAME

Plenty of stars never hit for the cycle, but Aaron Hill—shown here with the Toronto Blue Jays—did it twice in eleven days in 2012. KEITHALLISONPHOTO.COM

Rockies third baseman Nolan Arenado provided one of the most memorable completions of hitting for the cycle when he slugged a walk-off home run to finish the feat on June 18, 2017. KEITHALLISONPHOTO.COM

Before June 6, 2017, Scooter Gennett had never hit more than two home runs in a game. But that night, Gennett blasted four home runs for the Cincinnati Reds, making him just the 17th player to hit four homers in a game.

COURTESY OF THE CINCINNATI REDS

On May 30, 1894, Boston's Bobby Lowe set a standard which has been equaled 17 times, but never surpassed, when he slugged four home runs in a single game.

LIBRARY OF CONGRESS

Washington outfielder Bryce Harper became the fifth player to draw six walks in a game against the Chicago Cubs on May 8, 2016. The talented Harper will likely be pitched around many more times in years to come. KEITHALLISONPHOTO.COM

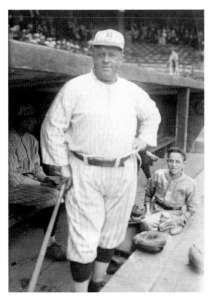

Washington third baseman Anthony Rendon had a cold start to 2017—until he blasted six hits, three home runs, and ten RBIs on April 30 against the New York Mets. Rendon finished 2017 as his best season to date. KEITHALLISONPHOTO.COM

Much beloved as the comical manager of the Brooklyn Dodgers—for years known as the Robins in his honor—Wilbert Robinson was also the first player to knock in ten or more runs in a nine-inning game. LIBRARY OF CONGRESS

Willson Contreras used his rocket throwing arm to transition into a catcher in the minor leagues. On the other side of home plate, he promptly slugged the first pitch he saw in the big leagues for a home run. KEITHALLISONPHOTO.COM

The father of the Super Slam, Roger Connor, is shown here at left, after his playing days with Washington Senator Goose Goslin. A few years before this photo, Connor's career record of 138 home runs was topped by Babe Ruth. LIBRARY OF CONGRESS

Shown here as he is best remembered, as the wily manager of the New York Giants, John McGraw was also an excellent player, stealing his way around the bases for the Baltimore Orioles on July 4, 1899. LIBRARY OF CONGRESS

Pictured are the only players to steal for the cycle in a single inning on four different occasions, Ty Cobb (left) and Honus Wagner (right). Similar in baserunning prowess, different in so many others ways, Cobb and Wagner were two-fifths of the Baseball Hall of Fame's original class of inductees. NEW YORK PUBLIC LIBRARY

Frank "Piggy" Ward reached base in 17 consecutive plate appearances, despite being traded in the middle of the streak. His record was unacknowledged for over a century before historians tracked it down. LIBRARY OF CONGRESS

The only man to ever steal six bases in two different MLB games, Hall of Fame second baseman Eddie Collins did so in a 12-day span in September 1912. It was almost 80 years before another player stole six bases in a game. LIBRARY OF CONGRESS

The most recent player to steal six bases in a game, Carl Crawford, shown here taking second against the Baltimore Orioles. Crawford's record base larceny occurred in 2009. KEITHALLISONPHOTO.COM

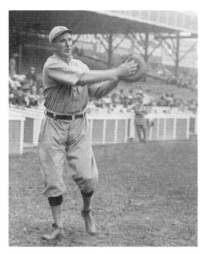

Catcher Johnny Kling had a hit in a dozen consecutive at bats in 1902. A career .272 hitter, Kling was an undervalued component of the Chicago Cubs' 1908 World Series title. LIBRARY OF CONGRESS

Pictured in his Red Sox uniform, Walt Dropo went on to tie the MLB record of getting hits in 12 consecutive at bats as a Detroit Tiger in 1952.
NATIONAL BASEBALL HALL OF FAME

Ken Griffey Jr. models the hitting form that allowed him to tie a record by blasting home runs in eight consecutive games in 1993. NATIONAL BASEBALL HALL OF FAME

Dale Long escaped being converted into a left-handed catcher, and in a memorable 1956 hot streak, he hit home runs in eight consecutive games.
NATIONAL BASEBALL HALL OF FAME

While Ted Williams's 1941 season of hitting .400 is the last one on record, Tony Gwynn might have joined the .400 club in 1994—had a players' strike not ended the season with him batting .394.
NATIONAL BASEBALL HALL OF FAME

Sixty-six years before José Canseco founded the 40/40 club, Ken Williams nearly reached the feat with the lowly St. Louis Browns.
LIBRARY OF CONGRESS

The only 40/40 player whose accomplishment isn't tainted by evidence of the use of performance-enhancing drugs, Alfonso Soriano had a long and arduous route to stardom. KEITHALLISONPHOTO.COM

The last batter to hit .400 in a major league season is still Ted Williams, who did so in 1941. On the last day of the season, with history in the balance, Williams was the beneficiary of helpful advice from umpire Bill McGowan that may have helped him get the hits to push him over the .400 mark. NATIONAL BASEBALL HALL OF FAME

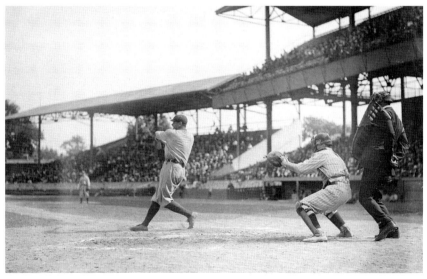

Shown here in 1920, the year of his dramatic 54-home-run power explosion, Babe Ruth was a Fitzgeraldian character who virtually founded America's love of power hitting. LIBRARY OF CONGRESS

The younger of a father/son pair of 50+-home-run sluggers, Prince Fielder battled through estrangement from his father, Cecil, before the relationship was healed. Father and son each finished with 319 career home runs.

How popular was Cleveland second baseman Napoleon Lajoie, shown here? Popular enough that the St. Louis Browns tried to throw the American League batting title in his favor in 1910, with disastrous results.

Even for the 1890s, outfielder "Wee Willie" Keeler was tiny. There was nothing small, however, about his 1897 hitting streak of 44 games—which remained the MLB record until 1941.

In 1894, Bill Dahlen had a 42-game hitting streak, then a hitless game, then another 28-game hitting streak.

LIBRARY OF CONGRESS

Among his other skills, Ty Cobb was a deceptively good power hitter. After telling a pair of sportswriters that he could hit home runs too, Cobb slugged three in a game in 1925, but years earlier, he showed enough power to win the 1909 Triple Crown, besting both leagues in batting average, home runs, and RBIs. LIBRARY OF CONGRESS

Forty-five years after the most recent MLB Triple Crown, Detroit Tiger star Miguel Cabrera accomplished the feat in 2012.

KEITHALLISONPHOTO.COM

Shown here modeling one of the most iconic batting stances of all time, Yankee legend Joe DiMaggio will always be remembered for his 56-game hitting streak in 1941.

NATIONAL BASEBALL HALL OF FAME

In 1967, Carl Yastrzemski dealt with the dueling pressures of a tremendous pennant race and a quest for the American League Triple Crown. He would up succeeding on both fronts. NATIONAL BASEBALL HALL OF FAME

Photographed here with 6'3" teammate "Long" John Reilly, pint-sized Hugh Nicol stole 138 bases in 1887, paving the way for runners like Lou Brock and Rickey Henderson. LIBRARY OF CONGRESS

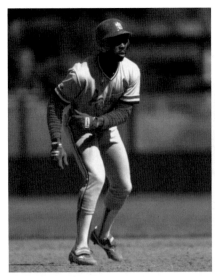

Cardinals speedster Vince Coleman stole over 100 bases in each of his first three major-league seasons—making him the last man to reach that mark in a single season. NATIONAL BASEBALL HALL OF FAME

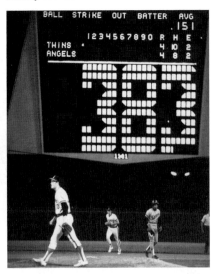

Nolan Ryan sets a modern major-league record for strikeouts in a season with 383 for the 1973 California Angels. He struck out 300 batters five more times in his career, with the last such season coming in 1989, when he turned 42 years old. NATIONAL BASEBALL HALL OF FAME

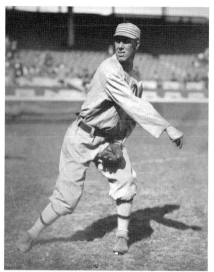

Denny McLain of the Detroit Tigers won 30 games in 1968, making him the only pitcher to reach 30 wins in a season in the last 83 years. McLain says the odds of another pitcher winning 30 are "less than one in a million." NATIONAL BASEBALL HALL OF FAME

In 1910, pitcher Jack Coombs was the first MLB hurler to throw 50+ consecutive scoreless innings. LIBRARY OF CONGRESS

In the Year of the Pitcher (1968), Dodger Don Drysdale set a new MLB record with 58⅔ consecutive scoreless innings—with a little help from an unusual call by umpire Harry Wendelstedt. NATIONAL BASEBALL HALL OF FAME

Jim Vaughn was saddled with the unfortunate nickname of Hippo, but in 1918, he won pitching's Triple Crown for the Chicago Cubs. LIBRARY OF CONGRESS

One of a pair of pitchers to win the pitching Triple Crown in 2011, then–Detroit Tigers ace Justin Verlander has been one of the most dominant players of the 21st century. KEITHALLISONPHOTO.COM

Adding his name to the lengthy list of L.A. Dodger aces, Clayton Kershaw claimed a pitching Triple Crown in the National League in 2011.

KEITHALLISONPHOTO.COM

Francisco Rodríguez, shown here with the Baltimore Orioles, not only topped 50 saves in 2008, but his season total of 62 set the current MLB record.

KEITHALLISONPHOTO.COM

Mickey Grasso on the first pitch. Pitcher Lou Sleater knew he dodged a bullet and admitted that the pitch "was straight down the pipe." The next time Dropo came up, he got the same pitch and lined another base hit. But the streak was over, and Dropo had his dozen.

In that 1952 season, Dropo came as near to recapturing his prior glory as he ever would. He hit .276 with 29 homers and 97 RBIs between the Red Sox and Tigers. But after that season, he would never again top 23 homers or a .281 average. Dropo stayed in the major leagues until 1961, batting against two legacies he couldn't reach—his brilliant rookie season and his perfect 12-at-bat run.

The dozen-hit mark looked pretty secure until in 2016, Red Sox second baseman Dustin Pedroia came within a base hit of equaling it. Pedroia's career is probably already more decorated than the other three men who reached the mark, and in August of 2016, he nearly joined them.

Pedroia singled in his last three at-bats on August 25th against Tampa Bay, and then added four consecutive singles during the next day's game at home against Kansas City. On August 27th, Pedroia again faced the Royals and made his try at history.

He opened the first inning with a solid single to center field for his eighth straight hit. He doubled to left-center in the second inning, singled to left-center in the fourth, and grounded another single up the middle in the sixth.

With 11 straight hits and a shot at the record on the line, Pedroia swung at the first pitch from Chien-Ming Wang in the eighth inning, and promptly grounded into a double play.

Pedroia claimed to be unaware of the record. He admitted he had heard the television broadcasters say something about it when he hurried by on his way to the bathroom, but denied any additional knowledge of the mark. His average went from .306 to .320 during his streak, even if he didn't quite make the ultimate goal.

If Pedroia can approach the mark that closely, surely another hitter can equal Dropo before another 65 years pass. It is a difficult feat to make, but if the record of those who have gone before confirms anything, it's that the record won't make or break a career. But there are worse ways to be remembered.

CHAPTER 18

HITTING A HOME RUN IN EIGHT CONSECUTIVE GAMES

Number of Times Accomplished: Three.

First Instance: Dale Long, Pittsburgh Pirates, 1956.

Most Recent Instance: Ken Griffey Jr., Seattle Mariners, 1993.

Likely Achievers: Griffey may have been the best player of the 1990s, and his 630 home runs attest to his legendary power stroke. Mattingly was nearly as potent of a hitter, albeit for a much shorter time frame, explaining his career total of "just" 222 home runs.

Surprises: Long never topped the 27 home runs he hit in 1956, and ended his career with 132 homers. A near miss worth noting was Texas outfielder Kevin Mench, who homered in seven straight games in 2006, and finished up with just 89 career homers.

Likelihood of Additional Occurrences: While it has been a quarter-century, three times in the 21st century, a player came within a game of joining this exclusive group. It stands to reason that sooner or later, another will succeed.

Dale Long of the Pittsburgh Pirates knew he would be part of something historic. It was such an inexplicable thing that nobody in baseball could really conceive of it. Branch Rickey was going to make Long a left-handed catcher. He worked at it during spring training, but after 12 at-bats with the Pirates, was sold to the St. Louis Browns. Within that same 1951 season, Long was sent to the minors, where he spent the next three seasons. Long played for 14 teams in 10 leagues before he finally stuck in the majors.

Ultimately, Dale Long did catch in two major-league games with the Cubs in 1958 (which made him the first left-handed catcher in the big leagues in 56 years). But by the time he returned to the Pirates in 1955, Long was a first baseman—and a first baseman who hit for power.

His mark wasn't destined to be as a left-handed catcher, but as one of the great streaky home-run threats of history.

Before Long, no one had ever homered in more than six consecutive games—that mark was reached by Ken Williams of the St. Louis Browns in 1922, and equaled by George Kelly of the 1924 New York Giants. Long would leave it behind easily. Long hit 16 home runs in 1955, and he slugged two on Opening Day in 1956. Entering play on May 19th, he had six home runs for the season, with none in his last dozen games.

In the eighth inning of that day's game at Forbes Field, Long connected for a two-run homer off Cubs reliever Jim Davis. It didn't mean much at the time, but it was the start of one of the most torrid hitting runs in baseball history.

The following day, the Milwaukee Braves came to Pittsburgh for a doubleheader. In the fifth inning of the first game, Long launched a three-run homer off Ray Crone. In the second game, Long hit his home run—a two-run blast off Warren Spahn—in the very first inning.

After an off day, the Pirates hosted the St. Louis Cardinals at Forbes Field on May 22nd. Long managed a solo homer in the sixth inning off Cardinal starter Herm Wehmeier. On the following day, Long made it five home runs in five games with a seventh-inning shot off reliever Lindy McDaniel.

Needing another home run to tie the existing MLB record, Long took his longball show on the road to Philadelphia's Connie Mack Stadium. He promptly tied the mark with his sixth home run in six consecutive games, this time a two-run bomb in the fourth inning against Curt Simmons. The next day, May 26th, Long nearly made history in the first inning, with a ringing double that just missed leaving the ballpark. Never to worry, in the eighth inning, Long turned on a Ben Flowers knuckleball and ripped the pitch over the right-center field wall. Even the fans in Philadelphia rose to applaud Long, who was met at home plate by the entire Pirate team, including the first and third base coaches.

With the record all his own, Long extended it even further. Back home in Forbes Field, Long faced the Brooklyn Dodgers and Carl

Erskine on May 28th. With his team trailing 2–1 in the fourth inning, Long caught up with an Erskine curveball and deposited it a few rows deep in the right field stands. Long shook his head in disbelief at his eighth home run in eight consecutive games. The next batter, Frank Thomas, was interrupted by the fan demand for a curtain call from Long, who was also roundly cheered when he took up his defensive position at first base in the next half-inning.

Long hit almost .500 (15 for 31) and knocked in 19 runs during his streak. His batting average was at .414 as play began on May 29th. One enterprising reporter asked Long, then with 14 home runs on the season, about his chances at Babe Ruth's single-season record of 60 home runs. For his part, Long got about four hours of sleep after the eighth game, heading off to New York for an appearance on *The Ed Sullivan Show*.

On May 29th, Long was finally stopped, as Don Newcombe held him to an 0-for-4 day in beating the Pirates 10–1. Long knew that he had lost the magical touch that had sustained him. "I was beginning to get weak," he admitted. "I couldn't get the bat around. I didn't feel comfortable anymore." Long essentially returned to an average major-league career, sprinkled with a few highlights. At least he wasn't remembered for being a left-handed catcher. In a 1987 interview, Long admitted, "As soon as I walk into a park, they say, 'Oh, here's the guy who homered in eight straight games,' and I automatically become the trivia question for the night." A few more answers to the question were also on the way.

Oddly enough, the next major leaguer to homer in eight straight games, like Long, was nearly a footnote to baseball history based on an odd position switch. Almost as unusual in the history of baseball as a left-handed catcher is a left-handed second baseman. And yet Don Mattingly almost made that move. Granted, Mattingly's switch wouldn't have been quite as jarring as Long's, as he would have played defense right-handed because he is ambidextrous. In fact, Mattingly did play second base left-handed in the 1983 Pine Tar Game, when Yankee manager Billy Martin angrily made the game something of a farce after Major League Baseball reversed its original ruling that Royals third baseman George Brett was out after hitting an apparent ninth-inning home run with an excess of pine tar on his bat. That appearance made Mattingly one of two left-handed second basemen in the last 35 years. He also made a spot appearance at third base in 1986, which was equally peculiar.

But like Long, Mattingly's ultimate spot in baseball history ended up not being defined by a few innings at an odd position. The then-mustachioed first baseman (Mattingly is now clean-shaven as the manager of the Miami Marlins) became one of the game's most popular players as a 23-year-old first baseman in 1984, when in his second season, he won the AL batting title by hitting .343, and also blasted 44 doubles and 23 home runs. Mattingly won the AL MVP award in 1985, and was then in the second year of a streak of six consecutive All-Star Game selections.

Mattingly had a strong power game (he hit 35 and 31 home runs in 1985 and 1986), but in 1987, he became part of a wave of baseballs flying out of ballparks. MLB hitters totaled 3,602 home runs in 1985 and 3,813 in 1986. But in 1987 (for no single obvious reason), the rates soared by almost 17 percent to 4,458 home runs. The trend would soon be reversed (to 3,180 total home runs in 1988), but for one glorious summer, power hitters were in the moment, and no one more so than Mattingly.

Mattingly, who missed a few weeks in June with an injury to his lower back, had eight home runs for the season in early July. On July 8th, the Yankees hosted the Minnesota Twins and Mattingly began his journey into baseball history. He turned around a Mike Smithson fastball in the first inning, hammering a three-run homer. In the sixth inning, he added a solo shot off reliever Juan Berenguer. Mattingly was suddenly red-hot.

The next day, the Chicago White Sox arrived in Yankee Stadium and promptly fell into the same pattern. Rich Dotson allowed a sixth-inning solo blast by Mattingly. That said, Dotson got off lightly compared to Joel McKeon, in the game in relief the next night, July 10th, when he faced Mattingly in the second inning with the bases loaded.

Mattingly took a pitch the other way, hitting a grand slam into the left field bleachers, his third slam of the season. The streak continued on July 11th, when Mattingly had three hits, including a solo blast to right field off José DeLeón. The following day, Mattingly started out 0-for-2, but hit a seventh-inning blast off Jim Winn to bring his streak to five games in a row with a home run. This was one short of the American League record, but Mattingly's momentum was stopped at this point for the All-Star Game.

Mattingly walked in two of his three plate appearances in the Midseason Classic, but was lucky that it was a mere exhibition game, because neither he, nor any other American Leaguer, managed a home run in the 2–0 shutout loss. But Mattingly then traveled to Arlington, Texas, to reopen pursuit of the homer streak mark.

Knuckleballer Charlie Hough became the victim for a sixth straight game with a homer, as Mattingly crushed a second-inning grand slam to right field. Not content with a day's work, he added a three-run shot to left off reliever Mitch Williams in the eighth inning. In an effort to set a new American League mark on July 17th, Mattingly narrowly missed a homer in the first inning off Bobby Witt, but in the sixth inning victimized Paul Kilgus for his seventh straight game with a homer.

On July 18th, Mattingly was ready to catch up with Dale Long. In the fourth inning, he swung on a José Guzmán sinker and lifted the pitch beyond the wall in left-center field, for a 10th home run in his last eight games—and an eighth consecutive game with a homer.

Yankee teammate Mike Pagliarulo later looked back and recalled that streak, and how he would joke with Mattingly about hitting home runs, only to watch Mattingly do it again and again. "You can't try to hit home runs," said Pagliarulo. "I mean, you can't do that—but he was actually doing it."

Mattingly could have claimed the home-run record for his own the next night in Texas, but it was the Rangers who got hot, routing the Yankees 20–3 as Mattingly was held to 2-for-4 with a single and a double. Mattingly denied any negative feelings when his streak was broken. "I've never felt pressure through this whole thing, really," he said after the game. Later, he admitted, "You hit ten home runs in eight days and see how you feel."

Back injuries would curtail Mattingly's career after 1995, but his years of New York glory made an impression on anyone who saw them. Undoubtedly, Mattingly ended up much better off than being the left-handed second baseman.

~

If Long and Mattingly played the game to get out of the shadows of odd positional moves, the third slugger in the eight-home-run club had his own shadows to deal with. This superstar had to emerge from the shadows of two World Series rings, a .296 average and 2,143 career hits, and three All-Star seasons. The shadow was cast by Cincinnati Reds outfielder Ken Griffey Sr., and it would be outmatched by Ken Griffey Jr.

It was appropriate that Ken Griffey Jr. was the son of a very good baseball player, because he played the game as if he was engineered to star at it. With one of the most beautiful left-handed swings the sport has ever featured, incredible speed, defensive ability, wisdom, and a glowing enthusiasm for the game, Griffey rewrote the baseball record book. But first, he had to get out of the shadow.

The top overall pick in the 1987 MLB Draft out of high school, the younger Griffey had his demons to battle. He knew the pressure that followed his name, and after a difficult rookie season in the minors (difficult in terms of off-the-field issues involving new life experiences as a 17-year-old professional; on the field, Griffey put up a .313/.445/.604 line) and some issues with his parents, in January 1988, the 17-year-old Griffey swallowed 277 aspirin in a suicide attempt.

Fortunately, medical help was promptly obtained, the issues between the young star and his family were resolved, and what could have been one of the biggest tragedies in baseball history was averted.

Griffey arrived in the major leagues at age 19, and was an All-Star the next year. At 21 (and 22 and 23), he knocked in 100 runs. At age

23, he hit 45 home runs in the 1993 season. And he also tied Long and Mattingly for consecutive games with a home run.

On July 20th, Griffey's Mariners had lost four games in a row. He went to see manager Lou Piniella before the game, and told the manager, "Skip, I'm going to take over tonight." Sure enough, that night, Griffey knocked in three runs as Seattle turned a 5–0 deficit into a 9–5 win. Included in the evening was an eighth-inning home run to right field for Griffey off Yankee lefty Paul Gibson. It was Griffey's 23rd home run of the year, and marked the start of his historic run.

The next day, Griffey hit a sixth-inning solo shot off Yankee Jimmy Key. On July 22nd, the Mariners moved on to Cleveland, where Griffey pulled a solo shot off Indian Jeff Mutis in a win. The following night, Griffey hit a sixth-inning bomb off Albie Lopez. The streak reached five games in a row on July 24th, as Junior victimized Indian Matt Young with a fifth-inning blast down the right field line.

On July 25th, Griffey's streak reached six, courtesy of an opposite-field shot in the fifth inning off Cleveland's José Mesa. The Indians were doubtlessly glad to see Griffey leave town, as he would bring the chase of history back home to Seattle. History continued early on July 26th, courtesy of a third-inning grand slam for Griffey off Minnesota's Kevin Tapani, which was measured at 441 feet. The next night, the Twins' Willie Banks had the Mariners' number, as he went seven strong innings in a 5–1 win. The one run was Griffey again—tying Long and Mattingly with eight straight games with a homer courtesy of a seventh-inning bomb to right field, which hit off the façade of the upper deck to the delight of 30,413 excited Seattle fans.

Like Long and Mattingly before him, Griffey could not get his ninth game with a homer. He had two hits the next day, but in his last at-bat, overswung on a hanging curveball and popped up to second base. "I tried too hard," Griffey admitted after the game. "I'm not disappointed," he said to the media, "I gave it my best shot. . . . I didn't want to let them down."

Even after his streak, Griffey did not think of himself as a home-run hitter, saying he might consider himself in that light once he hit 50 in a season.

He hit 56 home runs in both 1997 and 1998, and despite a disappointing end to his career after a series of nagging injuries, Griffey Jr. finished with 630 home runs, 13 All-Star selections, an MVP award, and induction into the Baseball Hall of Fame. Suffice it to say, he succeeded in overcoming almost anyone's expectations.

~

Since Griffey, a trio of players have had homers in seven consecutive games, only to fail in their effort to tie Long, Mattingly, and Griffey. Jim Thome in 2002, Barry Bonds in 2004, and Texas outfielder Kevin Mench in 2006 each nearly reached the summit of home-run consistency, only to fall short. Someday, another slugger will reach that elusive eighth game. And when they do, whatever odd legacy their career might have otherwise attained will be long-forgotten after another epic pursuit of baseball mastery.

CHAPTER 19

40/40 SEASON

Number of Times Accomplished: Four.

First Instance: José Canseco, Oakland A's, 1988.

Most Recent Instance: Alfonso Soriano, Washington Nationals, 2006.

Likely Achievers: Bonds and Rodriguez will go down in history as two of the premier (PED-aided) sluggers of all time. Both were also athletic, multi-tool players from their debuts.

Surprises: Soriano was a good player, but between playing a fair portion of his career in smaller markets, and having some definite limitations, he wouldn't have been the first guess of most fans as a 40/40 guy.

Likelihood of Additional Occurrences: Solid. It's been 11 years since the last 40/40 season, but with young players like Mike Trout, there's still a decent possibility.

It took 112 seasons of Major League Baseball for someone to reach the pinnacle of the seemingly dichotomous baseball skills of power and speed. The "40/40 club" wasn't really a thing for most of baseball's history. It took 44 years of Major League Baseball for Babe Ruth to become the first player to mash 40 home runs in a season. And even once that event occurred, baseball had muscular sluggers like Ruth or Lou Gehrig, and it had speedy base-stealers like Lou Brock or Maury Wills. But both together, 40 home runs and 40 steals in a season? It seemed impossible.

⌐⌐

Actually, six and a half decades before José Canseco brought the 40/40 season into national relevance, St. Louis Brown Ken Williams nearly nabbed such a campaign. The generally woebegone Browns won 93 games in 1922, narrowly missing the AL pennant, and Williams, who at 32 was in just his third full season as a regular, had the season of his career. He hit for a .332 average, mashed 39 home runs, knocked in 155 runs, and stole 37 bases. For that matter, Williams was caught stealing 20 times. Had he been only a slightly more successful baserunner, he could have climbed even closer to the yet unknown 40/40 plateau. Williams never replicated his 1922 season, and retired with the modest career totals of 196 home runs and 154 stolen bases.

No one approached a 40/40 season for more than three decades after Williams, but the 1950s brought about a generation of five-tool players who were the type of athletes that might accomplish such a feat. No less than Mickey Mantle commented years later, "If I'd known 40/40 was going to be a big deal, I'd have done it five or six times." Unfortunately, strategy in the 1950s was incredibly heavy on the three-run homer, and not at all on swiping bases. Only two players managed 40 stolen bases in a season in the entire 1950s—Luis Aparicio, a 5'9" shortstop who hit just 83 career home runs, swiped 56 bags in 1959, and Willie Mays reached 40 steals exactly in 1956. (As for Mantle, he never swiped more than 21 bases in a season.)

That 1956 season was the first of two consecutive challenges at 40/40 from the supremely talented Mays, who was both one of the best power hitters and baserunners of his (or any other) age. He slugged 36 home runs to go with his 40 steals in 1956, and the following season added 35 clouts and 38 stolen bases. Close, but no cigar.

Probably the best pre-Canseco 40/40 challenger, though, was Bobby Bonds. Between 1969 and 1978, Bonds had five 30/30 seasons and mounted a significant challenge to 40/40. In 1973, he missed by a single home run, hitting 39 blasts to go with 43 steals. In fact, he hit his 38th homer on September 9th, leaving him 21 games to hit two more. He reached 39 in the final game of the season. Bonds also had 37 homers and 41 stolen bases as a California Angel in 1977.

The 1980s brought about another round of multitalented players who made significant runs at 40/40—Dale Murphy of the Braves, Darryl Strawberry of the Mets, and Eric Davis of the Reds, who stole 50 bases and slugged his 37th homer in 1987 on September 17th, leaving him 16 games to hit three more. Unfortunately, injuries shortened his season, and Davis added no more homers.

After the numerous near-misses, the unifying theme for three-quarters of the 40/40 club's members is steroids. It turns out that athletes who can outslug and outrun the rest of Major League Baseball aren't often endowed by a benevolent creator with those gifts. No, the dual tandem of strength and speed is more often something that is a product of a laboratory, and a certain loose moral code about one of baseball's most malignant taboos.

José Canseco was a 20-year-old Cuban immigrant in 1984, a tall, skinny outfielder at High-A Modesto in the Oakland organization, when he discovered steroids. The A's had selected him in the 15th round of the 1982 MLB Draft, and he says that emotional disturbance over his mother's death led him to initially experiment with steroids. Canseco made his major-league debut in 1985, and by 1988, when he was a 240-pound outfielder, he says he was not only using steroids, but was injecting teammate Mark McGwire with them. Canseco hit 33 home runs in 1986 and 31 more in 1987, but stole just 15 bases in each of those seasons.

But in 1988, off to an excellent start, he told an interviewer in May, "If I don't get hurt, I . . . think I can hit 50 homers and steal 50 bases." When the interviewer pointed out that nobody had ever approached a 50/50 season, Canseco dialed back his prediction, "All right, then I think I can have a '40/40' season."

Canseco was a relentless self-promoter, the kind of player who used his success to endorse breakfast cereals and set up a 1-900 pay telephone number where fans could get updates on the daily minutiae of his life. The chase for 40/40 added some extra flash to an already glittering career.

On September 7th, Canseco hit a 454-foot blast in Texas for his 37th home run. He also had 35 stolen bases, and with the A's running away with the AL West division title, he could chase stats down the season's stretch. The home runs came easier, as Canseco reached 40 with a blast off Bret Saberhagen in Kansas City on September 18th.

On September 23rd, with eight more games to follow in Oakland's season, Canseco took aim at baseball history. He entered the game with 38 stolen bases, and after a first-inning single, he stole his 39th base on the second pitch to the next batter, McGwire. In perhaps the ultimate nod to his power-and-speed skills, in the fifth inning, Canseco, then with 41 homers for the year, did something he hadn't done all season. He bunted for a base hit. On the second pitch, he took off for second and easily beat the catcher's throw for his 40th stolen base. Canseco took second base out of the ground, and claimed it for his personal trophy collection, a signifier of an event so rare that Major League Baseball had never seen it before.

Oakland general manager Bob Watson noted after the game, "I told him he was going to have to live with [40/40]. People are going to expect him to do it every year. He said, 'No problem.' He wants to play like this every year."

Good intentions aside, 40/40 lightning did not strike twice for Canseco. He never again eclipsed 29 stolen bases in a season. He did slug 40 homers two more times, but by 1998, when he hit 46 bombs and swiped 29 bases, he did so as something of a clubhouse pariah, a .237 hitter who struck out 159 times and seemed to put the team's best interests far behind his own.

Canseco's steroid use was widely rumored long before he acknowledged same in his tell-all autobiography, *Juiced*, which was published in 2005. Back in 1988, respected *Washington Post* columnist Thomas Boswell called Canseco out, referring to him on a television appearance as "the most conspicuous example of a player who has made himself great with steroids." Canseco denied the charges, but in the 1988 ALCS, faced taunts from Boston Red Sox fans of "STER-OIDS! STER-OIDS!"

Not only did Canseco ultimately change his story, but he was only too quick to name many other names beside his own, and to spill as many salacious "secrets" as he thought might sell a few more copies of *Juiced*. When not battling law enforcement or showing up in reality television,

Canseco is widely held to be at the bottom of the baseball food chain. "He wasted more ability than most of us ever had," said an anonymous player of Canseco.

~

Alas, while Canseco was the first "juicer" to reach 40/40, he soon had company. If Canseco was, as Boswell contended, the most conspicuous player to make himself great with steroids, Barry Bonds was probably the first player to make himself superhuman with steroids. The son of near 40/40 star Bobby Bonds, as a lean young outfielder, Bonds was a Hall of Fame caliber player long before he ever began his experimentation with "the cream and the clear."

Of course, Bonds is also infamous for being a Hall of Fame jerk—notable for being voted off his college baseball team as a super-talented freshman before his coach manipulated the outcome of the situation to keep him around. The son of a star, the godson of the great Willie Mays, Bonds had the bloodlines of a star, and the ego to go with it.

His rise to baseball greatness began in Pittsburgh, where he helped spur an up-and-coming Pirates team to annual flirtation with the NL pennant beginning in 1990. At age 25, Bonds won his first MVP award, and hit 33 home runs while stealing 52 bases. After the 1992 season (when Bonds hit 34 homers and stole 39 bases), he became a free agent and headed to San Francisco, where he continued his ascent to the top of baseball.

In 1996, his fourth year with the Giants, Bonds entered 40/40 history. Bonds hit his 40th homer on September 17th, but at the time, he had only 31 stolen bases, leaving him only 11 games to steal nine more bases. He did it easily. In the Giants' ninth game, in Colorado on September 27th, Bonds had an RBI single in the third inning. On a 2-0 pitch to Glenallen Hill, Bonds took off for history, swiping the base ahead of catcher Jeff Reed's throw for his 40th theft of the season. The Giants ended the season at 68-94, and Bonds trade rumors circulated freely in the ensuing offseason, but Barry had made baseball history.

Unfortunately, Bonds's ensuing baseball history will be forever tainted by his usage of performance-enhancing drugs. Bonds maintained that he never used the drugs knowingly, but the law enforcement investigation of BALCO and Dr. Victor Conte produced a wealth of data that indicated that if Bonds had used steroids unknowingly, he worked as hard to not ask difficult questions as he did to become an excellent baseball player.

Many maintain that in 1998, Bonds watched Mark McGwire blast the MLB single-season home-run record, and became angry, both at the attention McGwire received ("They're just letting him do it because he's a white boy," Bonds allegedly said) and the fact that McGwire's hulking physique practically screamed his own use of performance-enhancing drugs. Around that time, Bonds allegedly began his own regimen.

The exact details remain unknown. Was Bonds using in 1996? Probably not, but the very fact that "probably" is needed speaks volumes. In 1997, Bonds nearly repeated his 40/40 performance, hitting 40 homers and stealing 37 bases. But his running game trickled down, to 28 steals in 1998 to 15 in 1999 to 11 by 2000. But by 2000, Bonds had moved on from speed.

In 2001, Bonds hit 73 home runs, destroying the single-season home-run mark. His once lithe physique was positively swollen, and even his head had grown to bizarre proportions. In 2007, Bonds took down Hank Aaron's career home-run record, ending his career with 762 home runs, although by that time, the Mitchell Report had ensured that Bonds would be less remembered for what he was—a truly top-level player before he touched a steroid—than as a symbol of greed, corruption, and excess.

~

The relative curse of 40/40 continued with the club's third entrant, Alex Rodriguez. A-Rod, an insanely talented Dominican American short-stop, who debuted in the major leagues at age 18, like Bonds was a player who would've gone into the Hall of Fame in his sleep, had he not also dallied with (and lied about) steroids.

While Rodriguez wasn't as surly as Bonds, he was every bit as image-conscious as Canseco, leading some of his teammates to call him "A-Fraud" behind his back. There can be little doubt that Rodriguez carried the baggage of projected success badly, but like the two 40/40 players who came before him, he did play some incredible baseball.

Rodriguez hit .358 at the age of 20 in 1996, when he first became a regular player for the Seattle Mariners. His power game was also strong—he ripped 36 homers in '96 and added 23 more in 1997. Meanwhile, he stole 15 bases in 1996 and managed 29 the following year. In 1998, playing most of the season at age 22, he had a historic year.

On September 9th, in the Mariners' 144th game, Rodriguez stole his 40th base of the season. He also had 39 home runs at that time, leaving him nearly three weeks to slug one more long ball. He needed barely half the time. On September 19th, in Anaheim, Rodriguez clubbed a first-inning home run on a line drive to right-center field off Jack McDowell, which clinched his 40/40 club membership. Rodriguez finished the year with 42 homers and 46 stolen bases.

Much of Rodriguez's 1998 thunder was stolen by the McGwire and Sosa home-run chase. Rodriguez moved on from Seattle to Texas after the 2000 season, and blasted 52 and 57 home runs in his first two years as a Ranger. While Rodriguez initially denied it, he later admitted that those totals were boosted by steroid use. Rodriguez was subsequently ensnared in controversy over the Biogenesis clinic, which may have prescribed him additional supplements during his late-career run with the New York Yankees.

As with Bonds, there is no significant evidence tying Rodriguez's 40/40 campaign to his later history of using performance-enhancing drugs. But there is at least a cloud of suspicion that lingers over the numbers.

Finally, in 2006, with baseball embroiled in the height of the PED scandal, another 40/40 player emerged, ironically, the only one whose career isn't tainted by a connection with steroid use. Unlike his predecessors, Alfonso Soriano was an unlikely candidate to be a 40/40 player.

Soriano hailed from San Pedro de Macoris, the Dominican town that has exported shortstops to MLB with shocking frequency. But if his hometown stood out, the young player did not. Soriano was slow, slow enough that he was nicknamed "Mule" as a youngster. He was skinny and awkward at the plate, coiling his body into a winding swing. So desperate was Soriano for baseball attention that he began his career in an unlikely place—Japan.

With MLB teams looking elsewhere, Soriano signed on with the Hiroshima Toyo Carp. He played one year in the Japanese minor league, and after going 2-for-17 in a brief trial with the big-league squad, Soriano found himself in a salary dispute. He "retired" from Japanese baseball, in an attempt to return to the United States, although the Carp advised all major-league teams that they would sue them if they negotiated with Soriano. After two months, MLB deemed Soriano a free agent, and he promptly signed a deal with the New York Yankees.

He remained thin and lithe, but his swing harnessed a surprising amount of whiplike power, and "The Mule" wasted little time announcing himself as a power-and-speed threat. In 2002, in his second full MLB season, Soriano stole 41 bases and hit 39 home runs. In fact, he played his last 11 games of the season with those 39 home runs, but just missed 40/40 status.

While Soriano's power and speed made him a desirable asset, he did have significant limitations as a player. He was a defensive liability and would rarely take walks. He finished third in the AL MVP voting in that 2002 campaign, but would never reach higher. Ironically, in February 2004, he was traded to the Texas Rangers—for Alex Rodriguez. (Soriano had also briefly been a teammate of José Canseco in 2000, when the former was a rookie and the latter was on his last MLB legs.)

Soriano was an All-Star twice in Texas, but then was traded to the Washington Nationals after the 2005 season. Soriano tangled with manager Frank Robinson in Washington. Mindful of Soriano's defensive struggles, Robinson wanted him to play left field. Soriano initially refused, but then decided he would try it. After the 2006 season, Soriano would be a free agent, and a good season—at a second position—would likely enhance his value.

Soriano certainly did nothing to hurt his value in 2006. He hit .277, only slightly above his career average of .270, and did strike out 160 times. But for the first time in his career, he took walks (67, significantly more than the 45 that was otherwise his single-season high). Mostly, Soriano slugged and ran.

He started at left field in the All-Star Game. At the All-Star break, Soriano had 27 home runs and 20 stolen bases. He did little to cool off in the second half of the season. On August 19th, Soriano hit his 40th home run of the season off Cole Hamels at Philadelphia. The night before, he had stolen his 30th base of the year. With almost 40 games to play, Soriano had plenty of time to run his way into history.

Leading off for the Nationals at home against Milwaukee on September 16th, Soriano singled to left field. On the 2-0 pitch to Felipe Lopez, Soriano broke for second base and had such a huge jump that he wasn't opposed with a throw. He had his 40th stolen base. Soriano had reached 40/40 with over two weeks to spare. He is also the only member of the 40/40 club to reach the feat at home, and the Washington crowd appreciated his exploits in appropriate fashion.

"There's a lot of players who can play this game, and it's a pretty amazing number," said Soriano afterward. "I'm happy and I'm proud of myself."

He finished the year with 46 homers and 41 stolen bases. After the season, he signed an eight-year, $136 million contract with the Chicago Cubs, where frequent injuries and the slow decline of his skills eventually forced him back to the New York Yankees. Soriano ended his career in 2014 with 412 home runs and 289 stolen bases.

The 40/40 club hasn't been reached in 11 seasons. Its siren song beckons those who are both strong and fast, but they would be wise to consider the wrecked careers that have gone before. Canseco, Bonds, and Rodriguez stand as cautionary tales—a warning that some records really just aren't possible. But then there is Soriano, by far the most "normal" of the four players—and a testimony that sometimes, it's a matter of being in the right place at the right time, perhaps with a smattering of contract motivation lumped in. If he can overcome obstacles like working through an awkward swing, a lack of foot speed, and getting lost in translation for a couple of seasons in the Land of the Rising Sun, a player can manage a clean 40/40 season . . . but it's not easy. In fact, it may take the stubbornness of "The Mule" to pull it off.

CHAPTER 20

HITTING .400

Number of Times Accomplished: 28 (15 of the 28 being pre-1900).

First Instance: Ross Barnes, Chicago White Stockings, 1876 (.429).

Most Recent Instance: Ted Williams, Boston Red Sox, 1941 (.406).

Likely Achievers: Not surprisingly, there aren't really any bums in the group. Fourteen of the 20 players who hit .400 are in the Hall of Fame. Standouts include Rogers Hornsby and Ty Cobb, who were the only players to hit .400 three times.

Surprises: Fred Dunlap, who hit .412 with the St. Louis Maroons in 1884, is the only .400 hitter with a lifetime batting average below .300.

Likelihood of Additional Occurrences: Never say never, but it has been 76 seasons. There are some strategic reasons it would be very difficult to hit .400 now.

If the old axiom about baseball's unforgiving nature holds true, that succeeding as a hitter 3 of 10 times at bat will make a player a Hall of Famer, then what does that say for a .400 hitter? What it says is that reaching .400, even for a single season, is as close to a guaranteed ticket to baseball immortality as can be obtained. With the exception of "Shoeless" Joe Jackson, every player who had a .400 season in the 20th century is now in the Hall of Fame. Time has done nothing to dull the allure of a .400 season, as more than three-quarters of a century has left the mark undisturbed.

The first player to hit .400 probably wouldn't have realized that the accomplishment would ever generate such a fuss. Ross Barnes had hit .400 three different times with the Boston Red Stockings of the National Association before joining the Chicago White Stockings in time for the National League's inaugural 1876 season. Barnes hit a robust .429, although he did so under very unusual circumstances. Under the rules of the time, if a ball landed in fair territory, even if it subsequently rolled foul, it was a fair ball. Accordingly, Barnes mastered the small-ball style of the day, and became adept at dropping down bunts that bounded into foul territory with enough English to make a pool shark envious. Led by Barnes's example, the White Stockings hit .337 as a team. The fair-foul rule changed to a modern understanding in 1877, and Barnes was never the same. At least, that was the traditional reading of baseball history. It doesn't make much sense, as Barnes led the NL not only in batting average, but slugging percentage, so unless he was somehow dropping down bunts for doubles and triples, he also could hit for power. The more likely culprit for the decline of Barnes's performance was that he suffered some sort of generalized "ague" during 1877 that drained him of his strength. Ultimately, for whatever reason, Barnes never broke .300 in his brief remaining career.

Similarly, in 1887, two more tainted entries to the .400 club arose in St. Louis Browns outfielder Tip O'Neill (not the future Speaker of the House) and Louisville outfielder Pete Browning. For some reason, in 1887, both the National League and the American Association credited walks as hits. O'Neill was then ruled to have "hit" .485 for the season. For historical purposes, only O'Neill and Browning are counted as .400 hitters, because their totals so project even without the bogus "walks as hits" classification. Cap Anson was considered a .400 hitter then, as were seven other players, but once their averages are corrected to modern scoring standards, they weren't in the .400 club.

Rules glitches aside, many more players did bat .400 in the formative years of baseball. Willie Keeler of "hit 'em where they ain't" fame managed the feat, as did other stars like Cobb, Lajoie, Delahanty, and Rogers Hornsby, whose legitimate .424 season in 1924 is generally regarded as the gold standard in modern baseball for batting average.

There were seven .400 seasons in the 1920s, and Bill Terry hit .401 in 1930, but otherwise, the decade yielded no other similarly high-average hitters. Perhaps the global effect of the rabbit ball and the home-run craze changed the game. Bill Terry's 1930 season would be the last .400 season, if not for some helpful advice from an unlikely source—an umpire.

⌒

The 1941 season stands on elevated footing in baseball history for many reasons, but the principal one is a pair of simultaneous hitting feats, neither of which has been equaled to date. Joe DiMaggio's 56-game hitting streak captivated the nation, and after that streak ended, Ted Williams's chase for .400 grabbed the attention of the baseball world.

Williams was hardly an inauspicious candidate to hit .400. Born in 1918, Williams played in the Pacific Coast League with the local San Diego Padres when he was still in high school. Picked up by Boston, he was sent to the minors for one season, where he won the American Association Triple Crown under the guidance of hitting coach Rogers Hornsby. Hornsby counseled Williams to wait on a good pitch—and perhaps no hitter ever has simultaneously demonstrated the ability to wait out a walk, or drive a single, or slug a home run quite like Williams.

As a 20-year-old rookie for most of the 1939 season, Williams hit .327, with 31 home runs, 145 runs batted in, and received 107 walks. His sweet left-handed swing was befitting a player who boldly admitted, "All I want out of life is that when I walk down the street folks will say, 'There goes the greatest hitter that ever lived.'"

The 1941 season was Ted Williams's best opportunity yet to move in on that goal. He hit .344 as a second-year player, but improved his game to another level in '41. Among a multitude of other extraordinary statistics from that miracle season, Williams took 147 walks—and struck out only 27 times.

For four weeks in May of 1941, Ted Williams went from a great baseball player to something approaching a superhuman. He entered play on May 3rd with a .308 average. In his next 24 games, Williams went 43 for 93 (.462) with six home runs and 21 runs batted in. He ended May hitting .429, and the race for a .400 season was on.

At the All-Star break, Ted was sitting at a robust .405. Just to keep things interesting, he hit a walkoff home run to win that midseason exhibition, and carried on his merry way toward history. The beginning of August found Ted at .409, and on the 1st of September, he entered play hitting .407. But late in the season, the pressure intensified. On the next-to-last day of the regular season, Ted took a 1-for-4 day against Philadelphia Athletics pitcher Roger Wolff. His average slipped to .39955. Ted had not dipped below .400 since July 24th. Suddenly, the season-ending doubleheader at Philadelphia on September 28, 1941, looked very, very interesting.

The easiest thing to have done would have been to sit out. After all, .39955 rounds to .400. But to the eternal credit of both Williams and Boston manager Joe Cronin, this wasn't going to happen. Cronin apparently did give Williams the option—either to sit out the entire series in Philadelphia, when he was solidly above .400, or to sit out the last day and allow his average to be rounded up. A few weeks past his 23rd birthday, Williams was reported to have stoically observed, "I want to have more than my toenails on the line."

It was good to talk the talk, but Sunday, September 28, would be the proving ground on whether Williams would become the 28th player in MLB history to hit .400. He later recalled that the night before "I went to bed early, but I just couldn't sleep. I tossed and turned and finally went to sleep, still thinking about that .400 average."

Another account had Williams chewing his fingernails and visibly trembling during the pregame. When Ted came to bat to lead off the top of the second inning, the pressure was on. Philadelphia catcher Frankie Hayes told Williams, "I wish you all the luck in the world today, but we're not giving you a damn thing." An unlikely ally was about to emerge. Granted, the game featured two teams well out of a pennant race (as usual, DiMaggio's Yankees had long since wrapped up the league flag), but few would have expected Williams's source of comfort to be home-plate umpire Bill McGowan.

McGowan was a well-respected umpire. He was 45 years old, having umpired 2,541 consecutive games before missing one late in 1940. He had worked four World Series and two All-Star Games, and would shortly be employed in the 1941 Fall Classic. For whatever reason, McGowan now felt some manner of empathy for the young Boston outfielder. Like Hayes, he would give Williams nothing—except some advice.

Williams later recalled, "Just as I stepped in, he called time and slowly walked around the plate, bent over and began dusting it off. Without looking up, he said, 'To hit .400 a batter has got to be loose. He has got to be loose.'" A word of practical advice that Williams set about putting into practice. He watched two balls from pitcher Dick Fowler, then blasted a clean single into right field.

Did Williams hit .400 because of McGowan? That may be a little too much credit to give the umpire. Still, it is telling that Williams, recalling the story years later, noted, "I'll never forget it." History would never forget it either, as Ted finished the doubleheader with five more hits, ending the season at .406, making him the last major-league player to conquer a .400 season.

~

Just because the ensuing years have lacked a successful conquest of .400 doesn't mean that players haven't tried. Thirty-nine years after Williams's amazing season, Kansas City Royals third baseman George Brett made his own run at history. Like Williams, Brett was a disciplined left-handed hitter, albeit one without quite as much power as Williams. He became a regular with the Royals in 1974 at the age of 21. Heading into 1980, he had been an All-Star four years in a row, and had finished second and third in the AL MVP voting during that span. However, he had never hit above .333 for a season coming into 1980. Indeed, even in a Hall of Fame career that included 3,154 hits, only in 1980 did Brett top a .335 average. The Elias Sports Bureau tabulated the odds of a career .300 hitter batting .400 over 600 plate appearances at 1 in 1.9 quadrillion. While Brett was better than a .300 hitter, he was still fighting very long odds. The longshot almost paid off.

Like Williams back in '41, Brett started slow in 1980. He finished April hitting .259 and the end of May saw him up to just .301. Brett started June hot, hitting .472 in nine games before being knocked out of action by an ankle injury. When he returned to the lineup in early July, he made that month count by hitting an absurd .494. Not content to rest on his laurels, he hit .430 in August. The end of July saw Brett's average at .390, and the end of August had it at .403. Another red-hot month would have put Brett into the .400 club.

"I sure hope he does it," quipped Ted Williams, "because I'm sick of people calling me every time someone gets close."

But alas, it was not to be. Brett slumped early in the month and while he rebounded to briefly push his average back to .400 on September 19th, he finished the season at .390. By how much did Brett miss .400? Mathematically speaking, if five outs had turned into hits, he would have reached the mark.

Brett recalled the swarm of media pressure, noting that he would do a press conference before and after every game, which he noted "alienated me from my teammates." Still, his ultimate recollection is a positive one.

"That whole summer . . . man, I was hot," Brett recalled. "No regrets. I had a good run."

⌒

The one run at .400 that left everyone with regrets came courtesy of Tony Gwynn in 1994. Like Williams and Brett, Gwynn was a sweet-swinging left-handed hitter who grew up in California. Unlike them, he was a squatty-built African American, whose physique disguised the fact that he was so athletic that he was drafted in the NBA by the San Diego Clippers in the same year that he was chosen by the San Diego Padres in the MLB Draft.

Gwynn was an amazingly consistent hitter. He hit .289 in a brief rookie season, but thereafter, never had a season where he hit under .309. He played his entire career with the Padres and finished with 3,141 hits and a .338 average. Gwynn won three consecutive NL batting crowns in the late 80s and hit an eye-popping .370 in 1987. But it was all a warmup for a glorious 1994 season—albeit a season that was prematurely shortened.

Gwynn turned 34 early in the 1994 season, but his production was still at peak levels. His incredible consistency as a hitter spilled over into the '94 season. Gwynn hit .395 in April, .392 in May, and .387 in June. He did have a minor slump in July, as he hit "only" .370. He compensated by beginning the month of August on a tear, hitting .475 through August 11th. His 3-for-5 performance that day placed his season batting average at .394, and it looked increasingly as if Gwynn might finally be the one to overtake Williams.

Except that he didn't bat again in 1994. Neither did anyone else. The labor strike that ended the season—and canceled the World Series for the first time in 90 years—did what few pitchers could do in 1994. It stopped Gwynn cold.

As with Brett, Gwynn chatted with Ted Williams during his chase. He later told a reporter that Williams had told him, "If I knew that hitting .400 would have been so damn important, I would have done it more often."

For Gwynn's part, he was confident that he would have made history. "I really believe I'd have hit .400," he admitted. "I was squaring the ball up nicely, hitting lefties, hitting righties. I would have given it a run."

Gwynn died of cancer in 2014 at the age of only 54. The chance to have a post-Williams .400 hitter may have died with his ill-fated 1994 season.

⌐

Since Gwynn, Larry Walker's .379 mark in 1999 is the closest anyone has come to .400. While it seems hardly impossible that another player will reach the mark, such a player hypothetically might need some advantages over his recent predecessors. Of the last three major challengers to .400, none were speedy players. A hitter like Ichiro Suzuki, who could beat out groundballs, would seem to have a leg up on the race to .400. Alas, even the great Ichiro topped out at .372.

Given the prevalence of the shift, a pull hitter like Ted Williams would now face a huge disadvantage in trying to reach .400. A modern hitter hoping for the mark must be able to hit the ball to all fields, or superior defensive scouting will rob a one-dimensional hitter of any chance.

Finally, as Bill McGowan told a nervous young Ted Williams, to hit .400, a batter has got to be loose. Could anybody stay loose in the face of more media attention than Williams could have ever imagined? Time will tell.

CHAPTER 21

HITTING 50 HOME RUNS IN A SEASON

Number of Times Accomplished: 45.

First Instance: Babe Ruth, New York Yankees, 1920 (54 homers).

Most Recent Instance: Giancarlo Stanton, Miami Marlins, 2017 (59 homers), and Aaron Judge, New York Yankees, 2017 (52 homers).

Likely Achievers: All-time leader Barry Bonds is on the list and third-place holder Babe Ruth pulled it off four times. Twenty-six of the 44 instances of 50 homers were by sluggers who topped 500 home runs for their career.

Surprises: PED suspect Brady Anderson (210 career home runs) and Cubs legend Hack Wilson (244) are among the more unlikely sluggers.

Likelihood of Additional Occurrences: There have already been four occurrences in the 2010s. While it won't be as common as it was in the 1990s or the 2000s (read: the PED era), baseballs should keep flying out of parks.

Future Hall of Fame pitchers Tom Glavine and John Smoltz proclaimed in a famous commercial, filmed around the era of the PED-aided home-run increase in the late 1990s, that "chicks dig the longball." Babe Ruth, the game's original legendary slugger, would second that.

Baseball fans also dig round numbers. Three hundred wins. Three thousand hits. Five hundred home runs. Three thousand strikeouts. Or, in the single-season context, 50 home runs. Not 49—although the 19 players who hit 49 homers were obviously just as capable as the men who added one more. They just didn't have 50. And that added boost of glamour means something.

⌐

It took until 1883 for a player to even reach double digits in home runs in a single season. And Harry Stovey's 14 homers probably weren't all that significant in the evolution of the game. The next season, Ned Williamson hit 27 bombs. More accurately—even with the dead ball—Williamson hit 27 long popups. Chicago played that season in Lake Front Park. In 1883, a ball hit over the short fence (186 feet in left field, 196 feet in right, and a not-so-gargantuan 300 feet in center) was a double. In 1884, it was a home run. Thus, Williamson went from two home runs in 1883 to 27 in 1884. The next year, Chicago moved to a new park . . . and Williamson dropped to three home runs. His record of 27 homers would remain the record for three and a half decades.

It stayed the record until a revolution named Babe Ruth took hold. Ruth became the very fulfillment of the home run. In the way that John Lennon famously said, "If you were trying to give rock and roll another name, you might call it Chuck Berry," so the same could be said of home runs and George Herman Ruth.

Ruth's story is well-known, but bears repeating as much to assure oneself of its essential facts as for anything else. In the American consciousness, Ruth appeared from thin air, much like the protagonist of *The Great Gatsby*. But like humble Jay Gatz, there was a reality behind Ruth, even if it was less glamorous than would be assumed.

Ruth was a more-or-less orphan from Baltimore, a child who grew up in his father's saloon until he was declared "incorrigible" and sent to St. Mary's Industrial School. Always large and tenderhearted (one of his St. Mary's classmates recalled a 16-year-old Ruth taking the rap for a window that the eight-year-old classmate had broken), Ruth grew into a man of gargantuan appetites—be they food and drink, sex, or just dominating the national pastime. Ruth lived his life at breakneck speed, as if he was always making up for the deprived childhood he left behind.

He was a pitcher before he was an outfielder, but he was so effective at the plate that he found himself being pulled from the mound to the batter's box. At the plate, as one biographer wrote, Ruth "ignored the fashion of the times, which was to protect the plate and punch out singles. He swung from the heels." And when he connected . . . well, it certainly didn't hurt that the ball during much of his ascent was the new "rabbit ball" with a solid cork center that more or less popped off the bat.

Ruth hit 29 home runs in 1919, his last year with the Boston Red Sox, which broke Williamson's old record. But the next year, 1920, he hit 54 homers. Of course, he was the first player to reach 50 home runs, but that really doesn't explain what happened. Of the other 15 major-league teams beside Ruth's Yankees, only the Phillies outhomered Ruth on his own. The second most prolific home-run hitter in 1920 was George Sisler, who hit 19 homers. One author notes, "For Barry Bonds to outdistance his peers in 2001 (when he set a new single season mark of 73 home runs) as Ruth did in 1920, Bonds would have needed to hit 431 homers."

Ruth never quite hit 431 homers in a season—it just felt like he did. He reached 50 four times, and on the last, in 1927, he reached 60 home runs. Ruth had opened the door to home-run glory, and while it was a rare feat—four times done in the 1930s, three in the 1940s, two in the 1950s, three in the 1960s, and once in the 1970s—it was a possibility.

Like Ruth, the next man to reach 50 home runs in a season came from virtually nothing. Lewis "Hack" Wilson is perhaps the most physically unlikely man to hit 50 home runs in a season. A 5'6" man with tiny feet—wearing perhaps a size 5½ shoe—Wilson was born to a pair of alcoholics who lived near Pittsburgh. His mother died when he was seven, and his father essentially abandoned Wilson to the woman who ran the boardinghouse where they lived. After a sixth grade education, Wilson dropped out of school to become a "printer's devil," which is to say he carried large amounts of lead in nearly insufferable heat. The rest of his short life was a fairly consistent battle with alcohol. Those who remembered Wilson told Wilson drinking stories the way that those who remember Ruth looked back on his hubris—the difference being that the Wilson stories don't tend to be funny.

Wilson played on various semi-pro and sandlot teams and was a catcher—until a broken leg forced him to move to the outfield. He was thick and squatty—a great many opined over the years that he was built like a beer keg. But Wilson could hit, and he proved it in 1930 with one of the finest seasons ever played. Since joining the Cubs in 1926, Wilson's power had steadily climbed—from 21 homers in 1926 to 39 in 1929. But in 1930, Wilson blasted 56 home runs and also managed to knock in 191 runs in the process. He hit .356 and posted an insane 1.177 OPS. Wilson never topped 23 home runs after 1930, and drank his way out of baseball by 1934.

In a radio interview shortly before his death in 1948, Wilson expressed remorse over basically drinking his life away. During the interview, he advised, "There are kids, in and out of baseball, who think because they have talent, they have the world by the tail. It isn't so." Wilson had talent, and in 1930, he had baseball by the tail, and even if he never reached that level again, he had one tremendous season to remember.

⌒

Perhaps the oddest of tandems to blast 50 home runs would be a father and son—similar in build and productivity, but differing in many other ways. There was little to indicate coming into 1990 that Cecil Fielder would hit 50 home runs. A behemoth slugger who was listed at 6'3", 230 pounds in his playing days, Fielder had shown power potential in the beginning of his major-league career in Toronto. He had 31 home runs in 506 at-bats, which sounds impressive until a look reveals that it took parts of four seasons for Fielder to get enough playing time to amass those at-bats.

In 1989, Fielder finally got to play and hit 38 home runs. That said, he hit them for the Hanshin Tigers of the Japanese Central League, who had purchased his contract from Toronto. After his amazing season, Fielder signed a free-agent deal with the Detroit Tigers and hoped to parlay his success abroad into a renewed chance back at home.

He made the most of that chance, crushing the ball through early 1990. After a three-home-run game in early June, Fielder arrived at the All-Star break with 28 home runs, some wondering whether he would break Roger Maris's then-record of 61 home runs set in 1961.

Fielder's pace cooled slightly, but on October 3rd, in the season's final game, Fielder drove a fourth-inning pitch from Steve Adkins off the facing of the upper deck of Yankee Stadium for his 50th home run of the season. At the time, Fielder was the 11th player in MLB history to reach the plateau, and was only the second to do so in the last 29 years. He added another homer in the eighth inning to cap his epic season. After the game, Fielder answered questions from the media with his wife and six-year-old son, Prince, on hand to be part of the festivities.

Fielder finished second to Rickey Henderson in the 1990 AL MVP voting, and he also finished second the following year to Cal Ripken, despite slugging 44 home runs. He was 26 years old when he gained a starting job in the big leagues, and his career ended when he was 34, but he mashed 319 home runs during that time.

Young Prince Fielder grew up very much in the shadow of his famous father. They even shared a McDonald's commercial in the early 90s, which showed Prince striking out Cecil in a backyard matchup before they adjourned to McDonald's for cheeseburgers. Prince grew to be even bigger than his father, slightly shorter than Cecil at 5'11" but a good bit heavier, as he sometimes neared 300 pounds. But much to the interest of baseball scouts, Prince had the same power as Cecil, although he learned to bat left-handed. He was chosen with the seventh overall pick by the Milwaukee Brewers in the 2002 Draft, and by the end of 2005, he had played his way to the big leagues.

Prince was a sensation. He turned 23 years old during the 2007 season and was named to the All-Star team. By the Midsummer Classic, Prince had slugged 29 home runs, although unlike his father back in 1990, few expected that he would break Barry Bonds's season record of 73 homers. He did, however, make a bit of history.

On September 25th, Prince and the Brewers hosted the Cardinals. In the first inning, he blasted a home run to right field off Braden Looper, which was his 49th of the season. In the seventh inning, he poked a drive to left field that snuck over the wall, and officially made the Fielders the first father-and-son tandem to each hit 50 home runs. (In case anyone is keeping score, Bobby Bonds never topped 39 homers, and Ken Griffey Sr. had a career best of 21 homers.) Prince also was the youngest player to hit 50 home runs in a season, breaking the old mark held by Willie Mays.

Unfortunately, after the game, much of the talk was not about the similarities between Cecil and Prince Fielder, but about the growing disconnect between the two of them. There had been some prior issues— many of them centering on how Cecil had negotiated Prince's contract. As the glory faded from Cecil's career, he found himself instigating controversy.

Earlier in the 2007 season, Cecil had commented that Prince had been a first-round draft pick only because of his father's name. There were more comments. "I don't think he's grown up yet," Cecil had said of Prince. "Until he can move on and talk to me like he's my son, we don't need to talk."

The feelings were mutual, as Prince confessed after his 50th home run that he really wanted to hit 52 to surpass Cecil's single-season best. He was asked about the MVP award and admitted, "It would be a cool award but that's not something I think about besides the fact my dad never did it. If I do get it, that shuts him up again."

Prince was asked about his father's comments and explained, "You've got to look at who's saying it. Let's be honest. He's not really the brightest guy."

It was a sad fact of life that instead of being able to celebrate the father/son moment together, the Fielders were sniping at each other. Prince finished with 50 home runs. He finished third in the MVP race, behind Matt Holliday and winner Jimmy Rollins.

Both the Fielders were struggling with other issues. Cecil went through financial trouble and a divorce. When a newspaper wrote that the financial trouble stemmed from a gambling addiction, he sued for libel. The suit was later dismissed. All was not well for Prince either. He had several excellent years in Milwaukee before he signed a hefty free-agent deal in Detroit before the 2012 season. Fielder was earning over $20 million per year, but his production dipped until Detroit traded him to Texas after the 2013 season. He missed almost all of the 2014 season with a neck injury, and this came on the heels of a split with his wife, Chanel (the two later reconciled).

But in the midst of the turmoil, Cecil and Prince quietly set about repairing the rift that had divided them. By mid-2015, they sat down for a joint interview in which they remembered some of their favorite moments of each other's careers. "I always knew he was going to be a special player," admitted Cecil. "If I can't be proud, nobody can be proud." For his part, Prince remembered seeing Cecil's 50th home run and the excitement of his father appearing in the playoffs for the New York Yankees.

Unfortunately, Prince's career came to a sudden and disappointing end at age 32. His neck injury flared up in mid-2016 and doctors advised him that he had to retire. Immediately. At a tearful press conference, Prince talked about his career—flanked by his two sons, Jaydn and Haven, whom he called "my two homies." He also credited Chanel, with whom he now hosts a television cooking show. Prince emotionally looked back on a life in which he had been in big-league locker rooms almost as far back as he could remember—often with his own father.

In one final irony, Cecil and Prince Fielder both hit exactly 319 career home runs. Fortunately, their relationship has returned to a place where Prince can say, "Obviously, it was supposed to go that way. It's a pretty cool thing."

⌒

Down the stretch of the 2017 season, two of the game's newest home-run kings added their names to the list of 50-homer sluggers. Miami Marlins star Giancarlo Stanton, a hulking 6'6", 245-pound outfielder, was already blasting major league home runs at the tender age of twenty. After the 2014 season, the normally frugal Marlins signed Stanton to the largest contract in MLB history—a 13-year, $325 million deal designed to keep the young star in the Marlin uniform for his career. For all his apparent skills, Stanton struggled to maintain health (batting just 279 times in 2015) and productivity (he hits .240 and missed over 40 games in 2016).

But in 2017, Stanton went on a torrid power streak, blasting tape-measure drives with stunning frequency. His prior career high was 37 homers in 2012 and 2014. Stanton bested that pace with his 38th home run of 2017 on August 8. August ended up being a memorable month for Stanton. His 18 home runs in August is a monthly total that has been bested only once in the entire history of MLB. He reached his 250th career home run in mid-August, at age 27, the sixth youngest player to ever reach that plateau. On August 27, he blasted an eighth-inning home run against San Diego Padres pitcher Clayton Richard, which was his 50th homer of the season.

Padres hitting coach Mark McGwire, who hit 50 homers on four different occasions, offered his perspective on Stanton's performance.

"He's in the zone," said McGwire. "It's called a beach ball. There's only a few guys who have played this game that know what that feeling is, and I can attest to it."

Stanton made a run at 60 homers, finishing his season with 59. Also joining the party was enormous Yankees outfielder Aaron Judge. At 6'7", 282 pounds, Judge is one of the largest everyday players in baseball history. Like a modern-day Babe Ruth, Judge used his enormous power to blast mammoth home runs—and, sometimes, to strike out.

In a 2016 cup of coffee with the Yankees, Judge batted .179 and struck out in 42 of his 84 at-bats. But in 2017, Judge exploded. He broke Joe DiMaggio's Yankee rookie home-run record on July 7. He was a starter in the All-Star Game and won the Home Run Derby. On September 25, he cranked his 50th home run, setting an MLB rookie home-run record. He did strike out 208 times, but hit .284 with 114 RBIs along with his 52 homers and led the Yankees to a playoff berth.

The sky is the limit for Stanton, Judge, and a coming generation of talented young sluggers. There will be plenty of home runs launched into that sky.

Chapter 22

SURVIVING SHENANIGANS TO WIN A LEAGUE BATTING TITLE

Number of Times Accomplished: Annually in each league (unlike every other accomplishment in this book, this feat is very much on a set schedule). Which is why we're going to focus on some of the instances where gamesmanship, hijinks, and even fixing plays have played a controversial role in the batting title.

First Instance: Ross Barnes, Chicago White Stockings, .429 in the 1876 National League.

Most Recent Instance: José Altuve, Houston Astros, .346, 2017 American League; Charlie Blackman, Colorado Rockies, .331, 2017 National League.

Most Unlucky: Over the years, 10 .400 hitters didn't win the batting title, although the last such instance was in 1922.

Luckiest: Carl Yastrzemski's .301 season to win the 1968 AL batting crown is still absurd, even in the so-called "Year of the Pitcher."

Likelihood of Controversy: Almost guaranteed, in light of the stories that follow.

Unlike the vast majority of feats in this book, a batting title is inherently a competition of a player and his peers. Nevertheless, the chase of the batting title seems a clear enough matter. The qualifying player (meaning only regular starters will meet the eligibility requirements) with the highest batting average wins the crown. What could be simpler? As it turns out, almost anything. Baseball's rules have been bent, broken, and reconfigured to allow or prevent players from winning batting titles. It has proven to be capable of introducing more controversy than any other baseball feat. Whether it's players sitting out, opponents fouling up things, or MLB getting in its own way, batting title battles can become anything but normal. Which is how an annual event becomes a rare feat—when it's subjected to some of the most unpredictable and unsportsmanlike shenanigans imaginable.

Probably the single most infamous batting title showdown of all time is the 1910 American League race between Ty Cobb of the Detroit Tigers and Napoleon Lajoie of the Cleveland Indians. The trouble probably began with a car—specifically, a 1910 Chalmers automobile, which would be awarded to the winner of the 1910 batting title. As the 1910 season ran down, it looked like Cobb, who was somewhere between vaguely unpopular and deeply hated, would edge out Lajoie, who was such a well-liked player that the Indians were called the Naps for a period after their leader and star second baseman.

With three games to go, Cobb was hanging around .382 and Lajoie at .376. Cobb took a 2-for-3 game and then basically took the rest of the season off. While varied excuses were offered for Cobb's conduct, the generally accepted conclusion was that he sat out to protect his lead for the batting title. Lajoie went 1-for-4 in the first of the three games, although many would later claim that his "hit" was a clear error by a left fielder who dropped an easy flyball. At the time, it seemed to matter little.

With Cobb sitting, Lajoie would need a minor miracle in the final day's doubleheader in St. Louis to catch the Georgia Peach. Instead, he got something else.

Lajoie tripled in his first at-bat in the early game. In the third inning, he grounded to shortstop, where Bobby Wallace misplayed the ball. It was called a hit, and Lajoie was 2-for-2. Meanwhile, Browns third baseman Red Corridon was defending against Lajoie from somewhere around Iowa, apparently on instructions from manager Jack O'Connor. Lajoie easily beat out a bunt, and on his next at-bat, again seeing Corridon playing in the region of the outfield, he bunted again for a hit.

In the second game, the pattern continued—Corridon played way too deep, and Lajoie bunted for hits. It happened in the first inning and again in the fifth, seventh, and ninth innings. A third-inning bunt was scored as an error, but Lajoie was initially credited with a sacrifice meaning that he had gone 8-for-8 on the day—and apparently won the batting title.

The race didn't just smell, it stunk to high heaven. And it was just getting started.

Official scorer Victor Parrish later admitted that he had been visited by a Browns coach, pleading for Lajoie's "sacrifice" to be scored as a hit. Parrish was later sent a note offering him a suit of clothes for such a decision. Parrish indicated that Lajoie had even telephoned, asking him to change his ruling.

AL president Ban Johnson ruled that Lajoie was 8-for-9, and lost the title to Cobb, .384944 to .384084. Even those totals were inaccurate—and some late-20th-century double-checkers noticed that Cobb had been credited erroneously with two extra hits. Manager O'Connor and the Browns coach were fired (and essentially blackballed from the major leagues), and the Chalmers Company decided it would present *two* cars—one each to Cobb and Lajoie. And an embarrassing chapter of baseball's history ended.

⌐⌐

If only Cobb and Lajoie marked the end of batting title chicanery, all would be well. Another sterling example surfaced in 1953, when the Cleveland Indians' Al Rosen was fighting for a batting title that would hand him the Triple Crown. His opposition was Mickey Vernon of the Washington Senators. The battle went down to the season's last day, with Rosen and the Indians playing the Tigers, while Vernon's Senators played the Athletics.

Rosen's game finished first, and he helped his cause with a solid 3-for-5 day. Vernon was 2-for-4 when Rosen's game finished, and word reached the Senators that if Vernon did not bat again, he would win the batting title.

Vernon didn't ask to be pulled out of the game—but his teammates took care of the batting title for him. In the Senators' last two innings, they sought to make sure Vernon was safely vested with the title. In the eighth inning, Mickey Grasso doubled and with what *The Sporting News* called "rare carelessness," allowed himself to be picked off. In the ninth inning, Kite Thomas singled and displayed a "super-obvious lack of judgment" in trying to stretch the hit to a double, and he was easily thrown out. The game ended with Vernon on deck—and holding the batting title.

Manager Bucky Harris was noted to have denied any conspiracy after the game—with a smile on his face. Ultimately, Rosen probably could have had a smile at the situation. Harris would have failed not only ethics, but also mathematics. Had Vernon made another out, he still would have won the batting title, and the pseudo–Cobb versus Lajoie fix was completely unnecessary.

At least the Rosen/Vernon race ends with a half-comic moment of irrelevance. Not so the 1976 AL batting race. Two Kansas City Royals, George Brett and Hal McRae, went down to the season's final games in a race for the crown. Brett is white and McRae is African American. That either had nothing or perhaps very much to do with how the race played out.

The title quest went down to the season's final game against the Minnesota Twins—in fact, to the very last inning. Brett and then McRae were due to hit. If both got hits—or if neither got a hit—McRae would win the title. The only way that Brett could win was if he got a hit, and McRae made an out.

Brett was up first and he lofted a fairly routine flyball to left field. Minnesota left fielder Steve Brye (who is white) was noted to run "toward the ball and it appeared that he would make a routine catch, but suddenly he stopped and the ball fell 10 to 15 feet in front of him." The ball then bounced high on Kansas City's artificial turf and went over Brye's head as Brett circled the bases with an inside-the-park home run. McRae met Brett at home plate with a smile and a handshake. McRae then grounded out to shortstop, clinching the batting title for Brett.

At that point, things got a little crazy. McRae had some comments for Twins manager Gene Mauch, apparently about Brye's suspicious defense on Brett's fungo-fly-turned-homer. He either raised a fist at Mauch or flipped him off, depending on which account is accurate. The narrative after the game then became first, whether the Twins had given Brett the title and second, why they would have done so.

Brye half-heartedly defended his awful defense, denying that Mauch had told him to play deep, and relating that he "didn't see it real good." Royals third baseman Dave Nelson told a reporter, "Brye is a good friend of mine but I can't believe in my heart that he made a good effort."

McRae confronted one obvious possibility of the situation.

"This is America, and not that much has changed," said the irate Royals slugger. "Too bad in 1976 things are still like that."

Others who felt that Brye's effort was lacking suggested other possibilities. Murray Chass of the *New York Times* suggested that the ill will toward McRae was based not on color, but on McRae's "aggressive style of play." He cited several examples of McRae's baserunning that would not likely endear him to opponents.

As for Brett, his comments made his own contempt for the situation clear.

"I think maybe the Twins made me a present of the batting championship," he said, also questioning the legitimacy of another hit he had during the final game. "[I]f they did, I feel just as bad about it as Hal does. This whole thing takes the edge off winning. I mean, I wanted to win, but I didn't want it to be this way."

For his own part, Mauch staunchly denied any ill will on his own part, calling the allegations "the worst thing that has happened to me in 35 years in baseball." The veteran manager continued, "I would never, never do anything to harm the integrity of baseball."

Twins veteran Rod Carew, who was third in the race, denied the racism angle as "a bunch of crap."

American League president Lee MacPhail investigated the matter and while he noted, "It is not always possible to know with certainty what governs men's actions," he did not find any plays "which were unfairly motivated."

In any case, as historians cast an eye back to the Cobb/Lajoie battle, it may be helpful to note that more egregious behavior could have occurred much more recently. Four decades have done little to clarify the controversial 1976 AL batting race.

⁓

Sometimes winning the batting title is a dramatic thrill, and other times, the champion is absent on awards day. That was the case in 1990, when St. Louis Cardinals outfielder Willie McGee was pursuing his second career NL batting title, and was trailing only Philadelphia's Len Dykstra, hitting .335 on August 29th. That day, McGee was traded to the AL champion Oakland A's.

But because McGee had over 502 plate appearances in the National League, his NL stats would qualify for the batting title—even if he couldn't do much about it.

"I can't help but see and I hear people talking about it, but that's the only way I know," McGee told reporters shortly after being traded. "It's not life or death. It it happens, fine. It's out of my control."

McGee hit .274 for the balance of his season with Oakland. He ended up with an overall mark of .324 for the season. Three players in the NL bested McGee's .324 average for 1990—Dodger Eddie Murray (.330), Met Dave Magadan (.328), and Dykstra (.325).

But in the National League, McGee reigned, as nobody could touch his .335 average from his NL at-bats. Willie McGee was the batting champion of the National League—a month after he was traded into the American League.

⁓

Much more common than Cobb/Lajoie or Brett/McRae type controversies or the oddball occurrences like McGee's absentee title are the mini-controversies when a player decides to simply sit to protect his lead. It's happened numerous times, but one recent example came in 2011. Mets third baseman Jose Reyes held a slim lead over Milwaukee outfielder Ryan Braun heading into the season's final games—Reyes was hitting .3358 and Braun was at .3345.

In the season's final game, Reyes led off the bottom of the first inning against the Cincinnati Reds and bunted for a single. Immediately, Mets manager Terry Collins sent in a pinch-runner for Reyes, who would not jeopardize his lead with further at-bats. Collins admitted after the game that he had removed Reyes at his request. For his part, Reyes was also honest about his motivation.

"I said, 'If I go 1-for-1, take me out of the game,'" Reyes said. "And I did that. If I went 0-for-1, maybe I'm still in the game until I get a hit. . . . I wanted to stay in the game, but (Mets fans) have to understand, too, what's going on. They have to feel happy about it if I win the batting title. I do that for the team, for the fans too, because they've been supporting me all the way through."

Others didn't see it quite the same way. Texas Rangers pitcher C. J. Wilson tweeted that the decision was "weak" and that he hoped Ryan Braun would go 5-for-5 to nab the title.

Indeed, the fact that Reyes did not further extend his lead left Braun an opening. A 3-for-4 game would have earned him the title, but instead he was 0-for-4. Braun noted that Reyes's exit had given him a chance—one he would not have been given had Reyes knocked a couple more hits. "I'm not really here to judge him," Braun argued after the game.

Sometimes the controversial side of a batting title isn't what happens on the field, but what happens off it. In 2012, Giants outfielder Melky Cabrera was having a career year, hitting .346, which led the National League on August 15th, when Cabrera was suspended for 50 games due to a drug test that revealed high levels of testosterone, consistent with the use of performance-enhancing drugs. While Cabrera had 501 plate appearances—one shy of the number needed to qualify for the batting title—he would still have won the title under Rule 10.22(a). That rule would allow the addition of a hypothetical hitless at-bat to qualify Cabrera (in other words, if he would have won the title with another hitless plate appearance, he would be declared the winner—Tony Gwynn was awarded the 1996 title under the same rule when he was four plate appearances shy of the requirement of 502).

But Cabrera requested on September 21st that Major League Baseball declare him ineligible for the batting title, and Commissioner Bud Selig did so. Giants catcher Buster Posey was awarded the title—although his average of .336 was well below Cabrera's. At least by getting ahead of the end of the season, the matter was resolved with a relatively minimal amount of fuss.

As long as players compete with the field to win a batting title, there will be controversy. Do opponents favor one player over another? When should or shouldn't a player sit? What about suspensions? These are some of the issues that make up the multitudinous unwritten rules of baseball—and will fuel arguments for years to come. It isn't enough to be good to win a batting title, sometimes you have to be on the right side of the shenanigans.

CHAPTER 23

HITTING STREAKS OF 40+ GAMES

Number of Times Accomplished: Six (or seven, see below).

First Instance: Disputable, but frequently considered to be Bill Dahlen, Chicago Colts, 1894.

Most Recent Instance: Pete Rose, Cincinnati Reds, 1978.

Likely Achievers: The list includes baseball's top two career hits leaders in Rose and Cobb, as well as other stars who are hardly surprising inclusions.

Surprises: Dahlen, a career .272 hitter, is definitely the outlier of the group, although he had a fine career.

Likelihood of Additional Occurrences: In the nearly four decades since Rose, many players have come close. There's a good likelihood that somebody will get a good bounce or a close call to make their way onto this list in the near future.

In 2003, *USA Today* ran a study of what exactly was the hardest thing to do in sports. The answer—hitting a baseball. For the men who have toiled in the game for decades, this was hardly a surprise. Facing the best pitchers in the world with world-class athletes playing defense behind them, it's hard enough to make contact, and even harder to get hits—which makes a hitting streak a fluke of the highest order that defies logic. But there are a few legendary hitters who have taken this defiance to extreme levels in managing 40+-game hitting streaks.

~

By the modern reckoning (more on this later), Bill Dahlen started this group in 1894. A 24-year-old shortstop, Dahlen had his career year in that season, hitting .359 with 15 home runs and 108 RBI. He strung together a 42-game hitting streak during the season. Dahlen stayed in the major leagues until age 41, but hit .300 only one more time after 1894. His career was ultimately marked by that lengthy hitting streak and by the frequency with which he was ejected from games—reportedly 65 total ejections both as a player and a manager.

One thing Dahlen had was a dose of bad luck. Not only did he hit in 42 consecutive games, but after the game his streak was stopped—a 13–11 win in which his team had 17 hits on August 7, 1894—he then started another 28-game hitting streak. Had Dahlen worked a bleeder through the infield on August 7th, he could have easily had a 71-game hitting streak.

⌒

Instead, Dahlen's hitting streak was a record for only a brief span. In the last game of 1896, Baltimore outfielder "Wee" Willie Keeler had a hit. There was nothing remarkable about this—Keeler was one of the best hitters in the game—but it quietly began a streak that Keeler would carry well into 1897.

Keeler was an unlikely candidate to become a baseball legend. For starters, there is the matter of size. Keeler (who was actually born William Henry O'Kelleher Jr.) was just 5'4½", tiny even by the standards of his era. Keeler's Orioles were a small team anyway, with future Hall of Famers like John McGraw (5'7") and Wilbert Robinson (5'8") on the roster. But Keeler was so exceptionally tiny that he had to craft his own hitting strategy to get around his diminutive stature. As one biographer noted, "[Keeler] had the speed to leg out infield singles, the bat control to drop down bunts, chops, and rollers in front of infielders, and when they moved in, the ability to loft a base hit over their heads." Keeler was a tiny man with a short, heavy bat (30 inches, 46 ounces) and he choked up so far at the plate that the photos are almost comical. Keeler's second most famous contribution to baseball was his description of his philosophy of batting—"Keep your eye clear and hit 'em where they ain't." His most famous contribution was his 19 seasons on the field of doing just that.

In 1897, Keeler was at his absolute best, batting .424, which included 46 extra-base hits, no small feat in the Dead Ball Era. Keeler just kept getting hits. Browns pitcher Duke Esper, facing Keeler once his streak had already reached 34 games, nearly shut him down, but a bunt single kept the streak rolling. On June 15th, against the Louisville Colonels, Keeler (counting that last game from 1896) broke Dahlen's record with 43 consecutive games with a hit. His streak reached 45 games against Pittsburgh on June 18th, when he singled, doubled, and tripled.

The next day, Keeler took an 0-for-4 afternoon against Pirate lefty Frank Killeen. His closest brush with a base hit was a soft grounder to third base, on which he was nipped at first. The streak was over, but Keeler and his inventive approach to solving a seemingly irreparable problem were just beginning to make their mark on baseball. Keeler retired in 1910 with 2,932 hits and was elected to the Hall of Fame posthumously in 1939. So universally enjoyed was Keeler that he even served as best man in the wedding of Bill Dahlen, a few years after breaking his hitting-streak record.

It would take a singular work ethic to break Keeler's hitting streak. For that matter, any player hitting in 40 or more consecutive games has to bring an incredible amount of attention to the daily tasks that make up baseball. But the man who would own hitting streaks was extraordinary even by the standards of major-league players. When asked once by columnist Jimmy Cannon why he played so hard, the player in question replied, "I always think, there might be somebody in the stands who's never seen me play."

An elegant 6'2" outfielder who was born to a pair of Italian immigrants as one of a trio of brothers who would play (and star) in the major leagues, Joe DiMaggio was always special. DiMaggio grew up near San Francisco and tore up the Pacific Coast League before the big leagues. At age 18, he amassed a 61-game hitting streak there in 1933, before moving on to New York in 1936.

Despite his multitude of skills and panache, DiMaggio still had to counter a culture that was almost obsessed with stereotypes. In 1939, less than a decade before Jackie Robinson would begin his own MLB circuit of slaying stereotypes, no less an observer of American culture than *Life* magazine heavy-handedly wrote of DiMaggio, "Although he learned Italian first, Joe, now twenty-four, speaks English without an accent and is otherwise well adapted to most U.S. mores. Instead of olive oil or smelly bear grease he keeps his hair slick with water. He never reeks of garlic and prefers chicken chow mein to spaghetti."

Of course, the reason *Life* felt compelled to contemplate DiMaggio in the first place is that he was a legendary player, perhaps one of the best all-around players in the history of the sport. Bridging the Yankee past of Ruth and Gehrig to the future of Mantle, DiMaggio was not so much a baseball star as an iconic figure of the late 1930s to early 1950s for a generation of New Yorkers. Oh, and there was the hitting.

DiMaggio on the surface seemed an unlikely candidate for a lengthy hitting streak. He was athletic, but tall and muscular, more inclined to rip home runs than chop out infield singles. He was also right-handed, which is significant because he is the sole member of the 40+-game club who wasn't either left-handed or a switch hitter. In his era—as they are today—right-handed pitchers were far more common. So DiMaggio hit against the platoon frequently, lost a step out of the batter's box, and wasn't one of the fastest players in the sport (30 career stolen bases).

In the summer of 1941, none of that mattered. On May 14th, the Cleveland Indians beat DiMaggio's Yankees 4–1 as Indians starter Mel Harder scattered six hits. DiMaggio didn't have one, which left him hitting .304 for the season. It is noteworthy in retrospect because DiMaggio got a hit in every game for the next two months.

On June 29th, DiMaggio's streak reached 42 games when he had a hit in the second game of a doubleheader. This surpassed George Sisler's 1922 mark of 41 games, which had been considered the "modern" record. On July 2nd, DiMaggio homered off Red Sox pitcher Dick Newsome, which made his streak 45 games, generally cited as breaking Wee Willie Keeler's streak (although as discussed before, Keeler's streak—when not restricted by single-season considerations—was actually 45 games). So in fact, it took until July 5th, when DiMaggio had two hits against the Philadelphia A's, for him to surpass Keeler.

DiMaggio rolled on, through the All-Star break, into mid-July. Across America, the common question of the day was whether DiMaggio got another hit. On July 16th in Cleveland, he had three hits, making his streak 56 consecutive games with a hit. The next night, DiMaggio's luck shifted. Indians third baseman Ken Keltner made two tough plays to rob him of potential hits, and the hitting streak came to an end.

The end of the streak was an admitted relief to DiMaggio, as his feat has been termed "the most extraordinary thing that ever happened in American sports" by noted baseball fan Stephen Jay Gould. For two months, sports fans could count on death, taxes, and DiMaggio. And as if to confirm that the streak was no fluke, DiMaggio had a 16-game streak immediately after Cleveland ended his historic run. But it wasn't all relief—years later, DiMaggio quietly admitted that "When my hitting streak was ended, I felt terrible. I felt as though I'd lost my best friend."

More than three-quarters of a century later, DiMaggio's streak is the one every hot hitter takes an imaginary aim toward. While the mark still stands, there have been times when a challenger made a legitimate run at it.

<hr />

While DiMaggio's skill set did not seem ideal for a legendary hit streak, his best challenger since was almost a prototype for the role. A scrappy switch-hitting third baseman with good speed, Pete Rose obviously didn't have any trouble cobbling together base hits, as he set the all-time MLB record with 4,256 of them. Rose was nicknamed "Charlie Hustle" for a reason. As his streak threatened DiMaggio's, popular sentiment backed Rose. But one night in Atlanta—under circumstances Rose himself called into question—his shot at the all-time record ended, although not until after Rose had joined the 40+-game club.

On June 13, 1978, Rose was 0-for-3 in a 1–0 win by his Reds over the Chicago Cubs. He was hitting an unremarkable .267 for the season and had gone without a hit in three of his previous four games. He wouldn't do that again for nearly two months.

By the end of June, the streak was 16 games and Rose's batting average was .293. On July 17th against the Expos, the streak reached 30 games, and Rose was hitting .304. In the first game of a doubleheader against the Phillies on July 28th, Rose doubled to run the streak to 40 games (and his average to .312). On July 31st, a sixth-inning single stretched Rose's streak to 44 games, tying him with Wee Willie Keeler for the second longest single-season streak in baseball history, which was also good for the all-time National League hitting streak record.

The next night, Rose's Reds were crushed 16–4 in Atlanta by the Braves. Rose walked in the first, lined out in the second, grounded to short to open the fifth inning, and hit into a double play in the seventh inning. With two out in the ninth inning, he came up with one last chance to extend the streak. The visiting fans in Atlanta's Fulton County Stadium stood and cheered for Rose, but he struck out on a 2-2 pitch from Gene Garber to end his streak at 44 games.

Bizarrely, Rose complained about the pitching he faced in the streak-busting game from Atlanta's Larry McWilliams and Garber. "Garber was pitching like it was the seventh game of the World Series," Rose said after the game. "He had a 16–4 lead. . . . Most pitchers in baseball just challenge a guy in that situation. He was just trying to in-and-out, up-and-down you."

It was an odd complaint for a player known for never taking nor giving any quarter, and whose diligent hustle had earned his way into the record books. For his part, Garber neatly summed it up.

"I had an idea he was hitting like it was the ninth inning of the World Series," he told reporters when advised of Rose's complaints. Of that, there could be little doubt.

One forgotten man in the list of lengthy hitting streaks is Denny Lyons, a 19th-century third baseman who somewhat made baseball history with the Philadelphia Athletics in 1887. Lyons had a 52-game hitting streak—kind of. A peculiar rule in effect for 1887 counted walks as base hits. The same statistical anomaly that led outfielder Tip O'Neill to hit either .487 or .492 allowed Lyons to conduct an epic hitting streak.

In games 22 and 44 of the 52-game hitting streak, Lyons didn't get any actual base hits, but he did get walks, which were counted as hits. Of course, not only was Lyons's streak ultimately discredited, but it generally went unmentioned even before MLB's 1968 rejiggering of the record book. Lyons's streak went unremarked upon until baseball researchers dug it out of the archives around a century after it occurred.

Lyons's name rarely appears on lists of hitting streaks, and it's not difficult to understand why. That said, Lyons's resume is legitimate under the rules of the time that he compiled the streak. DiMaggio never realized he was chasing Lyons, and by omitting his record from the accounts of hitting streaks, he is done a second disservice.

While no one has reached the 40-game plateau since Pete Rose, there have been those who approached it. Paul Molitor had a 39-game streak in 1987, and Jimmy Rollins of the Phillies put together a two-season 38-game streak in 2005 and 2006. There will likely be another 40-game streak—although the ensuing 16 games between reaching 40 and reaching DiMaggio's mark look incredibly daunting.

CHAPTER 24

WINNING THE TRIPLE CROWN (AS A BATTER)

Number of Times Accomplished: 17.

First Instance: Paul Hines, Providence Grays, 1878, National League.

Most Recent Instance: Miguel Cabrera, Detroit Tigers, 2012, American League.

Likely Achievers: Many of the claimants of possible Greatest of All Time status are on this list, including Mantle, Williams, Gehrig, Hornsby, and Cobb.

Surprises: A Triple Crown really can't be won by fluke. There are a few names on the list that are probably not exceptionally familiar to those who aren't followers of 19th or early 20th century baseball—Hines, Tip O'Neill, Heinie Zimmerman. But those three—plus active player Cabrera—are the only Triple Crown winners who aren't in the Hall of Fame.

Likelihood of Additional Occurrences: Before Cabrera's 2012 Crown, it had been 45 years since the last instance. It doesn't seem likely to become as common as it was in the 1930s, when four different players won the Crown. But another Triple Crown winner will probably pop up here and there.

The term *Triple Crown* comes from horse racing, which is altogether appropriate because only a baseball thoroughbred could post a league-leading batting average, home-run total, and number of RBIs. The modern usage of the term dates to the mid-1930s, after baseball's home-run explosion. Before that, a Triple Crown might be applied to other stats—batting average, runs scored, and hits, for instance. But once the usage became standardized, the Crown became a sort of prime baseball status symbol. It obviously requires a multifaceted player to top his league in all three categories. In fact, more Triple Crowns were actually won before the term was universally defined than in the 80-plus years since its meaning became common. But if early Triple Crown winners stumbled into the feat unaware, latter-day players became altogether aware of the significance of every hit, homer, and RBI down the September stretch.

‍⁓

The first Triple Crown was won by Paul Hines in the National League in 1878. Hines, who may or may not have also turned the first unassisted triple play (see chapter 1), certainly didn't chase home runs like a modern slugger—his league-leading total was a scant four homers. For that matter, Hines's achievement has to be somewhat devalued by the fact that his league played a 60-game schedule. By 1887, when the second Crown was won, seasons were more than twice as long, and baseballs occasionally flew out of ballparks.

‍⁓

For many years, James "Tip" O'Neill's unknown Triple Crown took a backseat to the fact that he hit almost .500 in 1887. Except that he really didn't. For whatever reason, baseball scorers counted walks as hits in 1887, so while O'Neill's average soared to .492, in the modern sense of the game, it was his on-base percentage that was soaring. This also doesn't account for the fact that walks took five balls in 1887, but strike-outs took four strikes as well.

All of this said, it's not like O'Neill won his Triple Crown on a scoring fluke. Even after the statistical record was corrected to align with modern understanding, O'Neill still hit a robust .435, an improvement of .033 over second-place finisher Pete Browning, and .067 above the third-place finisher. O'Neill hit 14 home runs, in a season in which he and Cincinnati's John Reilly (who hit 10 homers) were the only players in the American Association to reach double-figure totals. Had there been any drama over the Crown (and of course, it being not defined by the modern understanding for another 50 years, there was no drama), it would have come in the RBI race. O'Neill finished with 123, which was five more than Browning in second place. Nine batters knocked in 100 runs in the American Association in 1887.

O'Neill had been a pitcher before arm problems turned him into an outfielder. A career .326 hitter, O'Neill led the Association in almost every category in 1887—average, runs scored, hits, doubles, triples, home runs, and RBI. O'Neill was undoubtedly the best player in the American Association in 1887. Unfortunately, his ultimate legacy isn't as a Triple Crown winner, or as one of the first great Canadian baseball players, although he was both of those things.

In the fall of 1887, O'Neill's St. Louis Browns were scheduled to play the Cuban Giants, who, misnomer aside, were the first great African American baseball team. Shortly before the games were to be played, a group of Browns players presented team owner Chris Von Der Ahe with a letter—more specifically, O'Neill actually brought him the letter. It read:

> We, the undersigned members of the St. Louis Base-
> ball Club, do not agree to play against negroes to-
> morrow. We will cheerfully play against white people
> at any time, and think by refusing to play we are only
> doing what is right, taking everything into consider-
> ation and the shape the team is in at present.

Eight players, including O'Neill, signed the letter. The game was not played.

The Browns weren't the only players who felt that way—as many of contemporary star Cap Anson's comments and explosions certainly confirm. Many players, including manager and non-letter-signer Charlie Comiskey, downplayed the racial issue, and claimed that the team was simply overworked and tired. But whatever O'Neill and the Browns' true motives were, they played a role in the imposition and maintenance of a 60-year color line in big-league baseball. O'Neill helped bring about a stain on the sport of baseball that looms larger than any Triple Crown.

Another Triple Crown winner who might not find himself earning his way onto fans' Fantasy Dinner Party lists was the great Ty Cobb, who won the prize in 1909. While Charles Leerhsen's compelling 2015 biography of Cobb rebuts many of the more egregious catalog of Cobb's alleged complexities and failures, even Leerhsen readily admits, "Ty Cobb was a deep pool of brackish water."

Cobb's 1909 Triple Crown is especially remarkable because it wasn't just an American League achievement—no, Cobb led *both* major leagues in batting average, home runs, and RBIs. Frankly, the race wasn't especially close. Cobb's .377 average bettered the next highest average in the big leagues by 30 points. His 107 RBIs were seven ahead of Honus Wagner's second-place total. And finally, although nine home runs doesn't sound like much today, it was still two more than anyone else hit in the big leagues in 1909.

Indeed, after Leerhsen's biography, Cobb is perhaps more likely to be misremembered as a slap hitter than as an evil racist. Sure, Cobb's .366 lifetime batting average remains unequaled in subsequent history. But his split-grip, slap style of hitting was based more on aesthetic values than on limitations of skill. In 1925, he once told a pair of sportswriters, "They say I get my base-hits on infield grounders and little bunts. . . . I'll show you something today. I'm going for home runs for the first time in my career."

Cobb hit three home runs that day, and at least one account argues that he narrowly missed two more. The next day, he did hit two more homers. Cobb finished that 1925 season with a dozen homers, which tied his career high. But like Wade Boggs several generations later, Cobb had the power to hit home runs—he'd just rather destroy his competition otherwise.

Not unlike Cobb, the most recent player to win a Triple Crown in the National League didn't mind a good scrap with authority figures. Joe Medwick, as part of the St. Louis Cardinals' fabled Gashouse Gang, was labeled with the unfortunate nickname "Ducky Wucky." Lest anyone think the nickname made him soft, Medwick hated it—and preferred "Muscles" as his sobriquet of choice.

A 5'10" outfielder, Medwick is probably most famous for fighting with Detroit third baseman Marvin Owen in Game 7 of the 1934 World Series, which incited such bedlam in Michigan that MLB commissioner Kenesaw Mountain Landis ordered Medwick out of the game. The Cardinals won the game, 11–0, so Medwick laughed last.

He also had an incredible 1937 season. Generally more of a doubles hitter than a home-run slugger, Medwick cleanly led the NL in batting with a .374 mark, 10 points ahead of teammate Johnny Mize. He outright ran away with the RBI race, knocking in 154 runs, 39 more than Frank Demaree and 41 more than Mize. But home runs would be the toughest section of the Crown for Medwick. He otherwise never topped 23 homers in a season, and his work was cut out for him. The Giants' Mel Ott slugged his 31st homer of the year on September 14th. Medwick had 28 homers at that time. But the next day, he hit his 29th; on September 26th, he blasted his 30th homer, and on September 29th in Pittsburgh, he hit his 31st homer to tie Ott, which is where the competition finished.

Surprisingly, winning the Triple Crown didn't help Medwick out financially. The following year, Medwick's salary was $20,000. He led the league in RBIs again in 1938 with 122 (while hitting .322 and leading the NL in doubles with 47), and his salary was cut to $18,000. Medwick eventually protested enough that he was traded to the Brooklyn Dodgers. A week into that tenure, he was knocked unconscious by a fastball from a former Cardinal teammate, Bob Bowman.

Medwick was honored in 1968 with induction into the Baseball Hall of Fame. He seemingly fought everyone to earn his way into the baseball record book, and 80 years later, no one has matched his NL Triple Crown.

Every year, players face the pressure of the pennant race—and especially so before division play entered the fold in 1969 and doubled the number of playoff teams. Occasionally, players face the pressure of competing for the Triple Crown. But in 1967, Carl Yastrzemski dealt with both pressures in one fell swoop. As the season wound down, Yaz's Red Sox were in a four-way battle for the AL pennant, and the 27-year-old outfielder found himself in the race to top the batting average, home run, and RBI columns as well as the W-L columns.

The Red Sox hadn't won a pennant in 21 years, and in fact had finished in the bottom half of the American League for eight consecutive years heading into 1967. Meanwhile, Yastrzemski, a 5'11" lefty outfielder, was blossoming into a star. He had won a batting title before 1967, but had never eclipsed 20 home runs or 94 RBI in a prior season.

As the season headed down the stretch, Yaz went into overdrive, personally (along with ace pitcher Jim Lonborg) carrying Boston to the AL title. From September 1st through October 1st, Yastrzemski hit .417 with nine home runs and 26 RBIs—a month with an OPS of 1.265. He also mashed three home runs in the final six games of the season, which enabled him to tie Harmon Killebrew with 44 round-trippers. His .326 batting average and 121 RBI had given him clear-cut victories in both those categories.

Teammate George Scott later recalled, "Yaz hit 44 homers that year, and 43 of them meant something big for the team. It seemed like every time we needed a big play, the man stepped up and got it done." In the final 12 games of that 1967 season, Yaz batted .523 with 16 RBIs. Unbelievably, the bigger the situation, the better he got. In the season's last two games, both Red Sox wins—either of which could have thrown them into a three-way tie for the pennant had they been lost—he was 7-for-8 with six RBIs.

For his part, Yaz claimed no double intentions. "In '67, the Triple Crown was never even mentioned once," he recalled in 2012. "We were so involved in the pennant race, I didn't know I won the Triple Crown until the next day, when I read it in the paper."

At the time, Yaz's Triple Crown was the second in two years (Frank Robinson had won it the previous season) and the third in a dozen years. But for 45 years, no one else equaled the feat. It was beginning to look like Carl Yastrzemski would be the last Triple Crown winner. "Somebody's got to do it," he said in 2012. "I'm surprised it's gone this long."

In 2012, Miguel Cabrera became the first player in 45 years to even make a solid run at the Triple Crown. The 6'4" Venezuelan slugger had signed with the Florida Marlins at the age of 16. At the age of 20, he was the starting third baseman for the World Series champions. The next year, in his first full season in the majors, Cabrera raked 33 home runs and knocked in 112 runs. He went on to knock in 100 runs in each of the next 10 years, and to slug 30 or more homers in nine of the next 10.

Two weeks before the end of the 2012 season, Cabrera was leading the American League in batting average and RBIs and trailed Josh Hamilton by two in the home-run race. The mere fact of the chase was historic—Jayson Stark pointed out that since Yastrzemski, no one had even won two-thirds of the Crown and finished second in the other category.

But Cabrera was determined not to end his chase with being merely close. Cabrera homered on September 19th and again on the 22nd. With another homer on September 29th, he moved into the lead, and he hit a 44th homer on October 1st. This doesn't mean he won the title without suspense. In the final game of the year, Curtis Granderson of the Yankees hit two home runs, which pulled him to within one of Cabrera's mark. Potentially more serious, Angels rookie Mike Trout made a run at Cabrera's batting average of .330. After going 0-for-2 in the season finale, Cabrera was pulled from the game early. He ended up besting Trout by four points, and maintaining a one-homer margin over Granderson and Josh Hamilton.

"It was hard the last two days because everybody talked about it," Cabrera told reporters after the game. "I had to focus; I had to go out there and do the job."

Cabrera was content to allow the superlatives to flow in from elsewhere. The defeated Trout commented, "He's the best hitter in the game. . . . He had an unbelievable year."

MLB commissioner Bud Selig stated that the Crown was "a remarkable achievement that places [Cabrera] amongst an elite few in all of baseball history."

Through the middle of the 2017 season, Yankee rookie Aaron Judge looked like he might follow in Cabrera's footsteps. He ultimately tailed off, falling way behind the pack in batting average. But after 45 years of stagnancy, Cabrera gave a new generation of young stars a legend to chase. Long may they run.

CHAPTER 25

STEALING 100 BASES IN A SEASON

Number of Times Accomplished: 17 (nine of these seasons were pre-1892, with some wildly different "base stealing" scoring rules).

First Instance: Five different players stole 100 bases in 1887, three in the American Association and two in the National League. They were Hugh Nicol (138 steals), Arlie Latham (129), Charles Comiskey (117), John Montgomery Ward (111), and Jim Fogarty (102). Of course, you can put something of an asterisk on the whole group because of some truly bizarre scoring rules.

Most Recent Instance: Vince Coleman, St. Louis Cardinals, 1987.

Likely Achievers: All-time steals king Rickey Henderson broke the century mark three times. Runner-up Lou Brock is also on the list. Nineteenth-century star Billy Hamilton is third all-time in steals, and he entered the 100 club twice.

Surprises: Hugh Nicol stole 100 bases twice, but was a lifetime .235 hitter who is often forgotten. Jim Fogarty is another 19th-century player who is often overlooked—in part because he died of tuberculosis at the age of 27.

Likelihood of Additional Occurrences: It hasn't happened in 30 years, but it seems almost inevitable that another baseball revolution will bring speed back up the list of priorities—and statistics. But at present, Jose Reyes's 78 steals in 2007 is the closest challenge in this century.

Baseball tends to fixate on the duel between the pitcher, standing tall on the mound, ball in hand, and the batter, waiting at the plate, ready to slug the next pitch into oblivion. But it's not always a two-actor play. There is that third figure, the baserunner, edging away from first base, leaning toward second, feinting, jumping, always making the pitcher look over, the catcher get distracted, and everybody uncomfortable. Or at least, sometimes there is.

The history of baseball is one of eras, and some of those eras prominently feature the baserunner. The early years of baseball were one of those eras, but then the game swung toward sluggers and three-run homers. The fleet, crafty baserunner was a thing of the past, until the 1960s, 1970s, and 1980s brought the running game back. In the 21st century, speed has mostly again given way to power. But as surely as baseball ebbs and flows in cycles, the stolen base has had its days—and will have them again. Here, then, are a few of the masters of the tactic.

Again, in early baseball, the ball was dead, the defense was suspect, and the baserunner was of pivotal importance. Rarely is that more clear than in the story of outfielder Hugh Nicol, a Scottish immigrant who was born in 1858. Nicol was an athletic young man, although also a tiny one, given his listed height of 5'4". Nicol first surfaced in baseball in the minor leagues of his hometown, Rockford, Illinois, in 1878, and he soon made enough of an impression to earn his way onto the Chicago White Stockings in 1881. After two years as a part-time player (he hit .204 and .199 in those two years), Nicol was picked up by the St. Louis Browns. He played four years in St. Louis, but was then traded to the Cincinnati Red Stockings for catcher/first baseman Jack Boyle and $350.

No one has ever rained terror on baseball via baserunning quite the way that Nicol did in the American Association in 1887. Nicol hit only .215 that season, and had very little power (he slugged .267). But Nicol approached hitting like a man ahead of his time. A November 1887 newspaper article called Nicol "the base running star of the profession" and noted that the star himself "gives it as his opinion that a base on balls affects the game more than a base hit." The unknown sportswriter went on to state, "And he is right." For Nicol, at least, this was certainly true.

Nicol had 102 hits in 1887, but he also drew 86 walks, giving him a relatively robust .341 on-base percentage. Nicol was third in the American Association in walks that season, and he took full advantage of his opportunities on the basepaths. Nicol swiped 138 bases, a mark that still stands as the all-time MLB single-season record. Granted, there was plenty of base stealing in the 1887 American Association—the league's 10th-place finisher in stolen bases, 5'3" second baseman Cub Stricker, stole 86 bases. Further granted, part of the reasoning arose from the scoring rules of the time. Advancing on an error or going from first to third on a single could all constitute a stolen base. In fact, two players were actually credited with more steals than Nicol at the time—although subsequent revision of the stat book rendered him as the single-season king.

Regardless of all of this, Nicol was something else. One contemporary account indicates that Reds manager Gus Schmeltz was a big believer in Nicol's small-ball tactics, and had traded for him in an attempt to "infuse life and ginger into the team." The Reds had finished fifth in 1886, but Nicol helped boost the club to second place with his base-stealing exploits.

Nicol followed his 1887 success by stealing 103 more bases in 1888. However, over the long haul, he simply didn't hit enough to stick around, and his big-league career was over in 1890, when he was 32. Nicol's post-baseball career led him to Purdue University, where he became the school's first athletic director. Nicol would probably tell you that he walked his way there—one base on balls at a time.

<hr />

After 1891, it was over 70 years before anybody stole 100 bases again. Big innings and three-run homers took center stage after the ascent of Babe Ruth. For instance, in the entire 1940s, there were only three total individual seasons of 50+ stolen bases, topped out by George Case's 61 steals in 1943. And while the integration of the major leagues in

1947 would eventually change the game, the 1950s didn't mark the sea change. In the entire 1950s, the only single season of more than 40 stolen bases was Luis Aparicio's 56 steals for the 1959 Chicago "Go Go" White Sox, who ran at times to compensate for a complete lack of other offense.

Still, it was not until 1962 that the stolen base came back in any kind of meaningful way as an offensive weapon. Back in 1945, Arthur Daley of the *New York Times* had written, "[Ty] Cobb's ['modern'] record of 96 stolen bases in a season will probably never be broken, because modern ball has virtually eliminated the steal as a method of progression." In 1962, L.A. Dodger Maury Wills brought back the steal virtually single-handedly. Wills swiped 104 bases that season—not only more than triple the American League leader's total of 31 steals, but better than every other major-league *team* in stolen bases. Wills had stolen 50 bases in 1960, making him the first National League player in almost four decades to do so. But the following year, he stole 35 bases and was caught stealing 15 times. This wasn't an issue in '62, as Wills hit .299, led the league in triples, and ran the rest of the NL into submission en route to the league's MVP award. A *Sports Illustrated* writer noted during the historic season, "If the . . . Dodgers hold together and win the National League pennant, it may be said that they stole it. More accurately, a slight, almost frail Dodger stole it." The Dodgers didn't win the pennant, but Wills ran his way into history, breaking Cobb's "modern" record on September 23rd, when he stole two bases against the Cardinals, and becoming the first player since 1891 to steal 100 bases when he reached that mark on September 26th against Houston.

Wills stole 586 bases in his career, nearly reaching 100 once again in 1965, when he came up only six steals short. Wills is historically significant not only because of his career totals, but also because he showed a whole new generation of athletes how to make trouble on the basepaths. By the time Wills retired in 1972, another speedster had emerged.

⌐⌐

Lou Brock was a struggling young Chicago Cubs outfielder in 1964 when the Cubs traded him to the St. Louis Cardinals for journeyman pitcher Ernie Broglio. Brock had speed, but he had stolen just 50 bases in two and a half years as a Cub. In St. Louis, he was turned loose, and he promptly became the sport's all-time stolen base king—at least for a generation.

The late 60s Cardinals teams with Brock often ran their way into big innings like the teams of the late 19th and early 20th century. Of the nine seasons from 1966 to 1974, Brock led the National League in stolen bases eight times. Brock should have been on the back end of his career, as he turned 35 early in that season of 1974. But it was that summer that Brock truly ran wild. He ended up stealing 118 bases, demolishing the records of all but a handful of 19th-century players. On September 10th, he singled and stole second in the first inning of a game against the Phillies, which tied Wills's modern mark of 104 steals. In the seventh inning, he again singled, and with the home crowd plunged into excitement, promptly stole second to secure the modern record.

Brock had stolen just 50 bases in two and a half years as a Cub, but in 16 years as a Cardinal, he added 888 more steals, for a career record of 938, beyond even Sliding Billy Hamilton and the dead ball stars who had owned the stolen base record book. But records are made to be broken, and another legendary speedster was already on the way when Brock retired in 1979.

⌐⌐

On Christmas Day, 1958, Rickey Henderson was born in Chicago—more specifically, in the backseat of his family's car. He wouldn't often slow down, whether for obstetricians or opposing catchers. As a small child growing up on his grandmother's farm in Arkansas, Henderson practiced his speed by racing with chickens. "I'd chase them, then they'd chase me. Man, those chickens were fast. . . . I had to be fast to keep up with them, but there wasn't a chicken on that entire farm that could keep up with me."

Once he moved from Arkansas to California, Henderson became a superb two-sport prospect. Henderson would later recall a high school guidance counselor, Mrs. Tommie Wilkerson, who in an effort to cajole young Rickey into something approaching normal social behavior, bribed him with cash "rewards" for base hits. Or for stolen bases. Soon, Henderson's rewards would get much larger.

He was drafted by the hometown Oakland A's in the fourth round of the 1976 MLB Draft. Henderson's arrogance was always noticeable—not only was he the best, he knew he was the best, and he even walked like he knew it. But the arrogance didn't mean that he lacked for work ethic. As a minor leaguer, he worked before games with manager Tom Trebelhorn, who would later manage the Milwaukee Brewers. For his part, Trebelhorn later recalled, "I let him run; that was it. . . . The things we worked on were fairly routine, but he was a great student. He came early, he wanted to do well."

Henderson made it to Oakland in 1979. In 1980, he stole 100 bases. Henderson was a great baserunner—but he also was a superb player in all areas. He holds what is generally acknowledged to be the all-time record for home runs to lead off a game. He also hit out of a crouch, which shrunk his strike zone to tiny proportions, allowing for many walks. He was somewhat spotty as an outfielder, and he insisted on using a flamboyant sideways stabbing motion to catch many routine flyballs. But mostly, he just ran. And American League catchers looked like so many Arkansas chickens.

In 1982, 37 years after the *New York Times* had published a prediction that no one would steal 94 bases in a season, Henderson reached that mark—on July 26th, in the A's 99th game of the 1982 season. Rickey joined the 100-steals club on August 2nd—by far, the earliest that anyone had ever done so. He passed Maury Wills's total of 104 steals on August 8th. On August 27th, in Milwaukee, Henderson stole his 119th base of the year, surpassing Lou Brock's modern record. He celebrated by stealing three more bases in the same game.

Indeed, Henderson probably could have taken down Hugh Nicol's record, had it been acknowledged as a record by most media. He was 7-for-10 on stolen bases in September and October—which means he had 162 stolen base attempts in the season's first 133 games, as compared to 10 attempts in the last 28 games.

Henderson stole 108 bases in 1983, and while his steals numbers were not quite as astounding later in his career, he became a wiser, more careful baserunner. In 1988, he stole 93 bases and was caught just 13 times.

By 1991, Henderson was a defending AL MVP, had been a nine-time All-Star, and on May 1st, he stole his 939th career base, breaking Lou Brock's all-time record. The game was stopped, Henderson held the base aloft, and with characteristic self-promotion, proclaimed, "Today, I am the greatest of all time." The boy who outraced Arkansas chickens had grown into the man who stole 1,406 bases. He was the greatest.

If Rickey Henderson was the ultimate juxtaposition of power and speed, baseball still had not seen the guy who, maybe even more than Henderson, was a product of raw, unfettered speed. Vince Coleman was born in 1961 in Jacksonville, Florida, and is the last player to steal 100 bases in a season. Coleman, like Henderson, loved football as well as basketball. He was a kicker and punter on his college team at Florida A&M, even nailing a game-winning field goal to beat Division I-A University of Miami in 1979. Coleman was a 10th-round draft choice of the St. Louis Cardinals in 1982, and wasted no time blazing through the minor leagues.

After stealing 43 bases in 58 games of rookie ball in 1982, in 1983, Coleman moved up to Class A, where he hit .350 and stole 145 bases in 113 games. Lest anyone take that for a fluke, Coleman then swiped 101 bases for Triple-A Louisville in 1984.

Coleman moved to the big leagues in 1985. St. Louis played in cavernous Busch Stadium and had built a team of speedy slap hitters like

Ozzie Smith and Willie McGee. Coleman never hit as well as Rickey Henderson, totaling just 28 home runs in over 5,400 major-league at-bats. He hit .264 for his career, and didn't draw a ton of walks, as his on-base percentage was just .324. Comparatively, Henderson hit .279, but had a .401 on-base percentage.

But in 1985, Coleman led the Cardinals to the NL East division crown by stealing 110 bases, making him the only rookie to reach triple-digit steals in a single season. Unfortunately, in the NLCS, the fastest man in baseball was outrun—by the automatic tarp at Busch Stadium, which pinned his leg during pregame stretching exercises before Game 4. The Cardinals won the pennant, but lost the World Series as Coleman was sidelined due to his encounter with the tarp.

The injury didn't hurt Coleman's speed, as in 1986, he stole 107 bases and was caught just 14 times. He also hit .232, had a putrid .280 slugging percentage, and managed a .301 on-base percentage. Coleman led the National League in steals every season from 1985 to 1990, his last with the Cardinals. He even stole 109 bases in 1987, but never returned to triple figures again. In 1989, he stole 65 bases, but did make baseball history when he stole successfully 50 consecutive times without being caught.

Unfortunately, in 1991, Coleman signed a massive free-agent contract with the New York Mets, where he formed part of one of the most overpaid, underachieving teams in history. Coleman reached 50 steals in 1994 with the Kansas City Royals, but was never the player who laid waste to the National League in the late 80s. He retired in 1997, with 752 career stolen bases, sixth most of all time.

Since 1988, no player has stolen even 80 bases in a season. Marquis Grissom managed 78 steals in 1992, which was tied by Jose Reyes in 2007. But there have been no serious threats to join the 100-steals club.

Cincinnati Reds outfielder Billy Hamilton proved the circular nature of baseball when he became the next best threat to the club. Sharing a name with 19th-century thief Sliding Billy Hamilton, and a history as a two-sport standout like Rickey Henderson and Vince Coleman, Hamilton swiped 103 bases in Class-A Dayton in 2011, and totaled 155 steals in 2012 between Class-A Bakersfield and Double-A Pensacola. His blinding speed suggests 100-steal potential at the major-league level. But in the modern era, outs are considered too precious to gamble, even on a bet like Billy Hamilton. He has slowly improved, climbing from 56 steals in 2014 to 59 in 2017. It's a long way to go, but there's always a chance in baseball.

CHAPTER 26

STRIKING OUT 300 BATTERS
IN A SEASON

Number of Times Accomplished: 66 (31 of these were pre-1893).

First Instance: Three pitchers eclipsed 300 strikeouts in 1883—Tim Keefe (359), Jim Whitney (345), and Old Hoss Radbourn (315).

Most Recent Instance: Chris Sale of the Red Sox, 2017 (308).

Likely Achievers: Strikeout kings like Nolan Ryan (six times), Sandy Koufax (three times), and Walter Johnson (twice) are all on the list.

Surprises: At least in modern times, there's no real flukish way to strike out 300 hitters. The only surprises on the list are players whose names may be a bit less familiar than those above, simply because their careers were derailed—like J. R. Richard or Sam McDowell.

Likelihood of Additional Occurrences: Having a successful pitcher work enough innings to strike out 300 batters is something of a concern, and there had been a dozen-year gap since the last accomplishment before Clayton Kershaw joined the club in 2015. Still, at least for the moment, especially in light of Chris Sale's 2017 season, another 300-strikeout pitcher looks very possible.

It is one thing to have a game where your pitches are unhittable. Hitters may cut through the high fastball and be paralyzed by the breaking ball. But over the course of a full season, it's an onerous task to fool big-league hitters again and again. When it comes to strikeouts, at least in the post-1900 era, there is a magic number and it's 300. Only the best of pitching's best have put together seasons laden with enough strikeouts to join the 300 club. The list scans like a who's who of fireballers—Ryan, Koufax, (Walter) Johnson, (Randy) Johnson. But even within that talented club, the path to 300-strikeout seasons has never been easy.

"Kilroy was here."

Outside of baseball, it's a pop culture phrase, one that flourished during World War II, coming from some unknown Kilroy—possibly James J.—whose catchphrase attested to a very existential truth. The man writing the message was indeed present and accounted for.

It was the same on a baseball diamond, but instead of a scrawled message, Matthew Aloysius Kilroy made his mark with strikeouts. In the year of his greatest triumph, the pitcher worked from a four-foot-by-seven-foot rectangular box and delivered pitches from as little as 50 feet from home plate. The pitcher also had to throw *six* balls to walk a batter in that magical year of 1886. But while many pitchers flourished—to name one, Louisville pitcher Toad Ramsey was neck and neck with Kilroy all season long in strikeouts—the pitching message was that Kilroy was there.

A lefty who pitched for a last-place Baltimore team, Kilroy was a rookie who turned 20 years old during his historic season. As was the fashion of the time, Kilroy expected to pitch the entire game, every time out. He nearly did—starting 68 games and completing 66 of them. A 1917 newspaper article recalled that Kilroy reached double-digit strikeout totals 18 times in 1886 and that in 26 of his starts, the opposing team was held to four hits or fewer. Kilroy could have easily set a single-season no-hitter record as well as his historic strikeout mark.

On October 3rd against Louisville, Kilroy struck out four batters, and in so doing, surpassed Hugh Daily's previous single-season record of 483 strikeouts. In his next start, on October 6th against Pittsburgh, he struck out 11 more batters and pitched a no-hitter. Kilroy ended the season with a massive total of 513 strikeouts, 14 ahead of Louisville's Ramsey, and established a mark that will never be bested. Kilroy pitched 583 innings that season.

In the next season, baseball's rules changed to allow a fourth strike, and foul balls weren't counted as strikes. Batting averages soared and hitters ruled the day—except for Kilroy, whose strikeouts dipped to 217, but who was 46-19 for a Baltimore team that was 31-37 when he didn't pitch. Kilroy's famous left arm inevitably gave way to overuse, and after winning 121 games in his first four seasons, Kilroy won only 20 more for the rest of his career.

He was an afterthought by 1891, but no pitcher has ever approached 513 strikeouts. Kilroy was there—and looks safe to continue to be there in the baseball record book.

The first great strikeout king of the 20th century was one of the most eccentric characters the sport of baseball has ever seen. How eccentric? Eccentric enough that Bill James wondered in the late 1980s whether he was handicapped, going so far as to write that he "would have been as great a pitcher as Walter Johnson if only he had the sense that God gave a rabbit." But whatever issues surrounded the performance of George "Rube" Waddell, he was one of the great competitors and fastball pitchers of his era.

Waddell was a left-handed fireballer who was such an odd character that he once sat beside his new manager at a team meal and represented himself poorly enough that he was released before he ever played in a game. Modern scholarship appears to indicate that James may have overshot a bit on the extent of Waddell's eccentricities/possible signs of mental illness. That said, the case against him is well documented, if not entirely reliable.

Sam Crawford recalled manager Hughie Jennings distracting Waddell with children's toys. Christy Mathewson told a story about beating Waddell once by getting his mind focused on hunting and a particular bird dog that Mathewson owned. Even if Waddell's alleged propensity for chasing fire engines was apparently invented, he was at the very least an incredibly unusual man.

He also was a masterful strikeout pitcher, and once Waddell settled in under the steady eye of manager Connie Mack with the Philadelphia Athletics, the results were something to behold. Waddell was 29-32 with three different teams before he jumped to the A's in early 1902. He went 24-7 in 1902 with the A's, with a 2.05 ERA and a league-leading 210 strikeouts. The following year, he improved to 302 strikeouts, making him the first pitcher in 11 years to reach 300 Ks. This was immensely impressive in the true Dead Ball Era, because contact was so prized, and pitchers simply didn't record many strikeouts. This is perhaps best emphasized by pointing out that not only did Waddell's 302 strikeouts lead the league, but no other AL pitcher even reached 200 strikeouts that year—second place was held by Bill Donovan, with 187.

But in case 1903 didn't prove the point, Waddell had an even more spectacular 1904. He set what would become the "modern" record with 349 strikeouts, again posting a gap of 110 over his nearest competitor Jack Chesbro, who won 41 games that season. Waddell's strikeout total stood as the record (in post-19th-century terms) for over 60 years.

In 1905, Waddell nearly had a third consecutive 300-strikeout season. He settled for 27 wins, a 1.48 ERA, and a league-leading 287 strikeouts. He was injured late in the season, though, and would never be the same pitcher again. He was married three times in short succession, appears to have been an alcoholic, was out of the major leagues in 1910, and was dead within four more years. There have been other strikeout pitchers since, but none who marked the stage of baseball quite as vividly as Rube Waddell.

Following promising young careers in baseball—especially those of pitchers—is often an exercise in tragedy, but there may not be a single such story that is quite as sad as that of James Rodney Richard. The second overall pick in the 1969 MLB Draft, the 6'8" fireballer worked his way up the Houston Astros system, sticking full-time with the parent club in 1975. Richard had an overpowering fastball, but early in his career, he struggled to control it.

He won 20 games for Houston in 1976, his second full season. He won 18 games in each of the next three seasons, and had become one of the most consistent pitchers in baseball. In 1978, Richard struck out 303 batters. He did so while also leading the league in walks allowed with 141, and posting a 3.11 ERA. The next year, he improved markedly. While he continued to win 18 games, his ERA dropped to a league-leading 2.71, and his 313 strikeouts were recorded against just 98 walks. He struck out 15 hitters in two different games that season, and had 14 double-digit strikeout games.

Richard was off to an excellent start in 1980, posting a 10-4 mark, a 1.90 ERA, and 119 strikeouts in 113 innings. He had an odd injury around the All-Star break, and in his last start, was having trouble seeing his catcher's signals and moving his arm. Days later, Richard collapsed before a game with a near-fatal stroke. Richard would never return to the major leagues. He had multiple comeback attempts, but the damage of the stroke was too much to overcome.

Life after baseball was scarcely easier. Richard made some bad business deals, and became so destitute that in 1994, as he waited for his baseball pension to fully vest, he was homeless—living under a bridge near Houston. Fortunately, since that time, he has recovered, being active in his local community and church. Still, it was a long fall for Richard from back-to-back 300-strikeout seasons to being out of baseball and out of money.

～

Aside from the unusual members of the 300-strikeout club, the last half-century or so has seen the same trio of names dominate the list. Since 1960, there have been 30 seasons of 300+ strikeouts—and more than half come from the same trio of fireballers who battled control troubles and ultimately defined themselves as some of the greatest pitchers in the history of the game: Sandy Koufax, Nolan Ryan, and Randy Johnson.

Koufax was the hometown boy, born and raised in Brooklyn, making the Dodgers and inspiring a generation of local Jewish kids. He had a biting fastball and a vicious curve—but initially struggled to define where exactly they were going. In his first six big-league seasons, Koufax was 36-40 with a 4.10 ERA. While he had 683 strikeouts in his first 691⅔ innings pitched, he also allowed 405 walks.

Before the 1961 season, catcher Norm Sherry suggested to Koufax that he was simply trying too hard—that he should use a looser grip, mix in more off-speed pitches, and generally have a good time. Koufax did, but hitters did not. Hall of Famer Ernie Banks said of facing Koufax, "It was frightening. . . . In the end you knew you were going to be embarrassed."

From 1961 to 1966, Koufax led the NL in ERA five times. He led the league in wins three times, and in strikeouts four times. Three years—1963, 1965, and 1966—he reached 300 strikeouts for the season. In 1965, Koufax shattered Rube Waddell's record, picking up 382 strikeouts. Koufax had 21 double-figure strikeout games in that magical season, and pitched a one-hitter and a perfect game. Koufax finished the season with two remarkable feats—first, he declined to pitch Game 1 of the World Series because it fell on Yom Kippur, a courageous move rarely equaled by modern athletes of any faith, and second, he won the Series MVP anyway, as he won two games, and pitched a three-hit shutout to win Game 7.

Koufax retired after the 1966 season at just 30 years old, because of progressive arthritis that he feared would keep him from living a normal post-baseball life. Named one of the five greatest living players at the 2016 All-Star Game, Koufax's reputation continues to shine—even if his single-season strikeout mark does not.

⌁

Nolan Ryan was one of a bevy of talented young Mets pitchers of the late 1960s. The fastball that became known as "The Ryan Express" always featured prominently in his arsenal, but early in his career, so did a terrifying lack of control. Ryan was with the Mets for four seasons, going 29-38 with a 3.58 ERA. He had 493 strikeouts in 510 innings, but also allowed 344 walks—which got him traded to California for infielder Jim Fregosi after the 1971 season.

In California, Ryan emerged from the shadow of former teammates Tom Seaver, Jerry Koosman, and Gary Gentry. Pitching coach Tom Morgan worked with Ryan on his curveball, and Ryan also began what would be a career-long regimen of weightlifting. The results were instantaneous.

In 1972, Ryan won 19 games, lowered his ERA to 2.28, and led the American League with 329 strikeouts. This was the first of six 300-strikeout seasons in Ryan's career. He may have been at his best in the following season, when he won 21 games and broke Sandy Koufax's strikeout mark. Ryan pitched two no-hitters and a one-hitter that season, and broke the record by working 11 innings to strike out 16 Minnesota Twins to inch his total to 383 strikeouts. Oakland catcher Dave Duncan said of Ryan, "Ryan doesn't just get you out. He embarrasses you."

Ryan would embarrass hitters for decades, becoming a 300-game winner and baseball's all-time strikeout king, the only pitcher to strike out 5,000 batters in his career. In case another reminder was needed of his dominance, his sixth season with 300 strikeouts came in 1989, when Ryan turned 42 years old during the season. He never entirely conquered wildness—he is baseball's all-time walk leader as well as all-time strikeout leader. But no one was ever more durable or reached the strikeout pinnacles that Ryan set.

The one pitcher since Ryan who approached his record was—surprise, surprise—another hard thrower who had to grow into his stuff. And grow is an operative word for the 6'10" lefty who nearly broke Ryan's single-season mark. Randy Johnson is singularly intimidating—perhaps the most memorable image of the star called "The Big Unit" was when he nearly scared lefty hitter John Kruk to death with a fastball over his head in the 1994 All-Star Game. At least given the fact that it was an exhibition, Kruk could be candid about his fear. Other hitters just had to pretend they weren't horrified. Easier said than done.

Johnson was a second-round pick of the Expos in the 1985 draft, and he pitched briefly in the major leagues for Montreal. He was 3-4 with a 4.69 ERA in 11 appearances, walking 33 batters and striking out 51 in 55⅔ innings. And then Johnson was on his way to the Seattle Mariners, where he had the opportunity to become a legend. No less than Nolan Ryan recalled talking pitching with Johnson, advising him, as he had heard himself in the early 70s, that he should develop a secondary pitch and cut down on walks.

From 1992 to 1995, Johnson led the American League in strikeouts four years in a row. In 1993, he notched 308 strikeouts—the first of six such seasons he would log. Johnson had a very unusual feat in 1998, when he totaled 329 strikeouts, but did so between two different teams, Seattle and Houston. After that season, he signed with the Arizona Diamondbacks, where his best pitching was yet to come.

Between 1999 and 2002, Johnson logged four consecutive 300-strikeout seasons. In 2001, despite pitching "only" 249⅔ innings, Johnson made the closest ever run at Nolan Ryan's modern strikeout record, finishing 11 behind Ryan with 372 Ks. With some luck, Johnson might have caught Ryan—he won 21 games that season, but in three of his September starts, he fanned "only" six, eight, and six batters respectively. Had he matched his other three September starts, when he struck out 14, 10, and 16 hitters, the record would have been his.

That said, Johnson truly should have his own claim at the record anyway, because he logged a 5-1 postseason, including winning Game 7 of the World Series out of the bullpen. He struck out another 47 batters in 41⅓ more postseason innings.

For his career, Johnson won over 300 games and nearly became the second pitcher ever to reach 5,000 strikeouts (he retired 125 shy of that mark). Like Ryan and Koufax, he is a Hall of Famer, and each of the three has left a set of marks for future fireballers to pursue.

⌁

Before Clayton Kershaw's 301 strikeouts in 2015, it had been 13 years since any pitcher had joined the 300-strikeout club. But with the elevation of strikeouts in the modern game, the 300-K gap should continue to expand. Red Sox ace Chris Sale's 308 strikeouts in 2017 are the latest exhibit in the continuing growth potential in that area. That said, Nolan Ryan's 383 strikeouts looks almost as secure as Matt Kilroy's 513. But there's always another flamethrower, and when it comes to strikeouts, no word is the last word.

CHAPTER 27

WINNING 30 GAMES IN A SEASON

Number of Times Accomplished: Many before 1900, 21 after 1900, and only once since 1934.

First Instance: Four pitchers won 30+ games in 1876, the National League's first season—Al Spalding (47), George Bradley (45), Tommy Bond (31), and Jim Devlin (30).

Most Recent Instance: Denny McLain, Detroit Tigers, 1968.

Likely Achievers: Several of the biggest 19th-century stars, as well as other legends like Cy Young (five times, including twice in the 20th century), Christy Mathewson (four times), and Grover Cleveland Alexander (three times) won 30 games. The pickings get much slimmer after the Dead Ball Era.

Surprises: The most recent pitcher to achieve the feat, Denny McLain, had just 131 total MLB wins. Similarly, Jim Bagby had a 30-win season, but ended his career with 127 total victories. Devlin, while a star of the 19th century, was banned for gambling and amassed just 72 wins (although his career 1.90 ERA is impressive).

Likelihood of Additional Occurrences: It would take some bizarre new means of using pitchers. In the current five-man rotation, it's almost literally impossible.

It has been almost half a century since any MLB pitcher has won 30 games in a season. If 20 wins is a threshold for excellence, 30 wins has become all but impossible to understand. The reasons for the change are as simple as the shifts in pitcher usage in modern baseball. Once upon a time, it wasn't an especially big deal to win 30 games in a season.

Ask Charles "Old Hoss" Radbourn, who at the time believed he had won 30 games twice—in the same season. Modern statistics correct Radbourn's historic 1884 mark to a mere 59 wins, but it still boggles the mind. Radbourn started 73 games for the 1884 Providence Grays (of the 112 total games the Grays played). Essentially, Providence had two pitchers, but after Charlie Sweeney had arm and emotional problems,

Radbourn became the entire staff. He pitched a complete game in each start, adding in two additional relief appearances, for an arm-numbing 678⅔ innings pitched. Including the postseason, Radbourn actually won 62 games and pitched just over 700 innings, as he added three more triumphs in the 1884 World Series.

With his miraculous season coming just after the National League had made overhand pitching legal, Radbourn had numerous advantages that modern pitchers lack. In the Dead Ball Era, when six balls were needed for a walk, Radbourn coasted for much of his historic season. Teammate Paul Hines later said of him, "Rad had plenty of speed, but he never let it loose until it was absolutely necessary. That's why his arm lasted so many years." Others praised Radbourn's control, and even his resourcefulness. One man said of him, 25 years after his historic season, "Radbourne [sic], as sure as you live, in his day had everything the very best pitchers of today could boast of." Indeed, whatever the rules or advantages, starting (and thus completing) 41 of the last 51 games of Providence's season was a feat unequaled, even then. Radbourn's arm lasted another seven years until 1891, when he retired with 309 wins.

Sadly, pitching was about the only aspect of life that came easily to Radbourn. He was shot in the face by a hunting companion a few years after his career ended, and became something of a hermit after his disfigurement, likely due to the effects of syphilis on his health. He died at just 42 years old in 1897.

Research credits the four-man starting rotation with beginning in 1901, although it did not become widely accepted until around 1918. It is probably not coincidental that around 1901, winning 30 games became increasingly more unusual. For instance, even the super-durable Cy Young started more than 40 games only three times after 1900, and never more than 43 in any 20th-century season. With fewer appearances for starters, a 30-win season was suddenly much harder to come by.

After ten 30-win seasons in the 1900s, there were only seven 30-game winners in the 1910s. The only pitcher to reach the mark in the 1920s was Jim Bagby, who won 31 games in 1920. Bagby started only 38 games, but also benefited from 10 relief appearances, nine of which finished games, to reach his historic mark. After that, the mark went undisturbed for a decade, before Lefty Grove won 31 games in 1931. Three years later, Dizzy Dean reached 30 wins, winning three times in the Cardinals' last six games of 1934, including a shutout on the final day of the season to amass the mark.

While the mark was occasionally challenged, it was over a third of a century before another pitcher would reach 30 victories. And when he did, he didn't really fit with the staid, hardworking types who had come before him. No, the next (and as of yet, last) pitcher to win 30 games in a season was a different kind of guy, with his own motivations.

⌐⌐

Dennis Dale McLain was a pitcher destined to work to the beat of his own drummer. McLain was raised by a distant mother and a father who would routinely beat his son when he became frustrated with him. McLain later wrote that he felt close to his father in playing music—both the senior and junior McLain played the organ, and whatever crumbs of parental affection Denny remembered came from his work on the electric organ and the pitcher's mound.

McLain broke into the majors in 1963 at the age of 19, and while he was a competent pitcher, there was little to suggest that he would win 30 games. He did win 20 games and make the All-Star team in 1966, but a 20-14 record and a 3.92 ERA didn't exactly point to history.

For his part, McLain was incredibly gifted, but not especially single-minded in dedication to his craft. He told reporters at one point during his remarkable 1968 season, "I like the game, but I can't say I love it. I don't want to make baseball my career. I don't like the travel. Who needs it? I have always tried to imitate my life after Frank Sinatra and Arnold Palmer."

The talented but sometimes unfocused pitcher put together a season of epic proportions in 1968. It certainly helped that McLain's Tiger team was extraordinary—the Tigers had climbed from fifth in McLain's first season to the top of the American League, and would post a 103-59 mark in McLain's historic year. McLain remembered, "Black, white, green, yellow, we didn't have any issues on that team." The focus was on winning—something McLain continued doing plenty of into the summer and fall of '68.

It further helped that 1968 was itself dubbed "the Year of the Pitcher." Offenses were anemic, as Carl Yastrzemski won the batting title by hitting .301. But still, while plenty of pitchers were good in '68, none made history like McLain.

After a pair of no-decisions to open his season, McLain won his next five starts. He pitched a complete game each time, and never allowed more than two runs. Baltimore beat McLain on May 15th, but he then won his next four decisions. After a tough-luck loss to Cleveland in a 2–0 game, McLain then caught fire, winning his next nine starts. In the middle of that was the All-Star break, which McLain reached with a 16-2 record, a 2.09 ERA, and a growing consciousness that he could be doing something special.

McLain recalls thinking at the break that perhaps he could win 30 games. "Physically, I was in good shape, and mentally too. And we were in a pennant race, and there's nothing to get your juices flowing more than being in a pennant race."

On July 27th, McLain shut out the Orioles for his 20th victory against only three losses. He reached his 25th win on August 16th, in the Tigers' 121st game of the season. That was McLain's 31st start of the season, and he figured to make about 10 more, which left history well within his grasp.

It wasn't easy, though. McLain was hit hard in his next start, and admitted that he had pain in his shoulder "all the time." He went on to tell reporters, "When I go out to warm up, I have to throw sidearm at first because it pains so much. . . . Look, I want 30 as bad as anybody, but whether it's 30 or not I gotta think about next year, and I don't wanna throw my whole arm out in one year. If we get a good enough lead I'll take an extra day's rest. So far, between aspirins, pills, and rubdowns, I've been able to keep going." McLain lost his next start as well, and with only eight or so starts left, suddenly 30 wins looked a long way off.

It wasn't. McLain hit another one of his streaks, winning his next six starts. He made history on September 14th, at home against Oakland. McLain wasn't especially sharp, allowing four runs in nine innings, but when Detroit piled on a couple of runs in the bottom-of-the-ninth-inning win, McLain excitedly leaped up in the dugout and cracked his head. He had made history, and a mistimed jump was about his only mistake of the season.

The Tigers won the World Series in seven games, and Denny McLain, thanks to 31 wins, was in demand. He was booked in Las Vegas in the offseason, where he played shows with the "Denny McLain Trio" and admitted to his audience that he "would consider quitting baseball if he got a really good music offer." He spent a decent chunk of his offseason appearing on various television shows.

But just as the Tigers would not return to that 1968 form, the 336 innings McLain pitched would soon take their toll. McLain was also great in 1969, winning 24 games and another Cy Young Award, but that was the end of the line. McLain's off-field interests got him into trouble, as he was suspended for about half of the 1970 season due to associations with a series of gamblers and mobsters. In 1971, he lost 22 games. In 1972, at the age of 28, McLain threw his last pitches in the major leagues.

"I was told by any number of people, including Johnny Sain, that we all have so many pitches in our arm, and it's best to get as much as we can out of them, while we're having the opportunity to pitch. And he was right," said McLain. "Sooner or later, you get a problem here and a problem there, and then the problems just become compounded."

McLain's problems compounded after baseball, as well. He lost a young daughter in an auto accident, and was convicted on several criminal charges including embezzlement, money laundering, and mail fraud. After several years in prison, McLain has again rebounded, losing a large amount of weight and hosting a morning radio show in Detroit. His biggest claim to fame is being the last man to win 30 games, and as the 50th anniversary of that feat approaches, it may remain secure for some time to come.

"I can't imagine anybody winning 30, because they've changed the game so dramatically," said McLain. "Pitchers don't get to pitch and when they do, they don't get to pitch very much."

McLain started 41 games in both 1968 and 1969. He completed 51 of those 82 starts, and those numbers look increasingly like creatures of a different age. As baseball has evolved from a four-man to five-man starting rotation, and as pitchers rarely complete games, it has become almost mathematically impossible to approach 30 wins. If a pitcher starts 33 games, he needs not only great pitching, but an excellent team and a super bullpen to even entertain the vaguest thoughts of 30 wins. Of course, in this day and age, few pitchers even can stay healthy for 33 games. "We're having more Tommy John surgeries . . . and more arm and shoulder injuries than ever before," said McLain of modern baseball, an issue that he relates to not allowing pitchers' arms to mature in the minor leagues before overwork—and to the lowering of the mound after 1968.

Indeed, a better question for the 21st century might not be whether anyone else will join the 30-win club, as much as whether anyone can even approach the numbers of the last unsuccessful attempt at reaching McLain.

~

Bob Welch made his first appearance on the MLB radar in 1978 as a 21-year-old rookie pitcher who helped the Dodgers make their way to the National League pennant with a blazing fastball. Welch was 7-4 with a 2.02 ERA and was effective as both a starter and reliever. He also had a problem—a drinking problem.

Bob Welch became an alcoholic as a teenager. After the 1979 season, former Dodger pitcher Don Newcombe—himself a former alcoholic—cornered Welch and began asking him questions about his drinking.

What he heard rang enough alarm bells that Newcombe made some phone calls within the Dodger brass, and a week after New Year's Day 1980, Welch began 36 days of inpatient rehab at The Meadows in Wickenberg, Arizona.

To his credit, Welch never shied away from his problems, disclosing them to his teammates and the media in spring training, and writing about them extensively in his autobiography, *Five O'Clock Comes Early*, released in 1982.

Welch was a solid pitcher, making the All-Star team in 1980, and winning 13–15 games consistently for the Dodgers until after the 1987 season, when L.A. shipped him to the Oakland A's in a three-team trade. Oakland manager Tony La Russa and pitching coach Dave Duncan liked Welch's live arm, and felt that a split-fingered fastball could help his career have an Indian summer of sorts. While Welch won a career-high 17 games for pennant-winning Oakland teams in 1988 and 1989, nobody expected what happened in 1990. After all, Welch was 33 years old.

But Welch checked all of the boxes for a great season. He was in the prime of his career, pitching well for a talented Oakland team, which easily won a third straight American League pennant. Moreover, that A's team had a sublime bullpen—none of the top five relievers had an ERA over 2.97, and closer Dennis Eckersley allowed just five earned runs all season en route to an 0.61 ERA. Oakland scored runs with players like Henderson, Canseco, and McGwire. And Welch began to pile up wins.

Welch was 13-3 at the All-Star break, with a solid 2.91 ERA. He completed only two games all season, a pair of early-season shutouts. But he had only two no-decision starts, as Oakland's vaunted bullpen generally held up well. Welch reached 20 wins on August 17th, giving him a 20-4 mark at that time. However, already the five-man rotation was working against him. Welch was scheduled to make only nine more starts.

Welch had a couple of losses in August and September and never truly challenged McLain. But he did win 27 games, against only six losses—a mark that has itself now stood undisturbed for almost three decades. Indeed, just to challenge Welch's mark of 27 victories, a current pitcher would have to win 82 percent of his 33 scheduled regular season starts. A pitcher who made all 41 starts in a four-man rotation would have had to win just 73 percent of his starts to win 30 games.

For his part, Welch never re-created his 1990 form, going 12-13 with a 4.58 ERA in 1991, and finishing his career three years later. Welch ended up winning 211 games, and stayed active as a pitching instructor within the Oakland organization. An updated version of his autobiography was released in 2015, just after Welch suffered an untimely death when he fell at his home and fractured his neck.

So what about a current player winning 30 games in a season? While everything is theoretically possible, such a player would almost have to pitch in some alternate universe. Winning 30 games was a product of a four-man rotation and an era when starters pitched deep into games. Denny McLain opined, "The chances of it ever happening again are less than one in a million, I think." Indeed, baseball is about as likely to see another Old Hoss Radbourn as another 30-game winner.

CHAPTER 28

PITCHING 50+ CONSECUTIVE SCORELESS INNINGS

Number of Times Accomplished: Four.

First Instance: Jack Coombs, Philadelphia Athletics, 1910.

Most Recent Instance: Orel Hershiser, Los Angeles Dodgers, 1988.

Likely Achievers: Walter Johnson is the star of this group, although Don Drysdale joins him in the Hall of Fame.

Surprises: Jack Coombs and Orel Hershiser were both very good pitchers who had brief spans where they were untouchable. Neither is exactly shocking, but neither would have been among the first picks for this list.

Likelihood of Additional Occurrences: With the mark often recently approached, but never attained, a fifth pitcher to go 50+ scoreless innings seems likely to emerge within the next decade or so.

Even the best pitchers have trouble stringing together scoreless innings. Not only can the best hitters in professional baseball slug a ball out of the ballpark, they can bunch together a couple of hits and work tough walks. The fielders behind the pitcher can drop a flyball, or make an errant throw past the first baseman. The pitcher can lose the strike zone, leave one too many hittable pitches over the plate, or just generally be unlucky.

To pitch 50+ consecutive scoreless innings, a pitcher has to be skilled. He has to have good control, and not be prone to allowing home runs. But ultimately, he has to be lucky.

For some men, luck is in the era when they pitched. For Jack Coombs in 1910, home runs weren't a serious threat. The Boston Red Sox led the AL in home runs that season, with a total of 43—one about every four games. The league on the whole averaged a home run every nine games. For that matter, dead ball hitting in general was remarkably punchless. Not only did the league not hit for power, it didn't hit for much of anything else. The league batting average was .243 and the slugging percentage was .313. Two teams—the Browns and White Sox—didn't even hit .220.

Coombs played for the league's best team by far—his A's went 102-48 that season—and benefited from a manager who gave pitchers an especially long rope. Connie Mack's pitchers completed 123 of their 155 starts in 1910, so Coombs would not have to earn his streak six innings at a time like a modern starter likely would.

But still, Jack Coombs mowed down batters, and no advantages could negate that. Not only was Coombs a great pitcher in 1910, but he literally could be said to have written "the book" on baseball. A college graduate in an age when that was still a rarity among both the general population and the population of the major leagues, Coombs was known as "Colby Jack" because of his alma mater, Colby College, from which he had been accepted for graduate work at the Massachusetts Institute of Technology, before he gave chemistry a break in favor of curveballs.

Coombs arrived in the big leagues in 1906, celebrating by pitching a 24-inning complete game on September 1st of that year. He struck out 18 batters and allowed 15 hits, winning the game by a 4–1 count. He pitched through 1909 without much to distinguish his work, winning 10, 6, 7, and 12 games respectively for each of his first four seasons.

But in 1910, Coombs had a season to remember. He completed 35 of his 38 starts, winning 31 games and posting a meager 1.30 earned run average. As amazing as the season was, it wasn't until September that Coombs really caught fire. From September 5th to September 25th, he put together a history-making streak.

Coombs had won nine consecutive starts from mid-August to mid-September, and he didn't allow more than one run in any of the nine. But by September 20th, Coombs had amassed a 35-inning scoreless streak. The following day, Coombs faced off with Cleveland pitcher Harry Fanwell in an 11-inning scoreless tie that was called because of darkness. The no-decision ended Coombs's winning streak, but increased his scoreless inning streak to 46 in a row.

Coombs entered the 50+-scoreless-inning club in relief, oddly enough. On September 25th, Coombs entered a 1–1 tie from the bullpen in the ninth inning, facing White Sox star Ed Walsh. Coombs worked six more scoreless innings, and even began the game-winning rally in the 14th inning. The victory was his 30th of the 1910 season. Coombs then came back to start the second game of the doubleheader. He worked another scoreless inning before yielding three runs to Chicago in the second frame, ending the scoreless streak at 53 innings. Ring Lardner was among many who lauded Coombs's work, noting, "Coombs's performance is one of the wonders of the land. He has worked in turn, out of turn, and every other way, and he has a record that seldom has been approached."

Coombs was called Iron Man for his super 1910 work, which he finished with three World Series wins. His pitching paid a price for the 353 innings he hurled in 1910. By 1913, *Baseball Magazine* noted that Coombs had thrown so many curveballs "that his arm is actually shortened by the stiffening of the cords at the elbow."

Coombs won 158 games and finished his career in 1920. A much-beloved college coach at Duke University in his later years, Coombs authored an instructional book, *Baseball: Individual Play and Team Strategy* in 1938. Perhaps he instructed coaches to find a pitcher who would work 50+ scoreless innings—but probably not, because there haven't been many successors to Colby Jack.

Walter Johnson followed Coombs's feat with a similar streak of his own in 1913. Johnson, the fireballer of his (and perhaps any other) era again enjoyed the advantages of pitching in the Dead Ball Era. The Philadelphia A's led the 1913 American League totals with 33 home runs, and overall home-run totals were still around one per eight games played. In general hitting was a bit better, as the league batted .256, but still posted a humble .336 slugging percentage.

From his debut in the big leagues in 1907, Johnson already had one of the best fastballs of all time, but around 1913, he mixed in a good curveball, and the ensuing results were simply unfair. Johnson's win totals had increased from five to 14 back to 13 in 1909 (despite a 2.22 ERA, it was hard to win for the 42-110 Senators) up to 25 wins each in 1910 and 1911, 33 wins in 1912, and then 36 in 1913, which earned him American League MVP honors. Johnson pitched 11 shutouts, had a 1.14 ERA, and also put together a historic streak of his own.

Pitching on Opening Day of 1913, Johnson gave up a first-inning run to the Yankees before settling in to beat them 2–1. For any other pitcher, allowing a run would be unremarkable, but for Johnson, it was over a month before he allowed another run. Finishing the opening game with eight scoreless innings, Johnson followed with a six-hit shutout of the same Yankees in New York on April 19th. On April 23rd, he pitched a two-hitter against the Red Sox, and two days later, came in from the bullpen to pitch a scoreless ninth inning in a 5–4 win over Boston. When Johnson went to Philadelphia and pitched a four-hit, 10-strikeout shutout on April 30th, he finished the month with a 36-inning scoreless streak.

Clark Griffith again brought Johnson out of the bullpen on May 3rd, where he pitched 2⅔ scoreless innings to finish off a win at Boston. Two days later, he again entered in relief, and worked five scoreless innings in a 12-inning victory. In his next start in Chicago, Johnson pitched another two-hitter, bringing his streak to 52⅔ scoreless innings, just shy of Coombs's mark.

On May 14th, Johnson started at St. Louis. Staked to an early 6–0 lead, he faltered in the fourth inning, allowed a run, and ended his scoreless streak at 55⅔ innings. After that game, Johnson's ERA had climbed—to 0.30. In his first 59⅔ innings of 1913, Johnson posted an 8-0 record, allowed 36 hits and two runs, walked six batters, and struck out 47 batters. No pitcher ever began a season like that again. Even Johnson, who won 417 games, struck out 3,509 batters, and brought an elusive World Series title to Washington in 1924, couldn't replicate his 55⅔-inning scoreless streak. But two other pitchers could.

If 1910 and 1913 were friendly eras for pitchers, 1968 was a pitcher's dream. Maybe it was the size of the strike zone, maybe it was the tall mound, or maybe it was just the quality of pitchers who emerged up the ladder of organized baseball. Home runs were relatively common—a little more frequent than one every other game, but National League hitters batted .243 and had a .341 slugging percentage in "the Year of the Pitcher."

The pitching ace who truly shone that year was St. Louis right-hander Bob Gibson, whose 1.12 ERA bested even Walter Johnson's 1913 totals. And sure enough, Gibson strung together a 47⅔-inning scoreless streak, but he couldn't reach the 50 mark, much less the big-league record. Dodger right-hander Don Drysdale was the man who made scoreless history in 1968, but again, not without some significant luck and some questionable umpiring.

Drysdale was 1-3 with a 2.52 ERA on May 14th, when he began his streak. First, he two-hit the Cubs in a 1–0 shutout win. Four days later, he got another tough 1–0 victory, allowing only five hits to the Astros. The Dodgers managed to get him two runs on May 22nd, when he shut out the Cardinals on six hits. A fourth shutout followed four days later against the Astros, with another six-hitter. For the first eight innings, Drysdale's next start against the Giants was similarly uneventful. He had given up five hits, no runs, and no walks, and his scoreless streak had climbed to 44 innings.

But in the visiting half of the ninth inning, Willie McCovey drew a walk. After a Jim Ray Hart single, Drysdale walked Dave Marshall, which loaded the bases with no outs in the 3–0 game. Dick Dietz of the Giants came to bat, and history occurred—in a very unexpected way.

On a 2-2 count, Drysdale threw a slider that stayed inside and hit Dietz on the elbow, apparently ending the streak. But home-plate umpire Harry Wendelstedt invoked Rule 5.05(b) and indicated that Dietz had failed to attempt to get out of the way of the pitch. He ordered Dietz back to home plate and called ball three. A lengthy delay followed, in which Giants manager Herman Franks likely questioned Wendelstedt's ancestry and intelligence, but the call stood.

Still, Drysdale was far from out of the woods. On a 3-2 count, Dietz fouled off a pitch and then flied out to shallow left field, not deep enough to score a run. After an infield grounder led to a force-out at home, Drysdale got out of the jam with a popup to first base. The streak continued. Drysdale later wrote, "[T]here wasn't much doubt in my mind what was happening. I knew the rule . . . and it was obvious that Harry was exercising his right to make a judgment call." Still, even Drysdale admitted that the situation was "bizarre" and recalled that the pandemonium in Dodger Stadium after the last out "was almost like a World Series celebration."

On June 4th, back in Dodger Stadium, Drysdale faced the Pittsburgh Pirates, and first broke the NL scoreless streak of 46⅓ innings by Carl Hubbell, then broke 50 innings after the fifth frame, and ultimately finished off a sixth consecutive shutout, this one being a three-hitter.

The next start, on June 8th, saw Drysdale break Johnson's record before a sacrifice fly in the fifth inning ended his scoreless streak at 58⅔ innings. Interestingly, Philadelphia manager Gene Mauch asked home-plate umpire Augie Donatelli to search Drysdale at the end of that fifth inning, as the big right-hander had a reputation for throwing the occasional spitball. Drysdale was clean. Lucky, but clean.

The anemic Dodger offense ended up giving Drysdale enough runs to win just 14 games in 1968. It would take another lucky Dodger pitcher to join the 50-inning club—and win the Cy Young Award and World Series.

Orel Hershiser was a 17th-round draft pick, a born-again Christian who looked like a librarian, and for one magical summer and fall in 1988, the greatest pitcher in baseball. Hershiser had won 19 games in 1985 for Tommy Lasorda's Dodgers, but was coming off 14-14 and 16-16 campaigns before his run at history.

On August 30, 1988, Hershiser gave up two fifth-inning runs to the Montreal Expos before completing a 4–2 win. After that game, he was 18-8 on the season, with a 2.84 ERA. He looked likely to win 20 games, but would probably lose the Cy Young Award to Cincinnati lefty Danny Jackson, who won 23 games. But those four scoreless innings were a prelude to a scoreless September.

On September 5th, Hershiser four-hit the Atlanta Braves. In his next turn, on September 10th, he scattered seven hits in shutting out the Reds for his 20th win of the year. On September 14th, he had a 1–0 win over Atlanta. Hershiser had pitched a day early because his wife, Jamie, was about to give birth to their son.

With a new Hershiser to support, Orel won another 1–0 shutout in Houston on September 19th, boosting his scoreless streak to 40 consecutive innings. In his next start, on September 23rd at San Francisco, Hershiser had to be not only good—but also lucky.

In the third inning, José Uribe led off with a single. After a bunt single from pitcher Atlee Hammaker and a force-out, the Giants had runners at first and third with one out. The next batter, Ernest Riles, grounded to second base. Second baseman Steve Sax threw to shortstop Alfredo Griffin for a force-out, but Griffin's throw to first for an attempted double play went wide of the base and Riles was safe. The Giants had scored. Or had they?

Second base umpire Paul Runge intervened, calling not only the forced baserunner Brett Butler out, but also Riles. Hershiser did not hesitate. "I headed straight for the dugout before he changed his mind. I knew exactly what he was saying. Butler had apparently slid outside the baseline at Griffin and was out for interference. . . . [T]he run doesn't count, the streak stays alive."

When Hershiser reached the Dodger dugout, manager Lasorda promptly told him, "Drysdale got his break. Now you got yours."

Indeed he had. Hershiser finished the shutout, which ran the streak to 49 innings. In his final start of the regular season, at San Diego, he worked nine shutout innings, passing 50 innings with a scoreless first frame, but was matched by Padre pitcher Andy Hawkins. Hershiser went back to the mound for the 10th inning, and a shot to break Drysdale's mark.

Hershiser began the inning by tipping his cap toward Drysdale, who was present in the press box. Leadoff man Marvell Wynne reached base on a strike-three wild pitch. He was sacrificed to second, and after a groundout and an intentional walk, pinch-hitter Keith Moreland stood between Hershiser and a 59th scoreless inning. Moreland flied out harmlessly to right field and the record belonged to Hershiser.

"It couldn't have happened to a nicer kid," Drysdale told Hershiser after the game. For his part, Hershiser remained humble. In his autobiography, he listed the various ways a team can score and admitted, "Any one of those and hundreds of other things could have scored an innocuous run against us during my streak, and I would simply be a successful pitcher with a good record." Instead, Hershiser was a hero—and his standing wasn't exactly hurt by winning two more games in the World Series.

From the beginning of September on, Hershiser, including the NLCS and World Series, pitched 94⅔ innings, and posted an 0.46 ERA. He had been a bit lucky, but mostly, he had been dominant.

No other pitchers have reached 50 innings, much less challenged Hershiser's record. But there have been some close calls. Then-Dodger Zack Greinke put together a 45⅔-inning streak in 2015. The year before, Dodger lefty Clayton Kershaw piled up a 41-inning scoreless run. Someday, another pitcher will combine dominance and a touch of luck to reach 50 innings. But his work is certainly cut out for him.

CHAPTER 29

WINNING THE TRIPLE CROWN
(AS A PITCHER)

Number of Times Accomplished: 38.

First Instance: Tommy Bond, Boston Red Caps, 1877, National League.

Most Recent Instance: Justin Verlander, Detroit Tigers, 2011, American League. Clayton Kershaw, Los Angeles Dodgers, 2011, National League.

Likely Achievers: 27 of the 38 pitching Triple Crowns were won by current Hall of Famers—including Young, Mathewson, Johnson, Alexander, and Koufax. The gang is all here.

Surprises: There are a few mild surprises—from 19th-century players like Bond and Guy Hecker to early-20th-century guys like Hippo Vaughn and Bucky Walters to pitchers of the good-but-not great persuasion (such as Dwight Gooden and Jake Peavy.)

Likelihood of Additional Occurrences: Unlike the offensive equivalent, the pitching Triple Crown remains fairly common. There have been five winners in the 21st century and there's no reason to think there won't be another one soon.

Why should hitters have all the fun? If the artificial construct of the Triple Crown captured the imagination of multi-tool batters everywhere, surely there could be an equivalent variation for the men on the mound. And so three statistics for starting pitchers were tabbed, and lo, the classifiers of baseball found that it was good—wins, strikeouts, and ERA would make up the pitcher's Triple Crown. The pitching Crown has been more common than its hitting counterpart, with more than twice as many complete Crowns. Also, the longest run between Crown winners is 18 years, from 1945 to 1963. But as with the batters, a Triple Crown is a sign of outright dominance. There are many different stories among the Crown-winning mound men, but each had his season (or seasons) in the sun.

⌇

A 5'7" Irishman who threw underhanded doesn't seem like an obvious choice to be one of the first dominant pitchers in baseball history, but Tommy Bond was all of these things. Pitching was a very different science for Bond than it was for Johnson, Alexander, or Koufax. The rules of the time constrained him to pitching high or low pitches per the batter's request. He was supposed to throw underhanded, although *The Sporting News* noted years later, his pitching motion "more resembled side-arm motion than it did the submarine style of Carl Mays." Fouls were not strikes, and a batter got four strikes before he was called out.

It's not entirely clear exactly how Bond made his mark. As Rob Neyer wrote, "[A]ccounts of Bond's pitching style vary widely. It does seem that Bond was doing *something* different, though." Neyer indicated that Bond was apparently a hard-thrower as he was often referenced as a "cannon ball" pitcher. He was one of the pioneers of the curveball, and some sources even make the argument that Bond—and not Candy Cummings—actually invented the pitch.

In any case, in 1877, Bond's Boston Pilgrims posted a 42-18 record. Bond pitched 58 of those 60 games, and went 40-17. His 40 wins bested Jim Devlin by five—only three pitchers in the NL won 20 games. His strikeout total of 170 seems rather modest (particularly since he threw 521 innings), but not only did it lead the league, but he and Devlin (who had 141) were the only NL pitchers to strike out 100 batters. ERA was the closest of the categories, but Bond's 2.11 bested Terry Larkin of Brooklyn by three-hundredths of a run. It would be decades before anyone would speak of a pitcher's Triple Crown, but Bond laid claim to the first one in his best season.

Bond approached the same production for two more seasons, winning 40 again in 1878, and then 43 games in 1879. But thereafter, he was felled by arm trouble, and in 1884, he left the big leagues. Bond won 234 games and retired with a 2.14 ERA. He lived until 1941, and was celebrated as the last remaining player from the original National League in 1876.

In a 1936 article, a sportswriter noted that Bond "[r]ealizes [the] game has made rapid strides since days when he was playing, but believes there were just as good players in his time as there are today." Bond was still a regular at big-league parks in 1936, which means he may have seen parts of 20 other pitching Triple Crowns completed.

Few who study the game would argue that old-time baseball could be pretty cruel. A player with Native American heritage inevitably ended up as "Chief" and many who were deaf or had a speech impediment were branded "Dummy." Ernie Lombardi's outstanding proboscis made him "Schnozz." And Jim Vaughn, 1918 pitching Triple Crown winner, and a man of a few extra pounds, became "Hippo." Vaughn was listed at 215–230 pounds, but biographers have noted "evidence that he weighed close to 300 pounds later in his career" and "his lumbering side-to-side gait" as the genesis of the unusual nickname.

Vaughn's colorful nickname is one of the few things remembered about one of the most quietly effective left-handed pitchers of the 1910s. From 1914 to 1920, he won between 17 and 22 games each season, never topped a 2.87 ERA, and twice led the NL in strikeouts. The moment that put Vaughn on the historical baseball map came in 1917, when he lost the celebrated "double no-hitter" game as he and Cincinnati's Fred Toney each pitched nine-inning no-hitters against each other. In the 10th, Vaughn surrendered a hit and an unearned run, which wound up being the difference in the game.

The following year, Vaughn had a season to remember. Vaughn's Chicago Cubs raced to the 1918 NL pennant, finishing 10½ games ahead of the second-place New York Giants. Indeed, the Cubs were so dominant that not only did Hippo easily win the Triple Crown, but two of his nearest competitors were his teammates.

Vaughn won 22 games in 1918, two more than teammate Claude Hendrix, who was the league's only other 20-game winner. His 1.74 ERA was more than a quarter of an earned run per game ahead of second-place finisher Lefty Tyler—again, a fellow Cub. Finally, Vaughn's 148 strikeouts were 31 more than the runner-up in that category. Vaughn pitched eight shutouts that season—which was a league record for a lefty for a decade and a half. Unfortunately, Vaughn's brilliant season didn't help him much in the postseason. The Cubs lost the 1918 World Series to the Red Sox—that team's last title for 86 years—as Vaughn pitched three games, losing the first game 1–0 to Babe Ruth, dropping Game 3 by a 2–1 count to Carl Mays, and beating Sad Sam Jones 3–0 in the fifth game. In 27 Series innings, Vaughn posted a 1.00 ERA—and a 1-2 record.

After a rough start to 1921, Vaughn ended up pitching only in various minor and semi-pro leagues thereafter. Despite leaving the big leagues at age 33, he won 178 games and posted a career 2.49 ERA. Grover Cleveland Alexander later recalled, "Big Jim Vaughn used to pitch the particular kind of ball a batter liked best just to show him that he couldn't hit it. Nothing pleased him better than to strike a man out pitching to his strength." In 1918, Vaughn had to be very pleased.

⌒

In the mid 19th century, about the time that Abner Doubleday probably *wasn't* gathering the first baseball teams in a Cooperstown pasture, the poet John Greenleaf Whitter wrote his immortal lines, "For all sad words of tongue and pen/The saddest are these/What might have been." There's no indication that Whittier was a baseball fan, but his poem suggests an insight that would have served him well in that pastime.

In 1985, Dwight Gooden was 20 years old. The previous season, as a teenager, he had been an All-Star, the National League Rookie of the Year, and runner-up for the NL Cy Young Award. The next year, he was even better. Gooden was a smooth, 6'2" right-handed pitcher from

Tampa, Florida. With his elegant, textbook delivery and bullet fastball, he became a New York icon—in part because of what he did in 1985.

Gooden not only won the National League Triple Crown in a walk, he won it over both leagues. No one approached him in any category. Gooden led the NL with 24 victories, three more than his nearest NL competitor, and two more than any other active pitcher. His 1.53 ERA was two-fifths of a run better than runner-up John Tudor, and was almost a full run per nine innings lower than AL champ Dave Stieb. Finally, Gooden's 268 strikeouts were 54 more than the next highest total in the majors.

How could any pitcher be this good this quickly?

Alas, Gooden's ascent could not continue, and did not. His fastball, which had tremendous movement in 1984 and 1985, mysteriously flattened out, and became easier to hit. He never won more than 19 games again, nor did he come in at under a 2.84 ERA, and only once again would he top 200 strikeouts.

In 1986, after the Mets won the World Series, Gooden skipped the victory parade, during which he used illegal drugs. The following spring, he tested positive for cocaine and entered a rehab facility. In the mid-1990s, Gooden was twice suspended for positive cocaine drug screens, and on the latter occasion, his wife found him in his bedroom with a loaded gun to his head. While Gooden rebounded from that dark era of his life, he has struggled with legal issues and drug abuse throughout his life.

He finished his career with 194 wins and 2,293 strikeouts. But for anybody who saw Dwight Gooden in 1985, the story is less about what he did than about what he might have done. For one glorious season, his full range of potential was on display to all who watched. Clearly, it was difficult to be precocious and brilliant, and if Gooden couldn't live up to the standards he pitched to, neither could very many other pitchers.

In 2011, for the first time in almost 90 years, baseball celebrated two Triple Crown pitchers in a single season. In the American League, Detroit righty Justin Verlander accomplished the feat. In the National League, it was Los Angeles lefty Clayton Kershaw who added his name to the record book.

Verlander had been AL Rookie of the Year in 2006, before he stumbled to an 11-17, 4.84 season in 2008. He rebounded with a series of seasons that represented his career peak—culminating in his magical 2011 season. Verlander had always been good, but he had never topped 20 wins, and he had led the league in hit batters and wild pitches as many times as he had in strikeouts.

Verlander easily ran away with the wins title, as his 24 victories paced the field by a full five wins over C. C. Sabathia. His 250 strikeouts gave him a cushion of 20 over second-place finisher Sabathia. But ERA was a different matter, although it didn't look like it would be close. Jered Weaver, who was second to Verlander, made his final regular season start on September 23rd. He gave up two earned runs in 8⅓ innings, leaving his season ERA at 2.41 (or 2.4059, to be more precise). Verlander had a 2.29 ERA, so he looked like he would cruise home. But on September 24th, he gave up five earned runs to Baltimore in the first three innings of his start. Verlander then shut the door, completing seven innings. Final ERA: 2.40 (or 2.4024, to be more precise). Weaver was slated to make another start, but with no playoff implications on the line, he didn't do so. And in the end, had Verlander pitched one less scoreless inning, he would have lost the Crown on that rough final start. But, of course, he didn't.

Kershaw's Crown was no less impressive. The 6'4" lefty with the funky delivery and nasty stuff was just coming into his own in 2011. He had gone 5-5 as a rookie in 2008, then 8-8 in 2009 and 13-10 in 2010. Still, the signs were there—and Dodger manager Joe Torre compared the young lefty to a more familiar Dodger left-hander named Koufax. Kershaw won his Crown late, as he picked up victories in his last four starts of the season to tie Ian Kennedy with 21 wins. His ERA dropped from 2.45 at the beginning of September to 2.28 (and thus ahead of Roy

Halladay at 2.35) at the end of the season, and he piled up 36 strikeouts in his last five starts to finish the year at 248, 10 ahead of Cliff Lee of the Phillies. After his last start, he told reporters, "It's been an awesome year. I don't like to look at personal stuff too often, but now is the time I can start to look back a little bit."

Kershaw picked up the NL Cy Young Award for his brilliant season, and has had plenty of reason to look ahead as well as back since late 2011. He has yet to post an ERA higher than 2.53 in any subsequent season, and in 2013 and 2014, he won two-thirds of the Triple Crown. He has struggled with injuries, but with his 30th birthday yet to come, his victories approaching 150, and his strikeouts already over 2,000, Kershaw looks like a sure Hall of Famer.

Meanwhile, Verlander's path has been a bit more checkered. He won 17 games and was second for the Cy Young Award in 2012 and in 2016, but he has had some poor seasons as well. He was traded to the Houston Astros late in the 2017 season. Whether his career has a second wind or not is yet to be seen, but in 2011, he and Kershaw both turned baseball on its head.

CHAPTER 30

SAVING 50 GAMES IN A SEASON

Number of Times Accomplished: 16.

First Instance: Bobby Thigpen, Chicago White Sox, 1990.

Most Recent Instance: Jeurys Familia, New York Mets, 2016.

Likely Achievers: Considering that the first 50-save season was less than 30 years ago, there are still a surprising number of legendary names, like Mariano Rivera (twice), John Smoltz, and Dennis Eckersley on the list.

Surprises: Given the modern closer role, some of these pitchers were decent pitchers who had big seasons, like Rod Beck, Bobby Thigpen, or Mark Melancon.

Likelihood of Additional Occurrences: Five times in this decade, a pitcher has saved 50 games. Or, if you prefer, in the 27 seasons since it first happened, it's happened another 15 times. Given the evolution of the closer role, there's no reason to expect the trend to stop.

After the first eight innings of a game have elapsed, in walks the man with the sparkling uniform and (usually) a big fastball. He blows a few heaters past the other team, and wraps up another win. This is the essential job description for the modern closer, and the save is the currency by which his work is generally evaluated.

Chicago sportswriter Jerome Holtzman is generally credited as the father of the save, never mind that he himself disputed the honorary title. There were other writers who tracked saves even before Holtzman began doing so in 1960. But Holtzman standardized the task, creating the modern formula for what is or is not a save. MLB began tracking the save officially in 1969, and Ron Perranoski led baseball with 31 saves that season. The use of closers was very different from today—Perranoski pitched 75 times, finished a game 52 times, and worked $119\frac{2}{3}$ innings.

A few pitchers would meet or approach 30 saves per season, but it was not until Dan Quisenberry in 1983 that a 40-save season occurred.

Quiz was a submarine pitcher who saved 45 games—and pitched 139 innings to do so.

As the 80s progressed, teams began assigning one reliever to be the closer, responsible for finishing games in which they held a lead, and almost always for no more than one inning. Accordingly, save totals continued to increase, and it looked like a 50-save season might eventually be possible.

～

Jeff Torborg was the manager for the job, and a forkballing right-handed reliever named Bobby Thigpen became the fairly unlikely pitcher who made history. Thigpen became a closer for the White Sox in 1988, his second full major-league season, and he saved 34 games that year and again in 1989. But Thigpen's mediocre ERA stats (3.30 in 1988 and 3.76 in 1989) and the poor level of the White Sox (71 wins in 1988 and 69 wins in 1989) play made him an unlikely candidate for a save explosion.

Thigpen grew up in a single-parent home, as his father left his family early in his life, and his mother, Donna Jo, drove a school bus so that her children could attend a better school in their hometown of Aucilla, Florida. Thigpen learned a significant work ethic from his mother, and he used it to earn a junior college scholarship from his high school, which graduated 33 students his senior year. From there, it was on to Mississippi State, where he pitched for a team with an offensive murderers' row including future MLB stars Will Clark and Rafael Palmeiro before the White Sox drafted him in the fifth round of the 1985 MLB Draft.

Thigpen quietly made his way to the majors, resisting an effort from the White Sox to turn him into a starting pitcher. In 1990, he earned $325,000, a relatively modest figure that suggested the expectations held for him. For that matter, his White Sox were expected to remain near the bottom of the AL West in the final season of venerable Comiskey Park.

But the White Sox piled up wins, and Thigpen was there to close them out. Only eight times in 1990 did Torborg ask Thigpen to pitch two or more innings, a number that still seems high in light of the usage of 21st-century closers, but represented a much easier workload than previous relievers had endured. Thigpen ended up pitching in 77 games, working 88⅔ innings. The White Sox ended up going 65-12 in those 77 games.

Thigpen had five saves in April, and added 11 more in May, ending that month with a meager 2.08 ERA. June saw 10 more saves, and Thigpen added one more before the All-Star break, reaching the Midseason Classic with 27 saves to his credit. He was selected for his one and only All-Star appearance, although he was used as a setup man, pitching the seventh inning, but ultimately yielding the save to Oakland A's closer Dennis Eckersley, who himself finished 1990 with an 0.61 ERA and 48 saves.

Thigpen ended July with 32 saves, but then added 13 more in August, making it clear that he would get all opportunities to become MLB's first 50-save man. He made it look easy, notching his 47th save to set a new MLB record on September 3rd, and reaching 49 saves a week later. After the record-breaking save, catcher Carlton Fisk summed up Thigpen by noting that he was "special because he's just a guy, a regular guy. He's not goofy, not crazy, he has no peculiarities like some relievers. You like to see nice things happen to nice people."

Nice things would continue to happen for Thigpen on September 15th, when the White Sox hosted the Red Sox—and history—in Comiskey Park. Chicago jumped ahead to a 7–4 advantage, and in the ninth inning, Torborg called for Thigpen to close the game. Thigpen induced groundouts from Tom Brunansky and Mike Marshall before allowing a double to Tony Pena. He then faced pinch-hitter Danny Heep and struck him out on a 1-2 offering to end the game, and mark his 50th save.

The White Sox ended up winning 94 games, and Thigpen saved 57 of them. While he ended the season with a 1.83 ERA (and finished fourth in the voting for the Cy Young Award), it is worth noting that Thigpen blew eight saves, or he might have become the first pitcher to save 60 games in a season.

Unfortunately, Thigpen's season of good luck did not turn into a remarkable career. He sustained a back injury in a postseason tour of Japan, and while he was a closer for most of two more seasons, his pitching was nowhere near what it had been in 1990. Thigpen finished his MLB career in 1994, amassing a total of 201 saves, and is now a bullpen coach with the Chicago White Sox.

Thigpen is unlikely to end up in Cooperstown, but for one remarkable season, the boy whose mother had driven a bus every day answered his own near-daily call of duty, trudging to the mound again and again to save more games than any pitcher had before him.

In the more than a quarter-century since, only once has a pitcher surpassed Thigpen's totals. Francisco Rodríguez, a Venezuela import with a tough fastball, joined the Angels' bullpen at age 20. Nicknamed "K-Rod" for the abundance of strikeouts he induced (10.5 strikeouts per nine innings for his career as of this writing), Rodríguez put in his time as a setup man before becoming the full-time closer in 2005.

He saved 45, 47, and 40 games in his first three seasons as a closer, but those were humdrum years compared with 2008. As with Thigpen, the essential ingredients for a big season were in place—the Angels won 100 games and manager Mike Scioscia utilized K-Rod almost exclusively in one-inning appearances to close out wins.

Rodríguez pitched 76 times in 2008, finishing the game on 69 occasions. He never exceeded an inning all season long, finishing with 68⅓ innings. He saved 11 games in April and 10 more in May. Somehow, he added 17 more saves in June and the first half of July, arising at the All-Star break with 38 saves.

Like Thigpen almost two decades before, his fast start made it almost impossible for Rodríguez to not break the saves record. He amassed save number 40 on July 20th. He reached 50 saves on August 24th, making him only the ninth player ever to reach that total.

He tied Thigpen's mark of 57 saves on September 11th, and went for the record two nights later against the Mariners. Staked to a 5–2 lead, Rodríguez made things interesting by opening the ninth inning with a double by Miguel Cairo and a walk to Luis Valbuena. But he settled down by getting Ichiro Suzuki to ground into a force play, and then striking out Wladimir Balentien and Raúl Ibañez to make history with his 58th save of the season. Rodríguez gestured toward the sky, in a tribute to his deceased grandfather, and then fell to his knees on the mound.

"It's been an amazing year," said Rodríguez, who was careful to give tribute to his other bullpen mates who helped get him the opportunity to make history.

Rodríguez ended up with 62 saves in 2008 and a 2.24 ERA. He did blow seven more saves, but still finished third in the AL Cy Young vote and sixth in the AL MVP ballot.

Since his magical 2008 campaign, K-Rod has bounced around to the Mets, Brewers, Orioles, Brewers again, and as of this writing, the Tigers. He has been an All-Star three more times, but has only been a closer for part of his career. He reached 40 saves twice more—in 2014 and 2016 (44 each year). His 437 saves ranks fourth on the all-time MLB list, and nobody has approached his mark of 62 saves in a single season.

Within the handful of members of the 50-save club, there is a second, more specific club whose entire membership is a single man. As Rodríguez (seven blown saves) and Thigpen (eight) showed, even the best relievers occasionally fail in their task. Well, at least most do. Only once has a pitcher had a 50-save season without blowing a single save opportunity, and that was Eric Gagne in 2003.

Gagne, like so many closers do, began as a starter before transitioning to the bullpen before the 2002 season. In short order, he found himself comfortably established as the Dodgers' relief ace. He saved 52 games in 2002, and the scoreboard in Dodger Stadium flashed "GAME OVER" when he jogged in from the bullpen. Gagne had a live fastball, a sharp-dipping changeup, and an even slower curveball that enabled him to consistently keep hitters from getting comfortable. In fact, he would do a perfect job in 2003.

Gagne was picking up his 10th save of the year on May 4th when he allowed the first run he gave up all year long. By the All-Star break, Gagne had 31 saves and a sub-2.00 ERA. More impressively, he had not blown a save. A midseason article indicated that Gagne could be frequently used—by that point, Dodger manager Jim Tracy had once pitched him four days in a row, and at another point, six days out of seven. But Gagne used few pitches to blow away hitters.

For the season, he gave up a mind-blowing 37 hits in 82⅓ innings pitched. He walked 20 hitters and struck out 137. Gagne had been good in the first half, but he was superhuman in late 2003. He allowed a single earned run after the All-Star break, recording 24 more saves and managing an 0.24 second-half ERA in the process. Opposing hitters batted .146 in the first half of the season—and an even more pitiful .115 in the second half.

Gagne reached his 50th save on September 9th at Arizona. He racked up five more and finished the year without blowing a save. So dominant was Gagne that Dodger teammate Wilson Alvarez commented, "When he doesn't strike somebody out, you wonder what's wrong." Across multiple seasons, Gagne's consecutive saves converted streak went to 84 games, and he won the 2003 National League Cy Young Award.

Gagne had one more golden season, saving 45 games in 2004. But after that, a series of injuries, and the fallout of being named as a performance-enhancing-drug user in the Mitchell Report derailed his career. In fact, Gagne found headlines in 2012 when he indicated that 80 percent of his Dodger teammates had also used PEDs. Gagne last pitched in the major leagues in 2008, and of his career 187 saves, 152 came in his great run from 2002 to 2004.

Gagne's historically perfect season made him the last reliever to win a Cy Young Award. It also started another club for other relievers to shoot for. No one has converted so many saves in one season without blowing a single one.

It seems very likely that another pitcher will reach the 50-save mark soon. A tougher challenge will be joining Gagne in posting an unblemished 50-save season. Tampa Bay reliever Alex Colomé unsuccessfully made a good run at 50 saves in 2017, but given the number of excellent closers, and the close watch over the number of innings (and the tendency to shy away from using them in "dirty" innings, e.g., with men already on base), a new generation of closers will have something to aim for—and some of them will probably make it, sooner or later.

ACKNOWLEDGMENTS

One of the hardest things about writing a book is sitting down at the point when the ideas have finally hit paper and the fatigue of one's own words has set in and remembering all of the people who helped it get this far.

Thanks, as ever, to my wife, Julie. Marriage, much like baseball, is more about process than anybody outside it would like to believe. It isn't glamorous being kind and loving and dependable, but she does it every day, and my life is always immeasurably better for it. Thanks also to our kids, Natalie and Ryan, who grow into better people than their old man every day. I'm proud to know them, and can't wait to see what they have in store for the world. Love and gratitude go to the rest of my family and especially my mom, Liz, my sister, Teresa, and my kind and thoughtful in-laws.

Big-time gratitude goes out to Jessica Mendoza for helping out with the foreword. She's as big a star as any of the ones I wrote about, and it's an honor having my name alongside hers on this book. Ben Cafardo gets a first bump and/or high five as well for helping us connect.

Thanks to my friends at Cole, Loney & Cox, who helped me get the time to work this up, and who rarely failed to make me laugh. Work is also like baseball, in that the moments in between important things actually happening are how you know that you are where you are supposed to be.

Much love to my friends at Woodburn Baptist Church, who have provided fellowship and support. Pastors Tim, Rod, and Warren give me an example of excellence to follow, and my good friend Dennis Smith has always encouraged me to listen when I thought that maybe God was leading me down the path to spend more time studying baseball.

One of the best things about being a baseball writer is that you get lumped into a group with other people who are superb at this. I've gotten to talk with childhood heroes of mine like Fred Harris and John Hough Jr. Tim Wendel has always been selfless and helpful. Paul Dickson wrote a review of my last book so nice that if I could bake pies, I'd have made him one. Coming into this book, I didn't know much about 19th-century baseball, and I deeply appreciate all of the work that folks at SABR have done laying groundwork in that area. Guys like David Nemec and the late Charles Faber are giants to me. Other writers, like Bill James and Rob Neyer, never fail to entertain or inspire me. It's a good club of folks, and I'm glad to call them my brothers and sisters.

Thanks to the people who helped take this book from an idea to an actual tangible thing (or a series of files, if you're on an e-reader). With Keith Wallman and Rick Rinehart, I've been lucky enough to work with two great editors, and this book wouldn't be what it is without the input of both. Meredith Dias, Joshua Rosenberg, and Ryan Schroer were all invaluable at turning a manuscript into a book, which is even harder than it sounds.

Thanks to the guys who gave me some insight on what a few of these feats mean from the inside: Scooter Gennett, Drew Storen, Doug Dascenzo, Denny McLain, Fred Lynn, Aaron Hill, Brooks Conrad, and Mark Saccomanno. It was a pleasure speaking to each of them, and I hope I've done their stories justice. Thanks to the other folks who helped those interviews happen—Rob Butcher of the Reds, Alex Wilcox of the Cubs, Gilbert Martinez and Ryan Pollack from SABR, and Alex Trihias of the MLBPAA, who is more patient than anyone could ever expect. Thanks also to Jamie Ramsey, Jarrod Rollins, Christopher Browne, and the talented Keith Allison for photo help.

Appreciation to Matt Rothenberg, Cassidy Lent, John Horne, and all the good folks at the Baseball Hall of Fame's Giamatti Research Center. They are caretakers of treasure, and they know it, but are still incredibly polite and professional.

Thanks to every friend over the years who has supported me and my writing. If I started naming names, it would turn into another book. If you've read one of my books, you're a friend. It's that simple. Let's do this again.

—Joe Cox
September 2017

ENDNOTES

CHAPTER 1: TURNING AN UNASSISTED TRIPLE PLAY

2–3. Account of the play drawn from contemporaneous accounts cited by Hershberger, Marshall ("Analyzing Coverage of the Hines Triple Play"), Thorn ("Paul Hines and the Unassisted Triple Play" http://ourgame.mlblogs.com/paul-hines-and-the-unassisted-triple-play-220f56473f1a (5/5/15).), and an undated, unsourced article within Hines's file at the Hall of Fame Library by Mike Mulhern titled "Did Baseball's First Triple Crown Winner Also Make the Sport's First Unassisted Triple Play?"

2–3. Thorn's pro-unassisted article is "Paul Hines and the Unassisted Triple Play," http://ourgame.mlblogs.com/paul-hines-and-the-unassisted-triple-play-220f56473f1a (5/5/15).

3. Hershberger's article does not rule out an unassisted play, but leans against it.

3. "one of the most brilliant": *New York Clipper*, December 1879, as discussed by Marshall (*Baseball Research Journal*) and contained within Hines's file at the Hall of Fame Library.

3. "completing a brilliant triple play": *New York Clipper*, March 23, 1901, citing *Providence Journal*, May 9, 1878.

3. "The members of the [Providence] nine": Mulhern article in Hall of Fame Library, citing *Providence Journal*, May 9, 1878.

3. Macmillan crediting Hines with Triple Crown is per Mulhern.

3–4. Account of Ball's play is from *Naples* (Florida) *News*, July 10, 2009 and *Chicago Tribune*, July 20, 1909.

4. "ran right into my hands": *Naples News*, July 10, 2009.

4. Reaction and Cy Young's comments: Ibid.

4. "He had baseball sense": Ibid.

4. Ball's glove going to the Hall of Fame is per an unsourced column in Ball's file at the Baseball Hall of Fame dated March 20, 1953, written by Tom Magner, "Baseball's Hall of Fame to Get Neal Ball's Glove." The glove (as of time of writing) was still displayed.

4–5. Wambsganss's play and Runyon's account of same: *Washington Herald*, October 11, 1920.

6. "As soon as I saw the runners": Perkins, "Tulowitzki Turns Unassisted Triple Play," http://m.mlb.com/news/article/1937361/ (4/29/07).

6. "I just wanted to be sure": Ibid.

6. "It kind of just fell": Ibid.

7. Account of game per *New York Times*, August 24, 2009, as well as video on YouTube.

7. "It really is true": McQuade, "Eric Bruntlett's Unassisted Triple Play Was 7 Years Ago Today," www.phillymag.com/news/2016/08/23/eric-bruntless-unassisted-triple-play/(8/23/16).

7. Info on Bruntlett's retirement and post-baseball life: Ibid.

CHAPTER 2: PITCHING AN IMMACULATE INNING

10. Clarkson background info from Thompson, 31–32.

10. "a full head of steam": *Boston Globe*, June 5, 1889.

10. "was . . . made to knock three big holes": Ibid.

11. Account of Ragan's bizarre behavior is per *Boston Globe*, October 6, 1914.

11. "he exploded in the ninth": *Pittsburgh Press*, October 6, 1914.

12. Information on Koufax game from Aaron ("Sandy Koufax's First No-Hitter"), 212–13.

12. Conversation with Hemus is from *The Sporting News*, July 14, 1962.

12. "In essence, every pitcher": *Los Angeles Times*, July 1, 1962.

13. Contreras's game account is from viewing television broadcast on YouTube.

14. Storen's history from author's interview, July 1, 2017, and baseball-reference.com.

14. "It's a lot of full": Author's interview, July 1, 2017.

14. Game account is from viewing television broadcast on YouTube.

14. "I got the second strikeout": Author's interview, July 1, 2017.

15. "It's a rarity for me": Ibid.

15. "Being a . . . career reliever": Ibid.

15. "Throwing to your high school catcher": Ibid.

CHAPTER 3: STRIKING OUT 20 BATTERS IN A SINGLE GAME

18. Cheney game information is from Herlich, 25–26, as well as baseball-reference.com.

18. "That curveball of his": Herlich, 26.

18. "the greatest stuff I've seen": Ibid.

18. "I told him": Hines, 150.

19. "Back in those days": *Los Angeles Times,* November 3, 2001 (Cheney's obituary).

19. "it felt like someone": Herlich, 24.

19. Early history of Roger Clemens is from Bush (*Nuclear Powered Baseball*), 35–36.

19. "power control pitcher": Mayo, 200.

19. "He had velocity": Ibid.

19–20. Game account per Ibid., 197–207 as well as Pearlman, 92–100.

20. "If setting the record": Tan and Nowlin, 322.

20. PED issues discussed in Pearlman, 204 et seq. and Bush (*Nuclear Powered Baseball*), 42–43, and 47, among others.

21. Nitkowski story is from *New York Daily News*, May 6, 2008.

21. "I know I warmed up bad": Ibid.

21–22. Game account from official video *Chicago Cubs Legends*.

22. "He reminded me": Bush, "May 6, 1998: Kerry Wood Ties Major League Record with 20 Strikeouts," http://sabr.org/gamesproj/game/may-6-1998-kerry-wood-ties-major-league-record-20-strikeouts.

22. "That game was one": Ibid.

23. Wood on arm pain during game and being "worth it" is from Short, "Kerry Wood Says He Felt Something in Elbow During 20 Strikeout Game," http://mlb.nbcsports.com/2012/07/07/kerry-wood-says-he-felt-something-in-elbow-during-20-strikeout-game.

23. "Did we take advantage": *New York Daily News*, May 6, 2008.

23. "It set the bar": Ibid.

23. Game information from YouTube videos.

23. "Tonight . . . was a special night": Collier, "Roaring 20! Max Ties K Mark, Mauls Tigers," http://m.mlb.com/news/article/177612626/max-scherzer-ties-mark-with-20-strikeouts.

CHAPTER 4: TWO GRAND SLAMS IN ONE GAME

26. "Before the season": *The Sporting News*, June 4, 1936.

26. Lazzeri game account is per *New York Times*, May 25, 1936 and *Philadelphia Inquirer*, May 25, 1936. As an aside, baseball-reference has the first slam going to right field and the second to left. The *Inquirer* places the first to left field and the second to center.

26. "missed a fourth": *New York Times*, May 25, 1936, also confirmed by *Philadelphia Inquirer*, May 25, 1936.

26. "It will be many a day": *Brooklyn Daily Eagle*, May 25, 1936.

27–28. Cloninger game account from Huber, "July 3, 1966: Braves Pitcher Tony Cloninger Clouts Two Grand Slams," http://sabr.org/gamesproj/game/july-3-1966-braves-pitcher-tony-cloninger-clouts-two-grand-slams, and baseball-reference.com.

28. "I always told Bobby": *Ithaca Journal*, July 4, 1966.

28. "I didn't remember": Ibid.

28. "Funny thing, nobody asked": Huber ("July 3, 1966").

29. "I just want to enjoy": *Los Angeles Times*, April 24, 1999.

29. "I didn't think": Ibid.

29. "It's a thrill to witness": Ibid.

31. "[W]hen I was coming up": *Washington Post*, July 28, 2009.

31. "That's the beautiful thing": Ibid.

CHAPTER 5: FOUR STRIKEOUTS IN AN INNING

34. "was dull and stupid": *Philadelphia Inquirer*, October 1, 1885.

34. "dull, uninteresting, and poorly-played": *Pittsburgh Post-Gazette*, October 1, 1885.

34. "bad throws of missed third strikes": *Philadelphia Inquirer*, October 1, 1885.

34. The other source regarding the strikeouts and game information is Rothe.

34. Additional Mathews information from Nemec, Miklich, and McKenna.

35. Overall biography and "reputation as a 'money pitcher'": Marshall (*Deadball Stars*), 119–20.

35. Game account and "reaching for his fast drop": *Chicago Tribune*, October 15, 1908.

35. "a drop so sharp": Ibid.

35. "Not often does a pitcher": Ibid.

37. "That's the worst command": *Del Rio* (Texas) *News-Herald*, July 5, 1988.

37. "I thought he had": *New York Times*, July 5, 1988.

38. Info on Finley from Rushkin.

38. "I was really happy": Rushkin, 38.

39. "When he's on like that": *Binghamton* (New York) *Press and Sun-Bulletin*, May 13, 1999.

39. "That was the best forkball": *Los Angeles Times*, May 13, 1999.

39. Info on Finley's second game and "Maybe that will end up": *Los Angeles Times*, August 16, 1999.

39–40. Info on Finley's third game and "I was throwing everything": *Akron Beacon-Journal*, April 17, 2000.

CHAPTER 6: POSITION PLAYERS PITCHING

42. Info on Stanky and his plan to pitch Musial: *St. Louis Post-Dispatch*, August 6, 2014.

43. Account of Musial game is per *St. Louis Post-Dispatch*, September 29, 1952.

43. "I wanted to get it over": *St. Louis Post-Dispatch*, August 6, 2014.

43. "It's something that I've always": *Anniston* (Alabama) *Star*, August 20, 1997.

43. Anecdote from Nelson: Ibid.

43–44. Game account drawn from YouTube video footage of the inning.

44. "All of a sudden": *Anniston* (Alabama) *Star*, August 20, 1997.

44–45. Oquendo game account from Leach, 125–34.

44. "I don't think [Herzog]: Ibid., 129.

45. "I got in a lot": Ibid., 130.

45. "The guy had good stuff": *St. Louis Post-Dispatch*, May 16, 1988.

45. "We know our roles": *St. Louis Post-Dispatch*, May 14, 2013.

45. "I was hurt from head": Ibid.

46. "It hasn't come back": Ibid.

46. Dascenzo's comments on meeting requirements to pitch from author's interview, July 12, 2017.

46. Dascenzo 1990 game account based on YouTube video.

46. "I couldn't get the first": Author's interview, July 12, 2017.

47. "That's a pretty good line": Ibid.

47. "You want to throw the ball": Ibid.

47. "Anything that happened": Ibid.

CHAPTER 7: HITTING FOR THE CYCLE

49. "I didn't know what": Dickson, 416.

50. Foley game account is from *Buffalo Commercial*, May 26, 1882.

50. "should no longer lay claim": Ibid.

51. Foley career information and injury facts: Nemec ("Curry Foley"), 539.

51. Foley labor dispute and "shameful" treatment: McKenna, "Curry Foley," http://sabr. org/bioproj/person/d8a0584a.

52. "the heavy batting": *The* (Philadelphia) *Times*, July 31, 1883.

52. Knight game information is from Huber, "July 30, 1883: Philadelphia's Lon Knight Is First Player to Hit for a 'Natural' Cycle," http://sabr.org/gamesproj/game/ july-30-1883-philadelphias-lon-knight-first-player-hit-natural-cycle.

53. "There's no way to explain it": Author's interview, August 12, 2017.

53–54. Hill game accounts from baseball-reference, YouTube videos, and author's interview, August 12, 2017.

53. "It's human nature": Author's interview, August 12, 2017.

53. Williams tipping cap per Ibid.

54. "I remember not even having": Ibid.

54. "I hit it to right-center": Ibid.

54. "Baseball is so weird": Ibid.

55. Game account from YouTube video of broadcast.

55. "It crossed my mind" from BSN Denver Sports video of postgame comments at https://www.youtube.com/watch?v=FV6NYQZ6IJU&.

55. "Parra was telling me": Ibid.

55. "It's probably one of the best": *Chicago Tribune*, June 18, 2017.

55. "I've never done it": Ibid.

CHAPTER 8: HITTING FOUR HOME RUNS IN A GAME

57. Congress Street stadium info is per Faber ("Four for Bobby Lowe"), 249.

58. Lowe's fish dinner per *The Sporting News*, December 25, 1946.

58. Lowe's recollections of the game: *Detroit News*, May 31, 1944.

58. Lowe's $160 payday is per *The Sporting News*, December 25, 1946.

58. "[H]e got so tired of fish": Ibid.

58–59. Gehrig game account: Huber, "June 3, 1932: Lou Gehrig Hits Four Home Runs, Tony Lazzeri Hits for Cycle in Yankees Romp," https://sabr.org/gamesproj/game/ june-3-1932-lou-gehrig-hits-four-home-runs-tony-lazzeri-hits-cycle-yankees-romp.

59. Lowe's meeting with Gehrig: *Detroit News* (undated column circa June 1932, within Lowe's file at the Baseball Hall of Fame Library).

59. "I had hoped that": Ibid.

59. "It doesn't necessarily take": Ibid.

59. "I talked to some guys": Leach, 92.

59. "I was just trying": Ibid., 89.

60. "I didn't try": Ibid., 91.

60. "It was like when Michael Jordan": *The Sporting News*, September 20, 1993.

61. Hamilton's troubled early years are recounted well at Neyer (*Rob Neyer's Big Book*), 158–59. Hamilton wrote his own book, *Beyond Belief*, in 2008.

61–62. Game account per YouTube videos and Sullivan, "Hamilton Swings into History with Four Home Runs," http://m.mlb.com/news/article/30730042// (5/8/12).

62. "I prepared like any": Ibid.

62. "When I get away from it": Ibid.

62. Hamilton's relapse, trade from Angels detailed in Gonzalez, http://m.mlb.com/news/article/120843186/josh-hamilton-traded-to-texas-rangers-by-los-angeles-angels/ (4/27/15).

63. Gennett waiver is per *USA Today*, March 28, 2017.

63. "It was bittersweet": Author's interview, July 1, 2017.

63–64. Game account based on viewing of broadcast on MLBTV.com

63. "It was a pitch": Author's interview, July 1, 2017.

64. "I just tried to relax": Ibid.

64. "I never expected": Ibid.

64. "I ate a burger": Ibid.

64–65. Martinez game account per YouTube video.

65. "This at-bat": Gilbert, "JD-Back, Back, Back, Back! Martinez: 4 HRs." http://m.mlb.com/news/article/252494292/d-backs-jd-martinez-hits-four-home-runs/ (9/5/17).

65. "It's . . . one of those things": Ibid.

CHAPTER 9: SIX WALKS IN A GAME

68. "[T]here are more pleasant things": *Chicago Tribune*, August 23, 1891.

68. "may have been the exercising": Ibid.

68. "establishes a record": Ibid.

68. "the poor pitching of both": *Cincinnati Enquirer*, August 23, 1891.

69. Foxx game account is per *St. Louis Post-Dispatch*, June 17, 1938 and *The Sporting News*, June 23, 1938, with the latter reflecting that one walk (at least) was intentional.

69. "What good is a record": *The Sporting News*, June 23, 1938.

69–70. Thornton career and auto accident information is from Wancho, "Andre Thornton," http://sabr.org/bioproj/ person/8856996c (1/14/12).

71–72. Bagwell game account drawn from baseball-reference.com as well as *Galveston Daily-News*, August 22, 2009.

72. "Not really the record": Ibid.

72. "Walks are a pain": Ibid.

72–73. Harper game account is from baseball-reference.com and viewing the MLBTV broadcast of the game.

73. "They had a plan": *Washington Post*, May 8, 2016.

CHAPTER 10: KNOCKING IN 10 RUNS IN A GAME

76. "When I went into baseball": *The Sporting News*, December 23, 1959 (Bottomley's obituary).

76. "I don't have a regret": Ibid.

76–77. Bottomley game info is per *St. Louis Post-Dispatch*, September 17, 1924.

77. "You'll get no more chews" and accompanying story with Robinson: *The Sporting News*, December 23, 1959.

77–78. Weintraub information and background on anti-Semitic attitudes are from Berger, "Phil Weintraub," http://sabr.org/bioproj/person/ca37b853.

79. "I frankly don't know why": Ibid.

79. "It probably shows": Author's interview, August 11, 2017.

79. "When you're a rookie": Ibid.

79–80. Game account per Nahigian and YouTube video.

80. "That would have been my double": Author's interview, August 11, 2017.

80. Lynn's remaining career information per Nahigian, author's interview, August 11, 2017.

80. "He was like me": Author's interview, August 11, 2017.

80. "People come up to me": Ibid.

81. Garciaparra game account: *Argus-Leader* (Sioux Falls, SD), May 11, 1999.

81. "I was probably going": Ibid.

81. "I've never hit": Ibid.

CHAPTER 11: HOMERING ON FIRST PITCH FACED IN THE MAJOR LEAGUES

84. Mueller background information and injury: *Pittsburgh Post-Gazette*, January 26, 1928 (unsourced version of same article within Mueller's file at Hall of Fame Library is misdated January 1925).

84. "Home runs inside" and game account: *Pittsburgh Press*, May 8, 1922.

85. Mueller's subsequent injury and later career note per *Pittsburgh Post-Gazette*, January 26, 1928.

86. "When I hear that" and game account: (Minneapolis) *Star-Tribune*, July 24, 1964.

86. Information on Campaneris's game of playing all nine positions: (Long Beach, CA) *Independent*, September 9, 1965.

87. "I actually went off": Author's interview, September 6, 2017.

87. "a nice relationship": Ibid.

87. "hadn't touched a baseball": Ibid.

87. Clark's comments per Ibid.

87. "Literally, not only was I cold": Ibid.

88. "There's a Malcolm Gladwell book": Ibid. (The book is *Blink*.)

88. "If Dave Clark never said that'": Ibid.

88. Additional info on Saccomanno's game per *Indiana* (Pennsylvania) *Gazette*, September 9, 2008.

88. "He really made it big": Ibid.

89. Story of Contreras's transition to catcher: *Chicago Tribune*, March 4, 2016.

89. Account of Contreras game from review of MLBTV broadcast and *Chicago Tribune*, June 20, 2016.

90. "After I hit the homer": *Chicago Tribune*, June 20, 2016.

90. "I still feel like": Ibid.

CHAPTER 12: SIX HITS IN A GAME

92. "good batting and faulty umpiring": *Chicago Tribune*, June 28, 1876

92. "without doubt, one of the worst": *Chicago Inter-Ocean*, June 28, 1876.

92. Game account per Ibid.

92. Force as murder suspect is per Ball and Nemec, 456–57.

93. "choice cut of sirloin": Semchuck, "Wilbert Robinson," https://sabr.org/bioproj/person/5536caf5.

93. Game account is per Keenan ("Seven Hits in Seven Tries"), 237–38.

94. "the record of the season": *Sporting Life*, June 18, 1892, among others.

94. Robinson going into record books: Unsourced column by Damon Runyon dated August 1915 and unsourced and undated column by Ernest Lanigan which references Robinson's record "eluding historians and statisticians until round 1912 or 1913." Both columns were viewed within Robinson's file at the Hall of Fame Library.

94. Robinson's famous feats per Borst, 1304–5.

94. True grapefruit story (blame the pilot, not Stengel) in an unsourced article in the Baseball Hall of Fame's Robinson file, likely from *New York Herald Tribune*, December 4, 1957, as it was written by Harold Rosenthal.

95. Burnett game moved due to blue laws is per Dittmar, 118.

95. "one of the most spectacular": (Wilmington, DE) *News Journal*, July 11, 1932.

95. "a game the likes": Ibid.

96. Fridley biographical information from his file at the Baseball Hall of Fame Library.

97. Fridley's conversation with his wife is from an unsourced, undated column (apparently the week after this game) which is within his file at the Baseball Hall of Fame Library. He "wrote" the column under the name Jim (Fearless) Fridley.

97: "I got to the ballpark": Pepe, 190.

97. "[T]hat told me that day": Ibid.

98. Stennett asking to come out of the game is per Ibid.

98. Murtaugh joking about Robinson removing players is from *New York Times*, September 20, 1975.

98. Stennett's spot in the first all-black lineup is per Skornickel.

98. "I put the best athletes": Ibid.

99. Rendon game account is based on viewing of MLBTV broadcast.

99. "I was aware of some of it": Kerr, "Reactions from Anthony Rendon's Record Setting Day," http://www.masnsports.com/byron-kerr/2017/04/reactions-from-anthony-rendons-record-setting-day.html (4/30/17).

99. "No, I feel the same": Ibid.

CHAPTER 13: THE SUPER SLAM

102. Connor biographical information from Nemec ("Roger Connor"), 18–20.

102. Game account per *New York Clipper*, September 17, 1881.

102. "over the center fielder's head": *Troy Press*, September 12, 1881.

102. "a terrific drive to right": *Worcester Daily Spy*, September 12, 1881.

102. "notable for its lack": *Troy Daily Times*, undated in Husman, 133–34.

102. "the accidental hit": Ibid.

103. Ball hit out of Polo Grounds from an account within Kerr, 4–5. It is a superb book that is an excellent source on any aspect of Connor's life and career.

103. $500 collection for Connor: *Hartford Courant*, August 1, 2007.

103. Connor's loss of child, adoption are from Kerr, 92–93, 112–13.

103. Information on Connor's later life also from Kerr, especially 138–39, 162–63, and 174.

104. "down in Puerto Rico": *Pittsburgh Press*, July 26, 1956.

104–105. Account of play: Ibid.

104. "I all but tackled him": Ibid.

104. Bragan's comments on waiving the $25 fine are per *The Sporting News*, August 8, 1956.

104. "I say to Bobby": Markusen, 60.

105. "[h]is teammates mobbed him": Ibid.

105. "a Latin-American variety of showboating": Maraniss, 108.

105. "ran right over his manager": Ibid.

105. "excited the fans": Ibid.

105. An excellent reflection of Brosnan's comments and the double standard that Clemente faced is at Espada, "The Greatest Forgotten Home Run of All Time," http://lithub.com/the-greatest-forgotten-home-run-of-all-time/ (6/15/15).

105–106. Win expectancy, as with the game account, drawn from baseball-reference.com.

106. "being down eight runs early": Author's interview, August 24, 2017.

106. "it looked like he brought it back": *Atlanta Journal-Constitution*, May 20, 2010.

106. "I put my hands": Ibid.

106–107. "I don't know if": Ibid.

107. Celebration account is also per Ibid.

107. "That game was one of those games": Author's interview, August 24, 2017.

107. Tigers super slam information is per *Lansing State Journal*, July 1, 2014.

108. "I can't even remember": Ibid.

CHAPTER 14: STEALING FOR THE CYCLE IN ONE INNING

110. "the NL's best leadoff hitter" Jensen, 40.

110. "swung with a short": Ibid.

110. "It is the consensus": *Washington Evening Star*, July 5, 1899.

110–111. Account of the games is per *Baltimore Sun*, July 5, 1899.

111. "while 'Ducky' was engaged": Ibid.

111–112. Cobb's irascibility (or the contradictory evidence on same) is per the outstanding work of Leerhsen.

111–112. Cobb's baserunning is per Leerhsen, for example, 12–15.

112. "Cobb was always exerting": Ibid., 14.

112. "All the pretty slides": Ibid., 206.

112. "He was a gentle": James, 372. (Note that this text is from the 1986 edition and does not appear in the 21st-century edition.)

112. Cobb game info is per *Detroit Free Press*, July 13, 1911.

112. "he was about to move": Ibid.

113. Wagner 1899 game account per *Louisville Courier-Journal*, August 2, 1899.

113. "while Meekin was winding": Ibid.

113. Wagner 1909 game account per *Chicago Tribune*, May 3, 1909.

113. "actually hit the plate": Ibid.

113–114. Stynes game account based on viewing of broadcast video on YouTube.

115. Werth game account similarly based on YouTube video.

115. "If they're not going": *Philadelphia Daily News*, May 13, 2009.

115. "It was an embarrassing play": Ibid.

CHAPTER 15: STEALING SIX BASES IN A SINGLE GAME

118. Gore background info is per Grillo, 127–28.

118. Account of Gore's game: *Chicago Tribune*, June 25, 1881.

118. "Farrell . . . distinguished himself": Ibid.

119. "Women and wine": McMahon, 53.

119. Gore's memories of the holdout are from an unsourced 1937 article by J. Warren McEligot within Gore's file at the Hall of Fame Library.

119. Current equivalencies were calculated utilizing the Consumer Price Index (Urban) figures.

119. "I was stubborn": Unsourced McEligot article noted above.

119. Collins biographical information is from Mittermayer, 611–12.

120. Collins's September 11th game account per *Philadelphia Inquirer*, September 12, 1912 and *Detroit Free Press*, September 12, 1912.

120. Collins's September 22nd game account per *Philadelphia Inquirer*, September 23, 1912.

120–121. Additional Collins information is from Mittermayer, 611–13.

121. "I was mad at them": Franco, "Otis Nixon on the Art of Stealing Bases," YouTube video, posted March 12, 2015, https://www.youtube.com/watch?v=r7MZZJDdB00.

121. Nixon game account per baseball-reference.com and YouTube videos of his stolen bases.

121. Nixon drug information is per *New York Times*, September 17, 1991.

121. "They can't steal six": *Talking Chop Magazine*, "Interview with Former Braves Outfielder Otis Nixon," https://www.talkingchop.com/2010/12/24/1894966/interview-with-former-braves-outfielder-otis-nixon (12/24/10).

122. "I like to be like the old school guys": Sonnanstine, 79.

122–123. Game account taken from baseball-reference.com and YouTube video.

123. "I wish I had known": *New York Times*, May 4, 2009.

CHAPTER 16: GETTING ON BASE IN 17 CONSECUTIVE PLATE APPEARANCES

126. Ward game accounts are per McCotter, 43–44, and confirmed by handwritten notes (likely his) included within Ward's file at the Hall of Fame library.

126. Further game accounts also per McCotter.

127. Ward's fire heroics are mentioned in *Washington Post*, December 8, 1894, and additional information was provided by *Altoona* (Pennsylvania) *Tribune*, December 1, 1894.

127. "one of the greatest": *St. Louis Star and Times*, August 20, 1911.

127. "I tried to follow": *Seattle Post-Intelligencer*, August 6, 2003.

127. "It never is fair": *Los Angeles Times*, May 27, 1961.

128. Game accounts are per baseball-reference.com.

129. Thomas's approach of the record and the discussion of Holtzman and Siwoff is all per McCotter, 43.

CHAPTER 17: GETTING A HIT IN 12 CONSECUTIVE AT-BATS

132. Game accounts based on information with Kling's file at Hall of Fame Library.

132. "grand hitting": *Sporting Life*, September 6, 1902.

132. Kling's holdout discussed in unsourced article from August 31, 1952 within Kling's Hall of Fame library file, "When Chance Lost Big Chance."

133. Account of Higgins's streak: *The Sporting News*, June 30, 1938.

133. Belief that Speaker held record and Higgins's comments on perhaps going 0 for next 12 both per Ibid.

133–134. Racial issues with Higgins as manager are per Armour, "Mike Higgins," http://sabr.org/bioproj/person/dce16a07.

134. "He managed me for years": Ibid.

134–135. Dropo's streak accounts are per *Philadelphia Inquirer*, July 16, 1952.

135. "straight down the pipe" and Dropo's next hit are per *The Sporting News*, July 23, 1952.

135. Pedroia's unawareness of streak, hearing broadcasters when going to bathroom are per (Minneapolis) *Star-Tribune*, August 28, 2016.

CHAPTER 18: HITTING A HOME RUN IN EIGHT CONSECUTIVE GAMES

137. Long catching story is per an undated, unsourced magazine article "Dale Long's Hour of Glory" within Long's file at the Baseball Hall of Fame Library. The article appears to date from the late 50s, as it references Long playing last season for the Chicago Cubs.

137. Information on Long actually catching is per *Chicago Daily Tribune*, August 21, 1958.

138–139. Accounting of Long's home runs per undated article, apparently from *Milwaukee Journal*, " Road From Green Bay to Homer Record Was Torturous One for Long of Pirates," within Long's file at the Baseball Hall of Fame Library.

138. May 26th game is per *Pittsburgh Press*, May 27, 1956.

138–139. May 28th game is per unsourced newspaper article "Long Hits 8th Homer, Record" within Long's file at the Baseball Hall of Fame Library.

139. reporter asking about breaking Babe Ruth's record was from *New York Times*, May 30, 1956.

139. lack of sleep and *Ed Sullivan* is per an undated *New York Daily News* column within Long's Baseball Hall of Fame Library file (circa 1987).

139. "I was beginning to get weak": Undated, unsourced magazine article "Dale Long's Hour of Glory," cited above.

139. "As soon as I walk in": undated *New York Daily News* column, cited above.

139–140. Mattingly at second base and ambidextrity is per Shalin, 38.

140–141. Account of streak is per Shalin, 37–40 and baseball-reference.com.

141. "You can't try": Shalin, 40.

141. "I've never felt pressure": *New York Times*, July 20, 1987.

142. "You hit ten home runs": Ibid.

142. Griffey's suicide attempt is per Hawks, 50.

143. "Skip, I'm going to take": *The Sporting News*, August 9, 1993.

143. Griffey's streak per Ibid., YouTube videos, and baseball-reference.com.

143. "I tried too hard": *The Sporting News*, August 9, 1993.

143. "I gave it my best": Ibid.

CHAPTER 19: 40/40 SEASON

146. "If I'd known": *Washington Post*, July 23, 2006.

147. Link between Canseco's mother's death and his steroid use is per Canseco, 11.

147. Injecting McGwire is per Canseco, 74–75.

147. "If I don't get hurt" and ensuing 40/40 prediction is per *The Sporting News*, May 16, 1988.

148. 40/40 game account is per *The Sporting News*, October 3, 1988.

148. "I told him": Ibid.

148. Boswell/steroid accusations are per Dunn, 26.

149. "He wasted more ability": Bryant, 191.

149. Numerous examples of Bonds's issues in getting along with others (including the story of him being voted off his college team) documented within West, "Barry Bonds," http://sabr.org/bioproj/person/e79d202f (12/1/15).

150. BALCO investigation discussed at length in many sources, including Mitchell at 113–14, 118, etc.

150. Jealousy of McGwire and his attention as basis for steroid use is per Fainaru-Wada, 38–39.

150. "They're just letting him": Fainaru-Wada, x.

151. "A-Fraud" nickname is per Roberts, 7.

151. Steroid admission: *Baltimore Sun*, February 10, 2009.

151. Biogenesis issues, which resulted in a one-year suspension, documented at *Orlando Sentinel*, January 12, 2014.

152. Soriano's background, including "Mule" nickname per Wendel (*The New Face*), 190–91.

152. Japanese experiment and fallout per Ibid.

152–153. Soriano's issues with Robinson and left field per *Washington Times*, March 14, 2007.

153. "There's a lot of players": *Washington Times*, September 17, 2006.

CHAPTER 20: HITTING .400

156. On Barnes's .429 average, it's worth noting that he would have believed he barely broke .400, because the scoring rules of the time counted walks as outs. Both his average and his team's average in this chapter are quoted using modern methodology.

156. The belief that Barnes was a freakish creature of the fair/foul divide was widely propagated, notably by Lee Allen in *The National League Story*. It is well rebutted by Thorn, 82. It may be worth pointing out that we thus have the official historian of

Major League Baseball correcting a myth that was preserved in an official history of the National League.

157. Williams background information is per Nowlin, "Ted Williams," http://sabr.org/bioproj/person/35baa190.

157. "All I want out of life": Williams, 7.

158. "I want to have more": widely reported, among other places in *New York Times*, September 18, 2011.

158. "I went to bed early": Holway, 282.

158. Williams chewing off nails, etc., is per *The Sporting News*, October 9, 1941.

158. "I wish you all": Bradlee, 192.

159. "Just as I stepped in": Williams, 90.

159. Elias's 1.9 quadrillion to one odds are often cited as being odds they tabulated on Brett specifically. This isn't true. Original context is at *Battle Creek* (Michigan) *Enquirer*, August 31, 1980.

160. "I sure hope he does it": Singer, "Summer of .400: Brett Looks Back 30 Years Later," http://m.mlb.com/news/article/14748648// (9/17/10).

160. "That whole summer": Ibid.

160. "If I knew that hitting": Kenney, 47.

161. "I really believe": Ibid., 48.

CHAPTER 21: HITTING 50 HOME RUNS IN A SEASON

164. Williamson and Chicago's tiny ballpark info per Green, 99.

164. Lennon's famous quote was TV dialogue for the *Mike Douglas Show*, February 16, 1972. Doubtlessly, Lennon didn't write it. But he did say it.

164. An excellent summary of Ruth's troubled youth—and the rest of his career for that matter—can be found at Wood, "Babe Ruth," http://sabr.org/bioproj/person/9dcdd01c.

164. "ignored the fashion": Creamer, 76.

165. 431 homers figure is per Wood, "Babe Ruth," http://sabr.org/bioproj/person/9dcdd01c.

165. Wilson's biography culled from Schott, 176–81.

165–166. Wilson being built like a keg of beer is an oft-repeated comment, for instance, *Los Angeles Times*, January 16, 1964.

166. "There are kids": Schott, 180.

167. Fielder game account based on YouTube video.

167. Fielder's wife and son being in press conference per *Battle Creek* (Michigan) *Enquirer*, October 4, 1990.

167–168. Prince Fielder game information also based on YouTube video.

168. "I don't think he's grown up yet": *Washington Post*, June 22, 2007.

168. "It would be a cool award": *South Florida Sun Sentinel*, September 27, 2007.

168. "You've got to look at": *Indianapolis Star*, September 26, 2007.

168. Cecil's suit was against Jim Girard of the *Detroit News* for a 2004 article. Discussed, among many places, in *Philadelphia Inquirer*, December 1, 2004.

169. Prince's estrangement and potential divorce discussed at *Detroit Free Press*, August 18, 2013.

169. "I always knew": Sullivan, "Fielder's Memories Reciprocated by Famed Dad," http://m.mlb.com/news/article/131928284/prince-fielder-cecil-fielder-cherish-memories-of-watching-each-other-play/ (6/20/15).

169. Prince Fielder's press conference accounts per YouTube videos.

169. Post-retirement Fielder info and "Obviously, it was supposed": Crasnick, "Prince Fielder's Career Was Cut Short, But He's Still Cooking . . . Literally," www.espn.com/mlb/story/_/ id/18654365/former-texas-rangers-slugger-prince-fielder-opens-neck-injury-ended-baseball-career (2/10/17).

170. Stanton's 50th home run account per YouTube video.

170. "He's in the zone": *Miami Herald*, August 27, 2017.

CHAPTER 22: SURVIVING SHENANIGANS TO WIN A LEAGUE BATTING TITLE

172. Some background on the relative opinions of Browns manager Jack O'Connor on both men at Huhn, 104–5. While O'Connor's experience was probably relatively typical, it also became specifically important to the batting race.

172–173. Cobb/Lajoie race is per Huhn, 98–117 and Fleitz, 173–83.

173. Parrish's comments on the two contacts, from the Browns coach and Lajoie: Huhn, 118.

173. Ban Johnson's ruling per Fleitz, 183.

173–174. Rosen/Vernon chicanery per *The Sporting News*, October 7, 1953.

174. "rare carelessness": Ibid.

174. "super-obvious lack of judgment": Ibid.

174. Harris's reaction also per Ibid.

174–175. Brett/McRae game accounts per *The Sporting News*, October 16, 1976.

174. "toward the ball": Ibid.

175. "didn't see it real good": Ibid.

175. "Brye is a good friend": Ibid.

175. "aggressive style of play": *New York Times*, October 8, 1976.

175. "I think maybe": *The Sporting News*, October 8, 1976.

175. "the worst thing": Ibid.

175. "a bunch of crap": Ibid.

175–176. "It is not always possible": Ibid.

176. "I can't help but see": *Los Angeles Times*, October 5, 1990.

177. "I said, 'If I go'": *New York Daily News*, September 28, 2011.

177. Wilson's tweet per Ibid.

177. "I'm not really here to judge him": Ibid.

177–178. Cabrera situation per *Philadelphia Inquirer*, September 22, 2012.

CHAPTER 23: HITTING STREAKS OF 40+ GAMES

179. *USA Today* finding on hitting a baseball per *USA Today*, March 2, 2003.

179–180. Dahlen info per Spatz, 275–76.

180. Dahlen's 65 ejections: *Los Angeles Times*, May 25, 2007.

180–181. Keeler information per Skipper, 707–9.

180. "[Keeler] had the speed": Ibid., 707.

180. "Keep your eye clear": Aphorism is very widely quoted; Ibid. credits it to an interview with the *Brooklyn Eagle*.

181. Keeler streak info per Felber, 257–58.

181. Keeler as Dahlen's best man: *Brooklyn Daily Eagle,* December 21, 1903.

181. "I always think": Cramer, 234.

182. "Although he learned Italian first": Busch, 69.

182–183. Hitting streak information per Cramer, 161–86, baseball-reference.com, and Baldassaro, "Joe DiMaggio," https://sabr.org/bioproj/person/a48f1830.

183. "the most extraordinary thing": *New York Review of Books*, August 18, 1988.

183. "When my hitting streak": *New York Times*, August 6, 1978.

184. "Garber was pitching": Ibid.

184. "I had an idea": Ibid.

185. Denny Lyons info is per Voigt, 45–49.

CHAPTER 24: WINNING THE TRIPLE CROWN (AS A BATTER)

189. O'Neill's racist letter and mini-controversy: *St. Louis Globe-Democrat*, September 12, 1887.

190. "Ty Cobb was a deep pool": Leerhsen, 16.

190. Cobb's theory of the game and relevance of his play to same is documented, among other places, in Leerhsen, 307–9, 326–29.

190. "They say I get my base-hits": *The Sporting News*, December 27, 1961. Other accounts confirm the home runs, but don't indicate two additional near-misses, which doesn't seem to have any basis in fact.

191. Medwick stories are per Faber ("Joe Medwick"), 166–69.

192. "Yaz hit 44 homers" and general Yastrzemski info from Crehan and Nowlin, 46–49.

192–193. "In '67, the Triple Crown": FoxSports, "Yaz: Somebody Has to Win Triple Crown," www.foxsports.com/mlb/story/carl-yastrzemski-on-next-triple-crown-winner-somebodys-got-to-do-it-092612 (9/26/12)

193. "Somebody's got to do it": Ibid.

193. Stark's notes on Triple Crown are per Stark, "Miguel Cabrera's Triple Crown Chase," http://scorecenter.espn.go.com/blog/jayson-stark/post?id=67(9/19/12).

194. "It was hard": ESPN.com, "Miguel Cabrera Wins Triple Crown," www.espn.com/mlb/story/_/id/8458298/detroit-tigers-miguel-cabrera-wins-first-triple-crown-1967 (10/4/12).

194. "He's the best hitter": Ibid.

194. "a remarkable achievement": Ibid.

CHAPTER 25: STEALING 100 BASES IN A SEASON

196. Nicol background: Nemec ("Hugh Nicol"), 587–88.

196. "the base running star of the profession": An unsourced article dated November 9, 1887, located within Nicol's file at the Baseball Hall of Fame Library.

197. Harry Stovey and Arlie Latham initially credited with more steals than Nicol: Schmidt, 120.

197. "infuse life and ginger": Nemec ("Hugh Nicol"), 587.

197. Nicol's post-baseball career: Ibid., 588.

198. "Cobb's record of 96": *New York Times*, September 2, 1945.

198. "If the . . . Dodgers": Brody, 24.

199. Henderson being born in the back of the family car documented in many sources, including *San Francisco Chronicle*, June 9, 2000.

199–200. "I'd chase them": Henderson, 30.

200. Mrs. Wilkerson and her influence: Henderson, 64–65.

200. "I let him run": Roensch, 19.

200. Henderson's all-time record moment per YouTube video.

201. Coleman's two-sport skills and field goal to beat Miami: *New York Times*, June 12, 1985.

202. Tarp eating Coleman's leg recounted in *St. Louis Post-Dispatch*, October 12, 2015.

CHAPTER 26: STRIKING OUT 300 BATTERS IN A SEASON

206. Background information on Kilroy per Faber, "Matt Kilroy," https://sabr.org/bioproj/person/65e52675.

206. Kilroy game account per Keenan, "Matt Kilroy," 182–83.

207. "would have been": James, 445.

207. Crawford's story about Waddell: Ritter, 51.

207. Mathewson story documented at James, 445.

208–209. Richard's biography per VanDeMortal, 50–54.

209. Richard's decline and comeback: *Utica Observer-Dispatch*, June 14, 2015.

209–210. Koufax's biography and improvement: Aaron ("Sandy Koufax"), 198–209, improvement noted at 202.

210. "It was frightening": Aaron ("Sandy Koufax"), 198.

210. Not pitching on Yom Kippur per Aaron ("Sandy Koufax"), 205.

210–211. Ryan biography and improvement per Boston, "Nolan Ryan," https://sabr.org/bioproj/person/4af413ee (1/10/11).

211. "Ryan doesn't just get": Ibid.

212. Johnson biography, tips from Ryan per Wancho (*No-Hitters*), 436–41.

CHAPTER 27: WINNING 30 GAMES IN A SEASON

215–216. Radbourn's pitching down the stretch in 1884 documented by Nemec ("Charles Gardner Radbourn"), 59, which is careful to note that he didn't literally pitch every game, although he nearly did so.

216. "Rad had plenty of speed": Thorn and Holway, 81.

216. "Radbourne [sic], as sure as you live": Achorn, 234. (As an aside, this misspelling of Radbourn's name was common during his career.)

216. Radbourn's decline is per Ivor-Campbell, 132.

216. Origin of four-man rotation per Vaccaro, 30–32.

217. McLain's childhood reported in Wendel (*Summer of '68*), 58.

217. "I like the game": Schechter, 207.

218. "Black, white, green, yellow": Author's interview, July 23, 2017.

218. "Physically, I was in good shape": Ibid.

218–219. "When I go out to warm up": Schechter, 208.

219. "would consider quitting": McLain, quoting a contemporary report, 122.

219. "I was told": Author's interview, July 23, 2017.

219. McLain's problems after baseball per Armour (*Sock It to 'Em, Tigers*), 113.

219–220. Losing weight and radio show per author's interview, July 23, 2017.

220. "I can't imagine": Ibid.

220. "We're having more": Ibid.

220–221. Welch's alcoholism is documented in many places, including *The Sporting News*, March 22, 1980.

222. "The chances of it ever happening": Author's interview, July 23, 2017.

CHAPTER 28: PITCHING 50+ CONSECUTIVE SCORELESS INNINGS

224. Coombs's background and biography: Rogers, 614–17.

225. "Coombs' performance is one of the wonders": *Chicago Tribune*, September 25, 1910.

225. "that his arm": Lane, 66.

225. Later years of Coombs per Rogers, 617.

226. Johnson learning curve to complement fastball around 1913 is per Carey, 741.

228. Drysdale's famous inning described in Drysdale, 140–43.

228. "[T]here wasn't much doubt": Ibid., 141.

228. "bizarre": Ibid., 142.

228. "was almost like a World Series": Ibid., 141.

228–229. Drysdale checked by umpire Donatelli is detailed within *Los Angeles Times*, June 9, 1968, as well as Drysdale, 144–45.

229–230. Hershiser's streak detailed within Schechter, 303–17.

229–230. Hershiser's near-loss of streak described in Hershiser, 119–20.

230. "I headed straight": Ibid., 120.

230. "Drysdale got his break": Ibid.

230. "It couldn't have happened": Hershiser, 130.

230. "Any of those and hundreds": Ibid., 107.

CHAPTER 29: WINNING THE TRIPLE CROWN (AS A PITCHER)

234. "more resembled side-arm motion": *The Sporting News*, May 21, 1936.

234. "[A]ccounts of Bond's pitching": Neyer (*Neyer/James*), 61.

235. "[r]ealizes game has made rapid strides": *The Sporting News*, May 21, 1936.

235. Vaughn and his physical attributes: Finkel, 137.

235. "his lumbering side-to-side": Ibid.

236. "Big Jim Vaughn": Ibid.

237. Gooden's fastball flattening is per James and Neyer, 220.

237. Gooden's World Series parade story told in great detail at Gooden and Henican, xvi–xviii.

237. Gooden's drug troubles documented at Lichtenstein, 113–14, as well as many other places.

237. Gooden's suicide attempt documented at Gooden and Henican, 140.

238. Torre's comparisons of Kershaw to Koufax per *Los Angeles Times*, September 26, 2011.

239. "It's been an awesome year": Ibid.

CHAPTER 30: SAVING 50 GAMES IN A SEASON

241. Holtzman denying his status as inventor of the save: Deane, 104.

242. Thigpen biography: *The Sporting News*, September 10, 1990.

242. Thigpen's salary per baseball-reference.com

243. "special because he's just a guy": *The Sporting News*, September 17, 1990.

244. Thigpen's back injury discussed at *Los Angeles Times*, September 26, 2003.

245. "It's been an amazing year" and game account: *Reno Gazette-Journal*, September 14, 2008.

245–246. Accounts of Gagne's dominance and PED issues per *Los Angeles Times*, February 19, 2010.

246. "When he doesn't": *Los Angeles Times*, September 26, 2003.

BIBLIOGRAPHY

HALL OF FAME LIBRARY ARCHIVE COLLECTION
Earl Averill file
Neal Ball file
Ross Barnes file
Tommy Bond file
Jim Bottomley file
Tom Cheney file
John Clarkson file
Roger Connor file
Walt Dropo file
Don Drysdale file
Curry Foley file
Davy Force file
Jim Fridley file
George Gore file
Paul Hines file
Matt Kilroy file
Johnny Kling file
Dale Long file
Bobby Lowe file
Walter Mueller file
Hugh Nicol file
James "Tip" O'Neill file
Wilbert Robinson file
Frank "Piggy" Ward file

NEWSPAPERS AND MAGAZINES
Akron Beacon-Journal
Altoona (Pennsylvania) *Tribune*
Anniston (Alabama) *Star*
Argus-Leader (Sioux Falls, SD)
Atlanta Journal-Constitution
Baltimore Sun
Battle Creek (Michigan) *Enquirer*
Binghamton (New York) *Press and Sun-Bulletin*
Boston Globe

Brooklyn Daily Eagle
Buffalo Commercial
Chicago Daily Tribune
Chicago Inter-Ocean
Chicago Tribune
Cincinnati Enquirer
Del Rio (Texas) *News-Herald*
Detroit Free Press
Detroit News
Galveston Daily-News
Hartford Courant
(Long Beach, CA) *Independent*
Indiana (Pennsylvania) *Gazette*
Indianapolis Star
Ithaca (New York) *Journal*
Lansing State Journal
Los Angeles Times
Louisville Courier-Journal
Miami Herald
Naples (Florida) *News*
The (Wilmington, DE) *News Journal*
New York Clipper
New York Daily News
New York Herald Tribune
New York Review of Books
New York Times
Orlando Sentinel
Philadelphia Daily News
Philadelphia Inquirer
Pittsburgh Post-Gazette
Pittsburgh Press
Providence (Rhode Island) *Journal*
Reno Gazette-Journal
San Francisco Chronicle
Seattle Post-Intelligencer
South Florida Sun Sentinel
The Sporting Life
The Sporting News
(Minneapolis) *Star-Tribune*
St. Louis Globe-Democrat
St. Louis Post-Dispatch
St. Louis Star and Times

The (Philadelphia) *Times*
Troy Daily Times
Troy Press
USA Today
Utica Observer-Dispatch
Washington Evening Star
Washington Herald
Washington Post
Washington Times
Worcester Daily Spy

BOOKS AND ARTICLES

Aaron, Marc Z. "Sandy Koufax." In *No-Hitters*. Phoenix: Society for American Baseball Research, 2017.

Aaron, Marc Z. "Sandy Koufax's First No-Hitter." In *No-Hitters*. Phoenix: Society for American Baseball Research, 2017.

Achorn, Edward. *Fifty-nine in '84: Old Hoss Radbourn, Barehanded Baseball, and the Greatest Season a Pitcher Ever Had*. New York: Smithsonian Books, 2010.

Armour, Mark. "Denny McLain." In *Sock It to 'Em, Tigers: The Incredible Story of the 1968 Detroit Tigers*. Hanover, MA: Maple Street Press, 2008.

Ball, David, and David Nemec. "David W. Force." In *Major League Baseball Profiles, Volume 1: The Ballplayers Who Built the Game*. Lincoln: University of Nebraska Press, 2011.

Borst, William A. "Wilbert Robinson." In *Biographical Dictionary of American Sports, Q–Z*. Westport, CT: Greenwood Press, 2000.

Bradlee, Ben, Jr. *The Kid: The Immortal Life of Ted Williams*. New York: Little, Brown & Company, 2013.

Brody, Tom C. "A 'Snake-Sliding' Dodger Tries to Steal the Pennant." *Sports Illustrated*, October 1, 1962: 24–25.

Bryant, Howard. *Juicing the Game: Drugs, Power, and the Fight for the Soul of Major League Baseball*. New York: Penguin Group, 2005.

Busch, Noel F. "Joe DiMaggio: Baseball's Most Sensational Big-League Star Starts What Should Be His Best Year So Far." *Life Magazine*, May 1, 1939: 63–69.

Bush, Frederick C. "Roger Clemens." In *Nuclear Powered Baseball: Articles Inspired by The Simpsons Episode Homer At the Bat*. Phoenix: Society for American Baseball Research, 2016.

Canseco, Jose. *Juiced*. New York: Harper Collins, 2005.

Carey, Charles. "Walter Perry Johnson." In *Deadball Stars of the American League*. Dulles, VA: Brassey's, Inc., 2006.

Cramer, Richard Ben. *Joe DiMaggio: The Hero's Life*. New York: Touchstone, 2000.

Creamer, Robert W. *Babe: The Legend Comes to Life*. New York: Simon and Schuster, 2005.

Crehan, Herb, and Bill Nowlin. "Carl Yastrzemski." In '75: *The Red Sox Team That Saved Baseball.* Phoenix: Society for American Baseball Research, 2015.

Deane, Bill. *Baseball Myths: Debating, Debunking, and Disproving Tales from the Diamond.* Lanham, MD: Scarecrow Press, 2012.

Dickson, Paul. *The Dickson Baseball Dictionary Third Edition.* New York: W.W. Norton & Co., 2009.

Dittmar, Joseph. *The 100 Greatest Baseball Games of the 20th Century.* Jefferson, NC: McFarland and Company, 2000.

Drysdale, Don, with Bob Verdi. *Once a Bum, Always a Dodger.* New York: St. Martin's Press, 1990.

Dunn, Jeffrey. "Jose Canseco." In *Nuclear Powered Baseball: Articles Inspired by The Simpsons Episode Homer At the Bat.* Phoenix: Society for American Baseball Research, 2016.

Faber, Charles. "Four for Bobby Lowe." In *Inventing Baseball: The 100 Greatest Games of the 19th Century.* Phoenix: Society for American Baseball Research, 2013.

Faber, Charles. "Joe Medwick." In *The 1934 St. Louis Cardinals: The World Champion Gas House Gang.* Phoenix: Society for American Baseball Research, 2014.

Fainaru-Wada, Mark, and Lance Williams. *Game of Shadows: Barry Bonds, BALCO, and the Steroids Scandal That Rocked Professional Sports.* New York: Gotham Books, 2006.

Felber, Dave. "June 19, 1897: Wee Willie Keeler's 44-Game Hitting Streak Ends." In *Inventing Baseball: The 100 Greatest Games of the 19th Century.* Phoenix: Society for American Baseball Research, 2013.

Finkel, Jan. "James Leslie 'Hippo' Vaughn." In *Deadball Stars of the National League.* Dulles, VA: Brassey's, Inc., 2004.

Fleitz, David L. *Napoleon Lajoie: King of Ballplayers.* Jefferson, NC: McFarland & Company, 2013.

Gooden, Dwight, and Ellis Henican. *Doc: A Memoir.* New York: Houghton Mifflin, 2013.

Green, Christopher D. "Baseball's First Power Surge." *Baseball Research Journal* 40, no. 2 (Fall 2011): 99–103.

Grillo, Jerry. "George Gore's Theft Spree." In *Inventing Baseball: The 100 Greatest Games of the 19th Century.* Phoenix: Society for American Baseball Research, 2013.

Hawks, Emily. "Ken Griffey, Jr." In *Nuclear Powered Baseball: Articles Inspired by The Simpsons Episode Homer At the Bat.* Phoenix: Society for American Baseball Research, 2016.

Henderson, Rickey. *Off Base: Confessions of a Thief.* New York: Harper, 1993.

Herlich, Tim. "Tom Cheney." In *Sweet '60: The 1960 Pittsburgh Pirates.* Phoenix: Society for American Baseball Research, 2013.

Hershberger, Richard. "Revisiting the Hines Triple Play." *Baseball Research Journal* 45, no. 1 (Spring 2016): 96–101.

Hershiser, Orel, with Jerry B. Jenkins. *Out of the Blue.* Brentwood, TN: Wolgemuth & Hyatt, 1989.

Hines, Rick. "Tom Cheney: Baseball's Strikeout King for a Game." *Sports Collectors Digest*, July 26, 1991: 150–52.

Holway, John. *The Last .400 Hitter*. Dubuque, IA: William C. Brown, 1992.

Huhn, Rick. *The Chalmers Race: Ty Cobb, Napoleon Lajoie, and the Controversial 1910 Batting Title That Became a National Obsession*. Lincoln: University of Nebraska Press, 2014.

Husman, John R. "Roger Connor's Grand Slam." In *Inventing Baseball: The 100 Greatest Games of the 19th Century*. Phoenix: Society for American Baseball Research, 2013.

Ivor-Campbell, Frederick. "Charles Radbourn(e), Jr." In *Baseball's First Stars*. Cleveland: Society for American Baseball Research, 1996.

James, Bill. *The Bill James Historical Baseball Abstract*. New York: Villard Books, 1986.

James, Bill, and Rob Neyer. *The Neyer/James Guide to Pitchers: An Historical Compendium of Pitching, Pitchers, and Pitches*. New York: Fireside, 2004.

Jensen, Don. "John McGraw." In *Deadball Stars of the National League*. Dulles, VA: Brassey's, Inc., 2004.

Keenan, Jimmy. "Matt Kilroy, Strikeout King." In *Inventing Baseball: The 100 Greatest Games of the 19th Century*. Phoenix: Society for American Baseball Research, 2013.

Keenan, Jimmy. "Seven Hits in Seven Tries." In *Inventing Baseball: The 100 Greatest Games of the 19th Century*. Phoenix: Society for American Baseball Research, 2013.

Kenney, Kirk. *100 Things Padres Fans Should Know & Do Before They Die*. Chicago: Triumph Books, 2016.

Kerr, Roy. *Roger Connor: Home Run King of 19th Century Baseball*. Jefferson, NC: McFarland & Co, Inc., 2011.

Lane, F. C. "Pitching Science in All Its Angles." *Baseball Magazine*, November 1913: 52–66.

Leach, Matthew, with Stewart Shea. *Game of My Life St. Louis Cardinals: Memorable Stories of Cardinals Baseball*. New York: Sports Publishing, 2011.

Leehrsen, Charles. *Ty Cobb: A Terrible Beauty*. New York: Simon & Schuster, 2015.

Lichtenstein, Michael. *Ya Gotta Believe: The 40th Anniversary New York Mets Fan Book*. New York: St. Martin's, 2002.

Maraniss, David. *Clemente: The Passion and Grace of Baseball's Last Hero*. New York: Simon and Schuster, 2006.

Markusen, Bruce. *Roberto Clemente: The Great One*. New York: Sports Publishing, 2001.

Marshall, Brian. "Analyzing Coverage of the Hines Triple Play." *Baseball Research Journal* 45, no. 1 (Spring 2016): 102–8.

Marshall, Brian. "Orval Overall." In *Deadball Stars of the National League*. Dulles, VA: Brassey's, Inc., 2004.

Mayo, Jonathan. *Facing Clemens: Hitters on Confronting Baseball's Most Intimidating Pitcher*. Guilford, CT: Lyons Press, 2008.

McCotter, Trent. "Consecutive Times Reaching Base." *Baseball Research Journal* 35 (2006): 43–45.

McLain, Denny, with Eli Zaret. *I Told You I Wasn't Perfect*. Chicago: Triumph Books, 2007.

McMahon, William. "George F. Gore." In *Nineteenth Century Stars*. Kansas City: Society for American Baseball Research, 1989.

Mitchell, George J. *Report to the Commissioner of Baseball of an Independent Investigation into the Illegal Use of Steroids and Other Performance Enhancing Substances by Players in Major League Baseball*. DLA Piper US LLP, 12/13/2007.

Mittermayer, Paul F. "Edward Trowbridge Collins." In *Deadball Stars of the American League*. Dulles, VA: Brassey's, Inc., 2006.

Nahigian, Tim. "Fred Lynn." In *'75: The Red Sox Team That Saved Baseball*. Phoenix: Society for American Baseball Research, 2015.

Nemec, David. "Charles Gardner Radbourn." In *Major League Baseball Profiles, Volume 2: The Hall of Famers and Memorable Personalities Who Shaped the Game*. Lincoln: University of Nebraska Press, 2011.

Nemec, David. "Curry Foley." In *Major League Baseball Profiles, Volume 1: The Ballplayers Who Built the Game*. Lincoln: University of Nebraska Press, 2011.

Nemec, David. "Hugh Nicol." In *Major League Baseball Profiles, Volume 1: The Ballplayers Who Built the Game*. Lincoln: University of Nebraska Press, 2011.

Nemec, David, Eric Miklich, and Brian McKenna. "Robert T. 'Bobby' Mathews." In *Major League Baseball Profiles, Volume 1: The Ballplayers Who Built the Game*. Lincoln: University of Nebraska Press, 2011.

Nemec, David. "Roger Connor." In *Major League Baseball Profiles, Volume 2: The Hall of Famers and Memorable Personalities Who Shaped the Game*. Lincoln: University of Nebraska Press, 2011.

Neyer, Rob. *Rob Neyer's Big Book of Baseball Blunders*. New York: Fireside, 2006.

Neyer, Rob. "Tommy Bond." In *The Neyer/James Guide to Pitchers: An Historical Compendium of Pitching, Pitchers, and Pitches*. New York: Fireside, 2004.

Pearlman, Jeff. *The Rocket That Fell to Earth: Roger Clemens and the Race for Baseball Immortality*. New York: Harper, 2009.

Pepe, Phil. *Talkin' Baseball: An Oral History of Baseball in the 1970s*. New York: Ballantine Publishing Group, 1998.

Ritter, Lawrence. *The Glory of Their Times*. New York: Vintage Books, 1992.

Roberts, Selena. *A-Rod: The Many Lives of Alex Rodriguez*. New York: Harper Collins, 2009.

Roensch, Greg. *Baseball Superstars: Rickey Henderson*. New York: Chelsea House, 2008.

Rogers, C. Paul, III. "John Wesley Coombs." In *Deadball Stars of the American League*. Dulles, VA: Brassey's, Inc., 2006.

Rothe, Emil. "Fanning Four Batters in One Inning." *Baseball Research Journal* 5 (1976): 22.

Rushkin, Steve. "Chuckin'." *Sports Illustrated*, July 1, 1991: 34–43.

Schechter, Gabriel. *Unhittable: Baseball's Greatest Pitching Seasons*. Mattoon, IL: Charles April Publications, 2002.

Schmidt, Ray. "Hugh Nicol." In *Baseball's First Stars*. Cleveland: Society for American Baseball Research, 1996.

Schott, Thomas E. "Hack Wilson." In *Winning on the North Side: The 1929 Chicago Cubs*. Phoenix: Society for American Baseball Research, 2015.

Shalin, Mike. *Donnie Baseball: The Definitive Biography of Don Mattingly*. Chicago: Triumph Books, 2011.

Skipper, Doug. "Willie Keeler." In *Deadball Stars of the American League*. Dulles, VA: Brassey's, Inc., 2006.

Skornickel, George. "Characters with Character: Pittsburgh's All Black Lineup." *Baseball Research Journal* 40, no. 2 (Fall 2011): 42–43.

Sonnanstine, Andy, and Tucker Elliot. *Tampa Bay Rays IQ: The Ultimate Test of True Fandom*. Florida: Black Mesa Publishing, 2014.

Spatz, Lyle. "William Dahlen." In *Deadball Stars of the National League*. Dulles, VA: Brassey's, Inc., 2004.

Tan, Cecilia, and Bill Nowlin. "The First 20-K Game in the Majors." In *The 1986 Boston Red Sox: There Was More Than Game Six*. Phoenix: Society for American Baseball Research, 2016.

Thompson, Dick. "John Gibson Clarkson." In *Baseball's First Stars*. Cleveland: Society for American Baseball Research, 1996.

Thorn, John. "Ross Barnes." In *Major League Baseball Profiles, Volume 2: The Hall of Famers and Memorable Personalities Who Shaped the Game*. Lincoln: University of Nebraska Press, 2011.

Thorn, John, and John Holway. *The Pitcher*. New York: Prentice Hall, 1988.

Vaccaro, Frank. "Origins of the Pitching Rotation." *Baseball Research Journal* 40, no. 2 (Fall 2011): 27–35.

VanDeMortal, Dan. "The Saga of J. R. Richard's Debut." *The National Pastime* 34 (2014): 50–54.

Voigt, David Q. "Denny Lyons' 52 Game Hitting Streak." *The National Pastime* 13 (1993): 45–49.

Wancho, Joseph. "Randy Johnson." In *No-Hitters*. Phoenix: Society for American Baseball Research, 2017.

Wendel, Tim. *The New Face of Baseball: The One-Hundred-Year Rise and Triumph of Latinos in America's Favorite Sport*. New York: Phillip Leif Group, 2003.

Wendel, Tim. *Summer of '68: The Season That Changed America—And Baseball—Forever*. Boston: Da Capo Press, 2012.

Williams, Ted. *My Turn At Bat*. New York: Fireside, 1988.

INTERNET

Armour, Mark. "Mike Higgins." http://sabr.org/bioproj/person/dce16a07.

Baldassaro, Lawrence. "Joe DiMaggio." https://sabr.org/bioproj/person/a48f1830.

Berger, Ralph. "Phil Weintraub." http://sabr.org/bioproj/person/ca37b853.

Boston, Talmadge. "Nolan Ryan." https://sabr.org/bioproj/person/4af413ee (1/10/11).

BSN Denver Sports. "Nolan Arenado Cycles Via Walk-Off Homer." YouTube video. Posted June 18, 2017, https://www.youtube.com/watch?v=FV6NYQZ6IJU&.

Bush, Frederick C. "May 6, 1998: Kerry Wood Ties Major League Record with 20 Strikeouts." http://sabr.org/gamesproj/game/may-6-1998-kerry-wood-ties-major-league-record-20-strikeouts.

Collier, Jamal. "Roaring 20! Max Ties K Mark, Mauls Tigers." http://m.mlb.com/news/article/177612626/max-scherzer-ties-mark-with-20-strikeouts.

Crasnick, Jerry. "Prince Fielder's Career Was Cut Short, But He's Still Cooking . . . Literally." www.espn.com/mlb/story/_/id/18654365/former-texas-rangers-slugger-prince-fielder-opens-neck-injury-ended-baseball-career (2/10/17).

Espada, Martin. "The Greatest Forgotten Home Run of All Time." http://lithub.com/the-greatest-forgotten-home-run-of-all-time/ (6/15/15).

ESPN.com. "Miguel Cabrera Wins Triple Crown." www.espn.com/mlb/story/_/id/8458298/detroit-tigers-miguel-cabrera-wins-first-triple-crown-1967 (10/4/12).

Faber, Charles F. "Matt Kilroy." https://sabr.org/bioproj/person/65e52675.

FoxSports. "Yaz: Somebody Has to Win Triple Crown." http://www.foxsports.com/mlb/story/carl-yastrzemski-on-next-triple-crown-winner-somebodys-got-to-do-it-092612 (9/26/12).

Franco, David. "Otis Nixon on the Art of Stealing Bases." YouTube video. Posted March 12, 2015, www.youtube.com/watch?v=r7MZZJDdB00.

Gilbert, Steve. "JD-back, Back, Back, Back! Martinez: 4 HRs." http://m.mlb.com/news/article/252494292/d-backs-jd-martinez-hits-four-home-runs/ (9/5/17).

Gonzalez, Alden. "Trade Complete, Hamilton's Angels Tenure Ends." http://m.mlb.com/news/article/120843186/josh-hamilton-traded-to-texas-rangers-by-los-angeles-angels/ (4/27/15).

Huber, Mike. "July 3, 1966: Braves Pitcher Tony Cloninger Clouts Two Grand Slams." http://sabr.org/gamesproj/game/july-3-1966-braves-pitcher-tony-cloninger-clouts-two-grand-slams.

Huber, Mike. "July 30, 1883: Philadelphia's Lon Knight Is First Player to Hit for a 'Natural' Cycle." http://sabr.org/gamesproj/game/july-30-1883-philadelphias-lon-knight-first-player-hit-natural-cycle.

Huber, Mike. "June 3, 1932: Lou Gehrig Hits Four Home Runs, Tony Lazzeri Hits for Cycle in Yankees Romp." https://sabr.org/gamesproj/game/june-3-1932-lou-gehrig-hits-four-home-runs-tony-lazzeri-hits-cycle-yankees-romp.

Kerr, Byron. "Reactions from Anthony Rendon's Record Setting Day." http://www.masnsports.com/byron-kerr/2017/04/reactions-from-anthony-rendons-record-setting-day.html (4/30/17).

McKenna, Brian. "Curry Foley." http://sabr.org/bioproj/person/d8a0584a.

McQuade, Dan. "Eric Bruntlett's Unassisted Triple Play Was 7 Years Ago Today." www.phillymag.com/news/2016/08/23/eric-bruntless-unassisted-triple-play/ (8/23/16).

Nowlin, Bill. "Ted Williams." http://sabr.org/bioproj/person/35baa190.

Perkins, Owen. "Tulowitzki Turns Unassisted Triple Play." http://m.mlb.com/news/article/1937361/ (4/29/07).

Semchuck, Alex. "Wilbert Robinson." https://sabr.org/bioproj/person/5536caf5.

Short, D. J. "Kerry Wood Says He Felt Something in Elbow During 20 Strikeout Game." http://mlb.nbcsports.com/2012/07/07/kerry-wood-says-he-felt-something-in-elbow-during-20-strikeout-game.

Singer, Tom. "Summer of .400: Brett Looks Back 30 Years Later." http://m.mlb.com/news/article/14748648// (9/17/10).

Stark, Jayson. "Miguel Cabrera's Triple Crown Chase." http://scorecenter.espn.go.com/blog/jayson-stark/post?id=67(9/19/12).

Sullivan, T. R. "Fielder's Memories Reciprocated by Famed Dad." http://m.mlb.com/news/article/131928284/prince-fielder-cecil-fielder-cherish-memories-of-watching-each-other-play/ (6/20/15).

Sullivan, T. R. "Hamilton Swings into History with Four Home Runs." http://m.mlb.com/news/article/30730042// (5/8/12).

Talking Chop Magazine. "Interview with Former Braves Outfielder Otis Nixon." https://www.talkingchop.com/2010/12/24/1894966/interview-with-former-braves-outfielder-otis-nixon (12/24/10).

Thorn, John. "Paul Hines and the Unassisted Triple Play." http://ourgame.mlblogs.com/paul-hines-and-the-unassisted-triple-play-220f56473f1a (5/5/15).

Wancho, Joseph. "Andre Thornton." http://sabr.org/bioproj/person/8856996c (1/14/12).

West, Steve. "Barry Bonds." http://sabr.org/bioproj/person/e79d202f (12/1/15).

Wood, Allan. "Babe Ruth." http://sabr.org/bioproj/person/9dcdd01c.

INTERVIEWS

Brooks Conrad, August 24, 2017.

Doug Dascenzo, July 12, 2017.

Scooter Gennett, July 1, 2017.

Aaron Hill, August 12, 2017.

Fred Lynn, August 11, 2017.

Denny McLain, July 23, 2017.

Mark Saccomanno, September 6, 2017.

Drew Storen, July 1, 2017.

VIDEOS

Chicago Cubs Legends—Kerry Wood 20 Strikeouts. May 6, 1998. A&E Home Video, 2007.

ABOUT THE AUTHOR

Joe Cox is a member of the Society for American Baseball Research (SABR) and is the author of *Almost Perfect: The Heartbreaking Pursuit of Baseball's Holy Grail*, and has coauthored several other sports books. He lives with his wife and children near Bowling Green, Kentucky.